A highly personal but hugely readable chronicle of a quietly spoken genius, this is a no-punch-unpulled diary of a young man who found himself at the UK core of a vital new music which rattled the mainstream and shook the floors of jazz clubs from New York to London in the fifties. King's vividly remembered and often brutally detailed story makes a book whose appeal far exceeds the jazz cognescenti and is by turns funny, touching and, dare I say it, unputdownable!

A wonderful and historically fascinating self-portrait of an artist whose restless mind embraces far more than the achingly beautiful music he continues to produce.

Ian Shaw

Peter King paints a unique portrait of the London jazz scene over the past fifty years. Beautifully observed portraits of jazz legends (both American and British) are enhanced by fascinating anecdotes that give a rare insight into the art form that is jazz. The book could only have been written by a maestro of Peter King's stature and for me it was a complete 'page turner'. I couldn't put it down and read it in two sessions. I already have a place on the bookshelf for it, alongside *Music is my Mistress* (Duke Ellington), *Really the Blues* (Mezz Mezzrow), *Straight Life* (Art Pepper) and *Beneath the Underdog* (Charles Mingus).

Mike Figgis

Flying High

A Jazz Life and Beyond

Peter King

Foreword by Benny Golson

Cover design by Adam Yeldham of Raven Design.

Front cover photo of Peter King at the Theater De Tobbe, the Hague, in 1995 by Rene Laanen.
Back cover photo: Peter King with Archie Shepp, Queen Elizabeth Hall, London, 19 May 1997, by Peter Symes.
Photo page vi, Peter King by John Stoddart.

The publishers acknowledge with thanks the kind permission of copyright owners to reprint the photographs used in this book. Permissions have been sought in all cases where the identity of the copyright holders is known.

A CIP record for this book is available from the British Library.

ISBN 978-09550908-9-9

Published 2011 by Northway Publications,
39 Tytherton Road, London N19 4PZ, UK.
www.northwaybooks.com

Printed in Great Britain by CPI Antony Rowe, Chippenham, Wilts.

Contents

In memory of Linda

Foreword

I first heard Peter King play in 1964 at Ronnie Scott's Club in London. He was playing the tenor saxophone then, and, because of the way he mastered it, I readily assumed he was a tenor player. The way he played absolutely astounded me. He was bungee-jumping and sky-diving with the determination of a daredevil. Though I was overwhelmingly impressed, I somehow did not make myself known, but he left an indelible and lasting impression on my psyche that evening.

It was only a few years ago that we finally met. We were thrown together in a European saxophone group. It was then I began to know the length and breadth of this talented man. I discovered that he was really an alto saxophone player. However, the kind of saxophone he played was immaterial since the notes emanating always reflected the same thing – extraordinary talent underscored with a cognitive mind.

What makes Peter King who he is? I think I know. He draws upon boundless imagination. But why is this important? Actually, it's not only important but essential in the creative process. Creativity is essential to everything that moves ahead in the realm of time and concept. It's as a door to the future, a future that will always have an indistinguishable face, but because of curiosity and axiomatic talent, we can sometimes give it a face of our own making.

Imagination is preceded by curiosity. We intuitively think, 'What will happen if I do this?' 'Will this work with that?' Curiosity gives birth to imagination. If something comes into existence bereft of imagination, it is usually somewhat limp of conviction. But why is imagination ever so important? Because it's a precursor to giving 'birth' to creative thoughts – yes, creativity. It gets the monster up off the table as a living, breathing thing as we symbolically scream, 'It's alive!'

How does Peter King factor into all of this? He is the embodiment of these things. But don't all creative people experience and live this? Yes, of course, but not always on the deepest level possible. Peter does, which, in part, makes him distinctive, separate and aside from so many. I've heard his memorable rendition of 'Body and Soul', the most recorded song ever. It not only reaches the ear and heart, but goes to the deepest grotto of that heart's core. It's also a reflection of a plethora of *imperial dreams* causing his saxophone to speak with a voice like no other.

Peter is not satisfied with endlessly serving the same warmed-over dish time and again. Thus, he walks with one foot in the present and the other in the future, looking for things awaiting his discovery and giving them a name and direction never before known. This takes courage. New things, that is, things never before heard or seen, sometimes are met with disapproval because of unfamiliarity, suspicion and doubt. So, Peter, and those of similar ilk, must be brave of heart, but never arrogant because this fouls the air we breathe. He is aware of this, which explains his wonderful character as a man, a person, a functioning human being in a society of other humans. He is not only an exceptional saxophonist whom I admire, but a personal friend whom I hold in the highest esteem.

He is bent on moving ahead to the 'next something', whatever that might be. It's this mind-set that keeps him on the cutting edge of this music we lovingly call jazz. It's no easy feat, but he's mastered the ability to pull stars from out of the sky, taking them into precious possession as his own, and doing with them as he sees fit to the benefit of us all.

All of the foregoing is exemplified by his many recordings and performances that monumentalize who and what Peter King is. It's a part of his being that he is generously and mercifully sharing with all awaiting ears and hearts as he invites us to share his musical universe.

Real talent has no quadrilateral boundaries. Peter's talent, then, does not end with explorations of his saxophone. His pen readily obeys him also. He is a composer of consequence, having recently written a full-blown opera. A daunting undertaking which exists within another realm, dense of thought and concept on yet another level.

Though I've made use of many words here, no prolixity of words is really necessary in order to explain the likes of Peter King. He is a genius whose certainty far outweighs his doubts.

Benny Golson
New York City

Acknowledgements

This book could never have been written without the help and support of many people and I would like to acknowledge my debt of gratitude to them all. I wish I could list everyone but space does not permit, so my apologies to all those who are not mentioned.

Firstly, without Ann and Roger Cotterrell's faith in me this book may never have been published. Their patience, kindness and advice have been an enormous help, as has their knowledgeable and sensitive editing of my original manuscript. Working with Ann and Roger has been a fascinating and rewarding experience.

Writing a book, like writing an opera, takes many months of hard work and my dear friend, Julian Barry, was there for me throughout the long process of writing both this book and my opera *Zyklon*, for which he wrote the libretto. Julian has immense experience as a playwright and as a Hollywood screen writer. His wonderfully concise advice and continuing encouragement were invaluable. I'm also deeply indebted to Stacy Ann Ralph. Stacy not only read the first draft but also helped me improve my writing technique. Both Stacy and Julian gave me very useful and honest advice on certain issues that arose during the lengthy editing process. I also wish to thank my dear sister, Brenda Bainton, especially for her invaluable memories of my first days on this earth.

I am honoured and very grateful to Benny Golson for his eloquent foreword and I would also like to thank Ian Shaw and film director Mike Figgis for reading the original manuscript and then contributing glowing recommendations to help promote it.

My dear friend, Dr. Sheldon (Shelly) Hendler, deserves special thanks. He personally knew many of the jazz giants and was a close friend of Red Rodney and also his doctor. As well as doing brilliant work in medicine and biochemistry, Shelly is an excellent musician. He was a great source of information in writing the book, particularly the sections on Bud Powell, sharing with me his knowledge on Bud's medical condition and treatment. Through his contacts with the late Leon Parker, Charlie Parker's son, he also has a unique copy of Bird's complete medical records.

I'd also like to thank Verne Christensen, another great friend who lives in Kansas City and has great knowledge of the jazz scene there and its history. Without his energy, passion for jazz and promotional skills, I would never have been invited to play at the Charlie Parker celebrations in K.C., along with Max Roach, Milt Jackson and many other jazz legends.

Thanks are also due to the following friends who helped clarify the accuracy of facts in the text: Kim Parker helped with certain passages about her mother, Chan Parker. Tony Kinsey, Spike Wells, the late John Dankworth, Alec Dankworth, Stan and Clark Tracey, John Horler, John Miles, Martin Dilly, Del Cooper, Dennis Higgins and many others, all helped refresh my memory about events long in the past. Phil Woods shared with me his fascinating reminiscences of when he and other famous American musicians flew model aeroplanes in New York's Central Park, back in the early fifties. Special thanks too to Hardy Brodersen, who not only shared his experiences as a schoolboy friend of Lucky Thompson and Milt Jackson in Detroit, but also gave me information on famous Hollywood film stars of the forties and fifties who were also aeromodellers.

Last, but not least, I wish to thank all those friends who helped by reading the first draft of the manuscript and giving their opinion, encouragement and sometimes useful additional information. They include Michael Barham, Linda Masters, Haydn Bendall and Wally Evans (British representative for Yanigisawa saxophones and Rico Reeds).

1

'Blood on the walls! For Chrissakes, Pete, look, those are blood spots, all over the damned walls!'

'What d'you mean? What are you talking about?' I snapped back.

The guy who rented me the depressing room in Glebe Road, Barnes, where I was living, along with drummer Phil Seamen, was pointing to several small dark red spots all over parts of the wallpaper that formed a backdrop to the chaos that had become my life. He was accusing me of causing them! I tried frantically to dismiss his accusations but an awful truth had already forced its way into my mind. The monster that I thought I had under at least partial control, had in fact taken over my life. It was now destroying me and all my hopes of advancing my career as a musician. This could not be happening to me, could it? The truth is, it was.

When I decided to write this book I soon realised it would be difficult to tell my story truthfully without describing, for the first time, my struggle against a demon that almost wrecked my career and nearly killed me. This 'demonic shade' became such an all-pervading part of my life that it controlled almost everything I did. Having successfully rid myself of this threat to my very existence many years ago, I feel the time has come to bare my soul and finally lay its evil ghost to rest, once and for all. Writing this autobiography has not been an easy task. I have had to relive long forgotten nightmares as I delved back into the story of my life. It has also raised questions about how my experiences in infancy and in childhood may have affected the rest of my life.

Was it the terror of loud noises while, as a baby, I cowered night after night in the Anderson Shelter during the Blitz as the nearby ack-ack guns blazed away at the Nazi bombers above? Was it the fear of not living up to my elder brother's brilliant academic career? Was it the humiliation of still playing in Tubby Hayes' big band while everyone knew my wife at the time was blatantly sleeping with him?

Any one of these things could have eventually caused an over-sensitive person to seek solace in whatever could best take away the pain. But, difficult as they were for me, bad events are just part of any normal life. People adapt to them and survive much worse things without damage. Probably those events are just a way of justifying to myself why I took such a self-destructive wrong turn at a formative stage in my life.

But I overcame my demons – this book is about how music and musicians have given fulfilment, happiness and meaning to my life. Overall I've had wonderful experiences, I've made great friends and above all I had the long-term love of a woman who stayed by my side through good and bad times.

And yet still, as I write this, other horrific memories flood back into my mind and I wonder how on earth I arrived at that dreadful crisis in my life and how I ever fought my way back from the abyss that threatened to engulf me. We are all influenced by our experiences in childhood, but perhaps events long before we were even born can have profound effects on us too. After all fate is a strange thing – if my paternal grandfather had not been killed while working on the railroad in Harrisburg Pennsylvania, I might have been born an Amerian.

* * *

In 1912 my father, Edward Horace King was thirteen years old. His father and mother had decided the family should emigrate from West Ham, in the East End of London, to America. They crossed the Atlantic steerage class on one of the big trans-atlantic liners and took a train from New York to a new life in Harrisburg, Pennsylvania. Here my grandfather worked in the railway marshalling yards, riding the big shunting locomotives that prepared those amazingly long American freight trains for their journeys. He worked hard and things were looking good until, after only a few months, tragedy struck. As he stood on the front of one of the big locos one day, preparing to hook up wagons, the engine jolted over some points. He was thrown onto the track and the engine ran over him, killing him outright. It was quite a local tragedy and my grandmother, Amelia King, and my father were left to fend for themselves in a foreign country, three thousand miles from home. Eventually the Salvation Army helped them to get back to London as, although Dad managed to get work, he couldn't save enough to pay their passage. In later years, my mother and father would always give money to the Salvation Army if one of their bands played in the street. It was my dad's way of saying thanks.

Not long after my father's return to the UK, the First World War started and in 1916 he enlisted in the Grenadier Guards after a woman gave him a white feather. This obnoxious practice was rife during the so-called Great War. If a girl gave you a white feather it meant she thought you were a coward, because you had not volunteered for Kitchener's army. My father was just seventeen and therefore under age, but pride made him do what many other young men did. He lied about his age and enlisted. After basic training he was sent with the British Expeditionary Force to Belgium, where he was briefly involved in the second great battle of Ypres. He only managed three weeks in the trenches before being invalided out. Up to his waist in water, mud and corpses, he soon succumbed to what they called trench fever, caused by the filthy water, rats and rotting flesh, and as antibiotics were unknown then, this new strange illness could be a killer. Dad spent eighteen months in hospital recovering. He was also mustard-gassed. A gas shell landed in the trench, a few feet away from him, but didn't explode. The shell casing cracked, pouring its contents into the trench. The garlic-smelling, semi-liquid gas covered his hands, causing excruciatingly painful blisters. He also got some of the stuff in his lungs and suffered from a bad chest for the rest of his life.

I often wonder whether, in an opposing enemy trench, Adolf Hitler, then a young corporal in the German army, may have been close by. Hitler was also mustard gassed and temporarily blinded in Ypres. Once my father had recovered, he used to stand guard outside Buckingham Palace in his red Grenadier Guards uniform and bearskin hat. He told me that at six feet in height, he was the shortest guy in the squad and was nicknamed 'Shorty'. His seven feet three inches tall regimental sergeant major, who had a fourteen-inch 'handlebar' mustache, would pick on any poor soldier who forgot to get his 'short back and sides' bellowing out things like, 'Am I 'urting ya son? Well I oughta be 'cause I'm standing on yer ruddy hair!' Or, 'You may break your mother's heart but, you won't break mine!'

After his release from the army, Dad co-ran a shoe repair business until his partner did the dirty on him and left him without a viable business. He became a tea boy at Unilever House, where he worked his way up, eventually being promoted to advertising manager. By the time he retired, he had driven nearly a million accident-free miles as an advertising representative at Lever Brothers, without ever passing a driving test. He had to teach himself – Unilever gave him a brand new car one Friday night and just told him to get on with it! When driving tests were later introduced, anyone who had already learnt to drive was given a full licence without a test.

Not long after the war, he married Winifred Baldwin, my mother. She was the only surviving girl from twelve children. Her five sisters all died in childhood. Of her six brothers two were killed in the Great War and another also died young, of tuberculosis. My uncle Bill also suffered from TB later in life. That left my uncle George and my uncle Alf. My mother and her remaining brothers all died of heart disease in their sixties but my father's mother, Amelia, lived to the ripe old age of ninety-three. For most of her later years she was totally blind and profoundly deaf but she had a wonderful 'Cockney' spirit and would cheer herself up by endlessly singing old music hall songs. The only trouble was she took a wicked delight in singing them while her family were trying to watch television. Not being able to see or hear the new invention, she could not understand why anyone else should enjoy it better than singing along with her!

Uncle Alf had an important influence on my love of music. He was an excellent amateur pianist, could read music and played in the style of Charlie Kunz and Zez Confrey. I remember him teaching me to play 'God Save the King' with my nose, a trick he performed at parties. My mother played the piano quite well when she was young but my father, who played a bit of 'pub' piano, was the one sought after for sing-songs. I think my mother lost interest in the instrument, receiving so little encouragement. I hardly ever heard her play, although we always had sheet music and a piano in the house. She led a frustrated life in many ways, despite Dad being a loving husband and father.

My elder brother, Edward, was born in 1925 and my sister Brenda in 1929. Teddy was always the high-flyer in the family. Educated at Kingston Grammar School and the School of Oriental and African Studies, he was fluent in over forty languages, from Sanskrit to Lithuanian and from Swahili to Russian. In the Second World War he was in the Intelligence branch of the Royal Navy in the Far East as a member of Lord Mountbatten's staff, where his fluent Chinese was a great asset. I finally arrived, a late accident, in 1940.

In the mid-1930s my parents moved to a new semi-detached house in Tolworth, near Kingston upon Thames, Surrey. The area was being built up from virtually open fields into one of the many new outer London suburbs. The family settled into a contented lower middle class existence but then, in 1939, the Second World War broke out. Sometime in that November, I was conceived. For my parents and especially my mother, who was then in her forties, this must have been a shock and a considerable inconvenience. One can only speculate what traumatic thoughts went through her mind while she was carrying her new addition to the family. During the 'phoney war', anti-German propaganda was rife and I know she was badly

affected by a cinema newsreel purporting to show Nazi SS bay-
oneting mothers in the stomach at a maternity hospital in one
of the occupied countries. Total lies maybe, but my parents
wouldn't have known this at the time and in view of the scale of
Nazi atrocities by the end of the war, it might as well have been
true. People were expecting Hitler to invade Britain at any time
and the general fear and tension can only be imagined.

My mother went into labour just as the phoney war was drawing to a close and I arrived at 2 p.m. in the afternoon of 11
August. When my father returned to Kingston Hospital later
that evening he found the floors and stairs stained with blood
from casualties who had been hit by stray bombs. *Adler Tag*
(Eagle Day) with Hitler's all-out assault on the RAF followed on
13 August.

My mother always had a nervous disposition and – although I
seem to have inherited most of my genes from my father (I have
a strong resemblance to him even down to his slightly deformed
size twelve feet) – I definitely inherited my mother's genes as far
as my mental make up is concerned. On the first of many childhood visits to a psychiatrist, my parents were told my troubles
started in my mother's womb, before I was even born. Not a
good start for any kid.

I don't remember ever being frightened of bombs, but I did
have other fears, which I remember vividly from a very young
age – the kind of things that stick even in the mind of a baby.
One episode couldn't have helped much, though it has its funny
side. I don't recall it but my sister told me about it on my
sixtieth birthday. One night mom had bathed and powdered me,
changed my nappies, and generally tarted me up. Just as she
finished, the damned air raid siren sounded and we all trooped
down to the Anderson shelter in the garden. We had only been
there a short time when a stray bomb exploded in the allotment
next to the house. It was about fifty yards away and blew all the
windows out. That was frightening enough, but what made my
mother really blow her top was the fact that the shit from the

roof of the shelter showered down and covered us all from head to toe. Looking at her freshly bathed baby covered in filth, she saw red and screamed at the Nazi bombers, 'You bastards! I've only just bathed him!' She wasn't concerned about the blown-out windows nor the fact we had just missed annihilation. She was just incensed that those Nazi sods had dared to cover her baby in shit after all the work she had done cleaning him up!

My own earliest memories of the Blitz were of being woken up night after night to have my dressing gown put on before being carried to the garden shelter. The two things that really freaked me out were gas masks and loud noises. Apparently they tried to put me into one of those claustrophobic baby gas masks, the ones you put a whole child in. They never did manage it though, as my hysterical screams persuaded them I would rather take my chances without it. Later, when I was a toddler, they tried unsuccessfully to get me to wear one of the kids' gas masks. These were supposed to be less frightening than the adult ones, because they were brightly coloured and had Mickey Mouse or Donald Duck faces. But they didn't impress me one bit and, as I had realised by then that screaming blue murder usually made the grown-ups relent, I put up such a fight they gave up. My poor parents must have been beside themselves by now. Not only would I not wear any kind of gas protection, but I wouldn't let anyone else either. I wouldn't go near the shelter unless all the gas masks, Mickey Mouse or otherwise, had been removed. For a sensitive kid, those damned things were scary and people wearing them looked like the dreaded bogeymen that naughty kids were threatened with.

As a toddler it seems I also suffered from what they called 'night horrors'. These manifested themselves in strange ways, although I have no recollection of them. It seems that one night I was found trying to climb out of the upstairs bedroom window while still asleep. The other thing that scared me to death was any kind of loud noise. Except for the one stray bomb, we were fairly safe in Tolworth, but about two hundred yards away there was an anti-aircraft battery in the local park. The ack-ack guns made a horrendous din as they tried, mostly unsuccessfully, to shoot down the nightly raiders. I dreaded them and Mum used to cover my ears as best she could when they started up. Right up till my early teens I would jump a mile at things like fireworks or cars back-firing, because of those guns. It might not have been so bad if they had shot down a Heinkel or two, but the only thing they seemed any good at was terrifying the local kids.

My sister Brenda was educated at Surbiton High School for Girls, but wasn't too interested in furthering her education after she matriculated. In fact she suddenly decided she wanted to study aircraft maintenance, of all things. She had a textbook on the subject, full of wonderful diagrams and drawings of the inner workings of aircraft and engines. This and her wartime aircraft recognition books probably led to my fascination with aeroplanes. From the age of about four, I started learning how to spot planes, using the little silhouette plans in her books. I remember being upset just after the war when I asked my father why I never saw any Messerschmitt 109s or Heinkel 111s. Dad told me, 'Oh, you won't see any of them now, son.' The war was over and I had missed the fun, just when I was beginning to enjoy it!

Mum and I were evacuated a while in 1944, during the doodle bug raids on London: V1 flying bombs and V2 rockets rudely interrupted the comparative peace at home and caused much death and destruction late in the war. We lived in Gloucester with a family whose son, Paul, was a little older than me. He was the proud owner of a beautiful model locomotive, powered by real steam. He was like an elder brother to me. I sorely missed my real brother, who was always overseas somewhere. Paul would sometimes scrape pocket money together to buy wonderful-smelling purple liquid called methylated spirits, with which he would fire up the locomotive to show me how it worked. I was thrilled to bits and soon got into model trains myself, but all we could afford were the old Hornby clockwork kind. One night Paul tried to show me a model of a doodlebug he was making out of plasticine. His mum got really mad at him, telling him not to frighten me with such terrible things, as I was far too young. I couldn't understand what the fuss was about and told her I wasn't scared. After a conflab between his mum and mine, I was allowed to watch him finish his model. The seeds were sown for my later passion for model aeroplanes.

Once the war ended my parents had to think about my education. My first experience of primary school was miserable. I made few friends, learnt very little and was soon moved to a tiny private school, Berrylands College. I was much happier there. The headmaster, Mr Sylvester Savigear, was an intellectual oddball, with several young daughters, all named after Greek goddesses. He was a very good teacher and taught most of the subjects himself to the older pupils. The only problem was that, although it was a mixed school, it seemed biased towards the female students. We had to play netball and rounders instead of basketball and cricket, which I found embarrassing and frustrating. I had some good friends there though and one girl, who seemed to take a fancy to me, persuaded me to have lessons from her piano teacher. I hadn't yet fully appreciated the special attractions of the female sex, but I do remember two girls who aroused nascent adolescent feelings. One had beautiful long blond plaits and her name was Linda. I have loved that name ever since and my second wife turned out to be

At Berrylands College, ca. 1947

another Linda. I went every week to piano lessons and practised but my latent passion for music had not yet emerged. After a while the lessons stopped, but I always regret not continuing. The piano is difficult to learn once you grow older and a good knowledge of keyboard technique is invaluable for any serious musician, especially if you want to compose.

Eventually I passed the old eleven plus exam with flying colours and gained free entrance to Kingston Grammar School. This was my father's first choice as he wanted me to follow in my brother's footsteps. After the war, Dad's job no longer required him to travel and, although he had been promoted, his loss of a firm's car meant he was worse off financially than before. Teddy had been a private pupil at the school but my father could no longer afford to pay fees, so it was a relief when I passed and got a free place there. But this turned out to be a mixed blessing in the end and I felt a subtle but constant pressure to match my elder brother's illustrious career. This would eventually lead to a crisis and a serious clash between us.

By now my sister was a bright teenager. Brenda loved to dance, especially the jitterbug, and had a good collection of swing records. I remember hearing the Harry James band, the Squadronaires and Glenn Miller around the house. In the later part of the war, Brenda had a crush on a handsome RAF fighter pilot, Peter Hickson, and I remember tagging along with her to see his parents in Surbiton. They kept rabbits, a handy thing to have during wartime food rationing. I adored the little things but they probably ended up in the cooking pot, as rabbits were one of the few sources of meat in those days. Peter was tragically killed when his Tempest Mk 2 crashed while flying home from Germany, only a few weeks after the end of hostilities.

In the early 1950s Brenda fell in love with and married Alan Bainton, a handsome young blond-haired man with an endearing Wiltshire accent, who was a great dancer and jitterbug partner. He had been a paratrooper dropped into Denmark at the end of the war to fight the retreating Germans. Afterwards he served

PK's mother, sister Brenda, brother-in-law Alan and PK's father.

in Palestine, trying to keep the peace before the founding of the state of Israel. When, later, my second wife's mother first met him and learned that he had been a stonemason after his military service, she said, with a concerned look, 'Oh how wonderful. But I suppose that's a dying trade, isn't it?' She couldn't understand why we all fell about laughing, until the penny dropped and she burst out giggling herself. Maybe Alan had seen the light too because, shortly after marrying my sister, he enrolled at the Metropolitan Police Training College at Hendon and gave up stone masonry for good.

At Kingston Grammar, I did well with my studies for the first couple of years, mostly keeping near the top of the class. There wasn't much bullying either. I was in the 'A' stream, where the supposedly brightest kids were and most of the rougher boys were in the 'B' and 'C' streams. I made friends easily, something I had had trouble with earlier, being painfully shy, and I also began to enjoy sports.

As soon as we enrolled, we were asked if we wanted to take up a musical instrument. I had become very interested in my brother's classical record collection and would go round the house doing imitations of Benjamino Gigli, the great operatic tenor. God knows what that must have sounded like! I copied my brother's antics as he would flail his arms about 'conducting' his favourite recordings of Beethoven's *Fifth* and Handel's *Messiah*. I fell in love with the violin, and had fantasies of becoming a world famous violinist. In fact I was going through a phase of hero worship for anyone world famous. Just 'famous' didn't do it for me. My heroes ranged from Stanley Matthews through Don Bradman, Denis Compton and Captain Scott (the ill fated Antarctic explorer), to piano virtuoso Solomon (Solomon Cutner) and other musicians, sportsmen, explorers and artists. My father encouraged this, taking me to cup finals at Wembley, test matches at Lords and the Oval and telling me about his favourite heroes.

Once, when I was very young, Mum and Dad took me to a symphony concert at the Royal Albert Hall. The first half consisted of the usual classics, but the second ended with a contemporary piano concerto. My parents suggested we quietly leave before the concerto, as they feared the modern music would be hard going and were worried I would get bored and start fidgeting. To their astonishment, I didn't want to leave and listened, spellbound, to the whole piece. I think that was when they realised I might have some musical talent. I wish I could remember what that music was. It may have been a piano concerto by Béla Bartók, later to become my favourite composer. Whatever it was, I found the modern harmonies and rhythms fascinating.

A violin was acquired from the school and I started lessons. I really wanted to play the instrument, but I found it tough. In the early stages, the violin can make the most hideous noises. Nevertheless I persevered and even sat in the violin section of the school orchestra on one occasion. I also remember struggling with a simple string quartet when one of the masters invited some boys to his house for a musical evening. Nicknamed 'Gobbo' because he spat when he talked, he had been at Kingston Grammar since my brother was there. He had a slight limp but he could outrun any boy in the school and, when he got angry, he could hit your ear with a piece of chalk from thirty paces. He never missed and the chalk would fly at you so damned quick, you could never get out of the way in time! Unfortunately the violin idea, like the piano lessons, died a natural death, even though I always retained my love of the violin and for the sound of strings in general.

At school, problems started to appear when I had to decide whether to enter the third year in the arts or the science streams. Although I ended up as a musician, my interest then was more towards science but, because my brother had taken the arts route, I tried to do the same. This was a very bad move. It meant taking Greek and dropping chemistry and physics. I already hated Latin and things were not helped by the fact that the Latin master, Mr McIvor, was a nasty bit of work who also became our Greek master. He could have been an even bigger threat to me as he also taught the so-called music lessons. Actually these were simply choral singing classes and as I had a good ear, he didn't pick on me much, although he gave no real encouragement either. Boring as they were, those periods at least gave me some basic experience in reading music and using my ears. He left me alone in the music periods because he had ample opportunity to vent his spleen on me in the dreaded Greek classes. Boy, did he ever make up for it then! My total lack of interest in or understanding of Greek or Latin gave him plenty of opportunity to humiliate and terrorise me. It was so bad that in just one term I dropped ten or more places in the class and everyone realised that placing me in the arts stream had been a big mistake. I was quickly switched to the science curriculum but the loss of a whole term meant I had to catch up in physics and chemistry.

Actually I found this fairly easy. Science fascinated me, especially anything to do with aeroplanes. I was getting more and more interested in aerodynamics. But Mr McIvor got his own back on me for leaving his Greek classes by making the Latin lessons even more hellish than before. I started lying awake at nights, dreading the next day's Latin period. I struggled on for a year or so but I began to hate school and lost interest in the subjects I had to study.

By my second year I had become very keen on athletics and cricket, but two things put an end to all that. When the annual school athletics championships were held, I realised that, unlike all my friends in the same year, I was a couple of months older than the maximum qualifying age. The teacher told me not to worry and to enter with the rest of my classmates. The day of the competition came and I not only won four athletics events, running the winning last leg of the relay, but also broke the school 100 yards and long jump records for my age group. Suddenly I was a hero, but then came shame and disappointment. A few weeks later, a teacher came into the class and pulled me to one side. He was very embarrassed as he told me someone had lodged a complaint about my 'false' entrance qualifications. I was to be disqualified and all my medals taken away! They admitted a terrible mistake had been made and tried to mollify me with a gift of my choice to make amends. I chose an expensive set of Exacto modelling tools for my hobby, which was aeromodelling, so at least I got something out of the bastards. I covered my embarrassment as best I could and my classmates were very supportive but the episode left a bitter taste. Not only had I trained hard to win those events and lost my trophies, but I felt a cheat, even though it was not my fault.

I turned my energy to cricket practice. I was a natural fast bowler, although my batting was barely adequate. I was chosen for the school under-13 team and at my first ever match I annihilated the opposing batsmen, taking 9 wickets for just 28 runs. Honour was restored. I became a hero again and was assured this would win me my school colours. These allowed you to wear a special tie as a badge of honour and were only awarded for outstanding achievement. Monday assembly came and the headmaster called my name and praised my achievement. But, to my absolute disgust and that of my classmates, he decided I was too young to receive my colours! This double whammy was the last straw. With my declining interest in study and my rapid descent down the end-of-term class placing, I was heading towards a big crisis. I was almost bottom of the class now and terrified of being demoted into the 'B' stream, among the rougher kids and away from the friends I had made. I didn't know who to turn to or what to do, but I wanted out. At the end of that term in my fifth year I was determined to quit school and concentrate on my real interest, aerodynamics.

The first person I turned to for advice was a fellow-aeromodeller, Jack North. I had been making and flying models since I was about seven but it wasn't until I joined a proper club that I started to make real progress, designing machines and flying them in competitions. At Epsom Downs racecourse, to this day a well-known model flying site, I met some of our best flyers and they taught me how to become a serious competition flyer. I joined the Surbiton Model Aero Club and met my heroes, Pete Buskel and Mike Gaster, both of whom regularly represented Britain in the World Championships. Gaster finally became a world champion himself and went on to an illustrious career as a professor of theoretical aerodynamics. I later switched to the Croydon and DMAC, which is where I met Jack North, a top boffin at the National Physical Laboratory in Teddington who was heavily involved in the cutting edge of trans-, super- and hyper-sonic aerodynamic research. Jack went on to achieve international fame and recognition. A rather dour and intimidating man who didn't suffer fools gladly, he became a mentor and father-figure to me. In fact, at the age of fifteen, I was privy to some of the very latest theory and developments in this new field of research. Quite something for a teenage kid! Jack was famous for his pioneering work on colour schlieren photography, the technique that made it possible for the first time to observe and photograph supersonic shock waves in the wind tunnel. At the time, the National Physical Laboratory had some of the world's leading facilities, including revolutionary new shock tunnels. In these, controlled explosions created for a very brief duration air velocities approaching Mach 15 or more. High speed photography made it possible to analyse the airflow over the wind tunnel models at speeds in excess of 15,000 mph. Jack drummed into me the need for complete scientific rigour, a lesson that stayed with me for life. About thirty years later I bumped into him at a Duke Ellington concert and discovered to my amazement he was a lifelong jazz fan. I was always a little in awe of him, but he saw talent in me and took me under his wing. In many ways he had a quiet but profound and positive influence on my life.

When I explained to him that I wanted to get into aero-dynamics, he told me what I needed at that stage was just Ordinary level GCEs in Maths, Physics, English and one other subject. He recommended adding technical drawing, something not covered in the school curriculum. In those days, if you were a talented aeromodeller, the hands-on skill you acquired from successfully designing and flying models counted for a great deal; when it came to getting a job, that was worth almost as much as academic qualifications, vital as they were. My hope was that, after getting my 'O' levels, Jack could maybe help get me an apprenticeship at the National Physical Laboratory while I continued my studies at night school.

I told my parents about Jack's advice and how depressed I was at school. They could see I was going through a bad time and contacted the school. The upshot was that I visited the school psychiatrist, who decided I was suffering a mini nervous breakdown and was not in any state to continue my studies. He advised that I should leave school for a while and arranged for me to have free private tuition in the four subjects I wanted. For the next few months I studied hard at home for my 'O' levels. To everyone's great relief I passed with quite good marks in all four subjects. Things did not turn out the way I had planned, however, and a great change of direction was just around the corner.

Although my father let me leave school, he was not pleased and told me that if I quit now, it would have a permanent bad effect. I would find myself always quitting when the going got tough. Leaving school was a big decision to make at fifteen, especially as I knew there was a lot of truth in what he said. Things were compounded by a serious problem with my brother. Teddy was now a high ranking civil servant in Malaya. When he heard about my plan to leave school early, he was very angry and wrote to my father. In turn I was furious with my brother and wrote a long letter back, castigating him for making judgments about my life, when he was six thousand miles away and had no idea what I was going through. I also made nasty, unwarranted remarks about his wife Mary, who shared his view of the situation. I blamed him for my having spent my life trying to live up to his example and said it was his fault I had been pushed into the arts stream and that this was the cause of much of the problem. In reply to my outburst he demanded that I apologise to his wife, which I did reluctantly.

I had never been close to him, partly due to our age difference and partly because he was always away from home, at university or in some distant country. I had admired him from a distance and always got excited when he came home for a few days. Now, as far as I was concerned, he could stay in Malaya forever. Our rift mended after a while, but it was only a couple of years before he died that I finally shook off a constant need somehow to prove myself to him. It had been probably one of the strongest motivating forces in my life. Teddy retired to Malta and it was only when he belatedly started using email that I got really close to him. During his last two years on this earth I poured out my soul to him and he reciprocated, telling me, for the first time, how very proud of me he had been all along and how much he had grown to respect my talent as a musician. He even began collecting jazz records and sought my advice on what to listen to. It was a very moving time for both of us and I was terribly upset when he died suddenly of a heart attack.

While studying for my 'O' levels I rediscovered music, but this time it was not just another passing fad. I acquired my first

record player and rented a radio. My first passion was for Elvis
Presley. I bought his hit, 'Heartbreak Hotel', I read about his
fame, his pink suits and his pink Cadillac and was deeply
impressed with his glamorous and rebellious image. I started
trying to imitate him, even calling up a record company in the
hopes of getting 'discovered'. My hopes were dashed when they
told me I needed to send in a tape. I didn't own a tape recorder
and knew no musicians, so I quickly realised that being a
pop star was a stupid adolescent dream. For years after that I
kept my early infatuation for Elvis to myself and was very
embarrassed about it. It wasn't until much later that I realised it
wasn't such a bad thing after all. Listening to those early Presley
tracks now, I realise they introduced me to a watered down
'white' version of the blues, a musical form I became steeped in
for ever.

I would listen to my radio, turned down very quiet, under the
bed clothes at night and soon tuned into Willis Conover's *Jazz
Hour*, that wonderful nightly programme on American Forces
Network. At 11 p.m. there would be an hour of good quality
music by Frank Sinatra, Peggy Lee and all the top singers. This
was followed by *Jazz Hour*, which was a total revelation to me.
For the first time, I heard the whole panoply of jazz, from Louis
Armstrong to Charlie Parker. I was hooked and my interest in
science and aeronautics began to fade. I started to absorb all the
new sounds and read anything I could find about jazz.
Unfortunately I also learned too much about the destructive
lifestyles of people like Parker and Billie Holiday. In my impres-
sionable teens, I became infatuated with the image of black
musicians producing wonderful music whilst fighting racial
prejudice and often resorting to hard drugs to alleviate their suffering. The whole package had a fatal attraction for someone
who, having failed to gain academic qualifications, was looking
to rebel against his family's aspirations. My new passion would
later lead me into the lower depths of the human condition but,

thanks to my determination to excel as a jazz musician, it would also enable me to find my true calling.

The origins of my struggle with drug addiction probably began during this period. I became more and more aware of certain debilitating physical and mental symptoms and began to search for some kind of relief. I felt unable to cope with those perfectly normal feelings of unease that most people seem to take in their stride. Maybe the emotional problems I had suffered throughout my childhood were exacerbated during adolescence, but I felt as if I was lacking some of the normal physical and mental defence mechanisms that enable most people to cope with adult life. Our family doctor prescribed heavy barbiturates to my mother to help her insomnia so, even while still at school, I turned to him for help with my anxiety and depression, hoping for some kind of chemical relief. He was a Scot and had a typically humane approach – the kind of doctor you could always talk to. At first he gave me a mild sedative, which helped my anxiety to some extent but tended to make me even more depressed. After a while he tried me on Drinamyl, a combination of Dexedrine and phenol barbitone, often prescribed back then to relieve depression or to help lose weight. Dexedrine is a powerful stimulant and it helped my depression so much that I was soon asking for more. The doctor did his best to regulate my consumption.

There was one good bit of news though. I found I was to miss military service. Conscription was abandoned just a couple of months before I reached the call-up age. For once my age proved to be an advantage. Mind you, I had quite enjoyed the two years I was in the army and then the air cadet force at school. The idea had been to do basic training there but I think the military would have put us through it all again on call-up. I did get my lance corporal's stripe after the first year, and if I ever need it I still remember how to strip down, clean, oil and re-assemble a Lee Enfield .303 rifle, a wonderful old piece of kit that was still standard issue. Dad had one just the same, back in

World War One. I even fired a Lee Enfield once, but it was fitted with a smaller caliber 0.22 inch barrel. They told us the kick of a 0.303 would have been too strong for a fourteen-year-old. If I had stayed at school, I could have learnt to fly in the cadet force eventually. I still had a hankering to be a Spitfire pilot, but it was not to be.

At first I developed my passion for jazz in tandem with my love of aviation. I still vaguely wanted to become an aerodynamicist but gradually music gained the upper hand. However, it wasn't until I happened to see a film, *The Benny Goodman Story*, that I made the decision to become a professional musician. The movie was a typically bastardised Hollywood biopic, but at the time it had a profound effect on me. I loved the brash excitement of Harry James' trumpet which I had heard on my sister's records and which was heavily featured in the film. When I got home from the cinema, I was determined to play the trumpet, like James. Something odd happened while I was asleep, though, because when I woke the following morning all I could think about was Benny Goodman's clarinet playing. This badly-made movie was a kind of 'revelation on the road to Damascus'. It was not just the music but the lifestyle and the heroic struggles for recognition of the professional musician that captured my imagination. I had always believed that, for something I was really interested in, I had the capacity for hard work and attention to detail. Jack North had instilled in me the importance of application and scientific rigour. That lesson stood me in good stead when I applied it to music. That was it: I would be a professional jazz clarinet player, shit or bust, and would transfer all my enthusiasm and dedication from aerodynamics into playing jazz. At last, I seemed to have found my vocation in life.

2

'Pete, will you play at the opening of my new club?'
Ronnie Scott

Having decided to play the clarinet, how was I going to start?
My parents were only just reconciled to the fact I wanted to
study to be an aerodynamicist, although I think they had serious
doubts about how I was going to achieve this. After having
paid for piano and then violin lessons, all to no avail, they were
hardly going to pay for a clarinet and more lessons to satisfy
what they considered another passing craze. I knew I had to do
this with no help, at least until I could prove I had some chance
of making a success at my new vocation. I started to look for
jazz records and an old friend from prep school, John Callinan,
who also shared my early interest in model aeroplanes, obtained
some old 78s from his sister. He would bring her record player
over and we would listen to the few jazz records in her collection. The one that I remember best was a Louis Armstrong All
Stars live concert with Edmond Hall on clarinet. Hall made a
big impression on me and I began learning his and everyone
else's solos, by ear. Most of my spare time was now spent soak-
ing up everything I could about jazz. I learned every note from
each new record I got my hands on and would lie in bed at night
humming improvised solos under my breath and imagining I
was playing onstage. Not just clarinet solos but all the other
instruments as well. I would pretend I was playing a real concert
and visualise every aspect of the performance, down to the
announcements and the applause. In fact without realising it I
must have been using a 'visualisation' technique similar to that
used today by modern sportsmen and women.

One often hears references to this psychological method, but
very little about what it means in practice. There is a lot more

to it than visualising yourself winning Wimbledon or an Olympic medal. Sure, you have to 'see' yourself at the winning moment, but that gives no idea of the whole method. It's an extremely difficult and exact discipline that involves visualising (with all five senses) every minute detail of the task ahead.

As a Formula One fan, I can give an example from that sport. The great Ayrton Senna would sit on his bed the night before a Grand Prix and visualise the next day's race in its entirety. He would run through every possible scenario in the race including any possible incidents, planning how he would handle them and get into the lead. He used the technique for his legendary, last qualifying lap at Monaco one year. He had one flying lap left, with ten minutes to go to put the car in pole position. After telling his mechanics that the set-up of the car was fine, he sat motionless in the car in an almost trance-like state and visualised his next and last lap. He told his stunned engineers exactly how he could gain 0.1 sec on the entry to turn three, 0.2 seconds on the apex of turn five, 0.3 seconds on the exit of turn eight and so on, until he had mentally driven the whole lap. He calmly said he could gain a total of 1.2 seconds over his previous lap, a massive amount in F1 where you are normally talking about tenths of a second. The amazing thing was that he then went out and knocked exactly 1.2 seconds off his previous time and put the car on pole by almost a second. His qualifying time was so unbelievable that an enquiry was called by the other teams, who claimed there must be something wrong with the circuit's electronic timing equipment. Of course it was working normally. Ron Dennis, Ayrton's boss at McLaren, was heard to remark sarcastically, 'It's not the equipment they should blame. They should blame the bloody driver!' This is what visualisation really means. Senna could remember every detail of every lap in a race, down to what the oil pressure was in turn 7 on lap 45: the minutest details like that.

I have used the digression to make a point about learning to play jazz. When I started there was no one teaching jazz and virtually no decent books to refer to. We had to make our own way and success was a lot to do with how much you wanted to play and how much you were prepared to search for your own path. I guess, if I was able to make progress, it was because I realised the only way was to use my ears, my imagination and to do anything it took to achieve my goal. I'm sure my nightly efforts, imagining myself playing onstage and making up solos in my head, were an invaluable aid, in spite of my feelings of slight embarrassment about my strange bedtime fantasies! I have always believed that if you want to play jazz, you need to be able to sing solos and hear music in your mind, even before you buy your first instrument. These days young musicians are taught so much about which notes and scales to play on which chords, but they are seldom told just to listen and sing things in their head that sound good with the music they hear. Original musical ideas come from something beyond the mechanics of correct notes for particular chords. If the idea is good, the notes will work with the harmony. A strong melodic phrase can even have the power to convince you a 'wrong' note is right. If you have talent and you listen hard and long enough to good jazz performances, you acquire an instinct for what works and what doesn't. But even when you grasp this, you must, of course, still work hard at learning your way around the horn, honing your ears and your technique. If I hadn't realised this when I started I would never have made progress at all.

Having already begun playing in my head, I had to figure out a way to get my hands on an instrument. With no immediate help from my parents I looked to my model-making skills. If I could draw and scale up plans for models and make them, could-n't I use my skills to make a clarinet? First I needed to find out how a clarinet worked and what the correct dimensions of the instrument were. The local library was a great help. I found a book on the clarinet that had fingering charts and good clear photos of side and plan views. It also gave the exact overall length of the instrument. Armed with this information it was fairly easy to work out a scale factor from the photos and draw up a set of plans, complete with the correct positions for the tone holes. This was the easy part. Making the thing was a different matter. The first problem was I didn't possess a lathe. The only way I could make the cylindrical body was to use a piece of wooden dowel, saw it into two halves lengthways, hollow the two halves out with a wood carving tool and then join them back together again. It was tough going but I managed to produce the body of the instrument and something that vaguely resembled a mouthpiece. I knew right from the start that the biggest problem was going to be the keywork parts. Sawing and filing them out of mild steel would be best, but it would take months with the few hand tools I had. The other option was to make them from aluminium and attach them to the necessary brass tubes. Aluminium was much easier to work with a file and hacksaw, and the rods and rod holders could be made from piano wire and brass tubing. As I had foreseen, the problem then was to join the keys to the brass tubes through which the axle rods would go. I could solder steel to brass but you cannot solder aluminium. If epoxy adhesives had been around then there would not have been a problem, but the only thing available was a useless glue called Liquid Metal. This revolting stuff was supposed to set into a substance that could join metal to metal. It did at first but any kind of strain on the joint made it fall apart. This was to be my undoing, but not before I had made the top three keys, put pads in them and fixed a reed to the mouthpiece. Believe it or not, I got real notes out of the contraption! Only the middle G, G-sharp, A and B-flat, but real notes! Before I could get any further, the keys all fell off! To my intense frustration I had to give up. However, I still had the body of the clarinet and a fingering chart, so I set myself to learning the fingering, silently practising scales on what was, for all intents and purposes, a short length of broom stick with imaginary keys.

My parents watched all this with incredulity tinged with pity and one morning Mum told me she had had a word with Dad and they had decided that I might be serious about wanting to play the clarinet after all; if I could find one cheap enough, they would buy it for me. I had already seen an old Simple System B-flat clarinet on sale in a local secondhand shop for £4 10 shillings and I became its proud owner.

My home-made clarinet was consigned to the dustbin. A couple of days later I took the new horn with me on a family visit to Uncle Alf's house in Boston Manor. He was the pianist of the family so I figured he could give me some tips. At first we couldn't understand why, when I played a note, it was always a tone away from what uncle was playing on the piano. He assured me there was probably nothing wrong with my expensive new acquisition and I soon discovered the clarinet was a transposing instrument and I would have to play the piano parts a tone up.

I threw myself into learning the instrument, working through exercise books I had found, trying to copy what I heard on my few records and having a go at improvising simple solos. I made rapid progress and the clarinet seemed a lot more natural to play than the violin or piano. As there was no way my parents could afford to send me to music college, I compensated by working twice as hard at home. In any case I knew you couldn't learn much about jazz in an academy. In those days the music establishment viewed jazz as not worth serious study. So I figured I must find out about every aspect of music myself and searched the library for all the books I could find on the instrument and the theory of music. I borrowed dreary old tomes on harmony and counterpoint and found them as intimidating as Latin had been at school. However, I also discovered the Otto Langley *Tutor for Clarinet*, an excellent book covering every aspect of the instrument. There was no mention of jazz in it but, along with progressive exercises in all keys, the book had fine duets and difficult passages from the classical repertoire. There was enough there to keep me occupied for years. I was finally on my way but the time had come to look for my first, and what turned out to be my last, 'proper' job. Learning the clarinet was all right, but my parents insisted I should get a job and earn some money.

With only four 'O' level GCEs and any thoughts of further study far from my mind, my options were limited. An offer came up that didn't sound too bad if I could pass the interview. The Directorate of Colonial Surveys (soon renamed the Directorate of Overseas Surveys, DOS) was looking for trainee cartographers. The offices were right on my doorstep and the work sounded tolerably interesting. I got through the interview and was offered the job at £4 per week. As a civil servant I had to sign the Official Secrets Act. This all sounded intriguing and I wondered what top-secret government work I might get involved in. I knew I would be working on maps and poring over aerial photographs: maybe one day I would be secretly parachuted into some distant enemy territory if I played my cards right. The reality was, of course, very different; every civil servant, even the tea lady, had to sign the Official Secrets Act.

I started, as a lowly trainee, processing aerial photographs. I was given a pile of them, with an overlap of about forty per cent between each. The idea was to place them together and squint at them through a small plastic viewer. The photos were moved about until you could see the whole terrain in wonderful 3D. The mountains jumped out at you, as if you were seeing them from the aeroplane itself. Then you had to find two points of reference, such as a tree, road or bend in a river, and mark them very accurately by pricking both photos with a special compass point. Then you had to draw a ring, in chinagraph pencil, around the tiny pricks in the paper, so they could easily be located in a later process. I enjoyed it at first, but eight hours a day squinting through that damned viewer soon began to drive me crazy. The work was not so bad if you were dealing with mountainous country but all I ever got were flat areas of featureless jungle. Finding any kind of reference points, when every tree looks the same, is almost impossible. Others seemed to be able to do it but, as my boss pointed out, I couldn't.

My workmates were a good bunch but I spent more and more time going AWOL to the toilet or sneaking extra tea breaks. This didn't go down too well with my superior but he gave me one last chance, in the photo writing room. This was a long darkened room filled with 'light desks' – big drawing boards made of glass with a bright light that shone through a huge glass negative of a map. You had to re-touch the negatives in fine detail with a brown, opaque ink. Staring through a magnifying glass at the blinding white map lines, in a darkened room all day, was worse than squinting through the 3D viewers. At one end of the room was a big storage rack containing dozens of the glass maps. Each one, we were told, was worth several thousand pounds. There must have been two hundred or more. In the end I constantly had to stop myself from getting up and smashing the whole damned lot. After about a year, I knew I would never be any good at the work and that the sack was imminent, so I handed in my resignation. My father's words about 'quitting when the going gets tough' began to haunt me again but, while I was at DOS, I did meet two people there who helped to get my career in music started.

I had got to know one of the younger guys, in another depart-ment, who took me to a local youth club some evenings. I wasn't keen at first, as rough characters hung around the place, but maybe there was a chance of meeting some girls. I didn't have any luck in that department, but it did help me to loosen up a bit. Even though I had good friends at school, I always had a tendency to shyness in a crowd and still found it difficult to mix with people of my own age, especially girls. My interests and sensibilities made me more at home with older people like my aeromodelling friends than with the average teenager. When my new-found mate heard I was learning the clarinet, he told me about an older guy at DOS who was a trumpet player and had a band. He urged me to go with him to a pub in Kingston called the Swan and sit in with his friend's group. I told him I had only been playing three months and there was no way I could play with a band yet. But he insisted. Finally I bucked up courage and we went down to the place one Saturday night. The trumpet player, Alan Rosewell, had a dixieland outfit and played pretty good New Orleans-style trumpet. I was scared even to enter this dark, steamy back room, let alone think of trying to play with what sounded to me like a damned good jazz band. I figured I wouldn't get asked to play anyway, so I sat and listened to the music.

In the interval I was introduced to Alan, and to my consternation, he asked me to sit in for a number during the next set. I tried to explain I had only just started learning the clarinet, but he brushed that aside and my mate egged me on. There was not much I could do but get up and probably make a fool of myself. He called an old tune called 'Ice Cream' which I'd never heard before but it was in B-flat, a key I had practised in a bit, so I noodled away in the ensemble as best I could. Suddenly Alan looked in my direction and told me to take the next solo chorus. Shaking with fear I did my best to hear the simple harmonies and managed to produce half reasonable noises, until I realised I had no idea when to stop playing. I nearly panicked, but there was a point in the music that sounded like it might be a good place. I wound up my solo, expecting to be laughed off the stage. Instead, people applauded enthusiastically. The band carried on and I returned to my tentative ensemble role. Alan thanked me and I left the stage to more applause as the regular clarinettist returned to finish the gig. I had survived my first attempt to play in public but then, at the end of the night when everyone was packing up their instruments, Alan came over to me, explained that his regular clarinettist was leaving and asked me to join the band, starting the following Saturday. I couldn't believe it, but he was serious. I was to show up for a rehearsal.

Sure that I would now be 'found out', I nervously kept the appointment. Alan called a tune I didn't know. 'That's OK,' he said. 'Go and see the banjo player and he'll show you the chords.' Having little idea what he meant I went over to the amiable guy, wearing 'mouldy fig' sandals and a huge sweater. He pulled from his pocket a little notebook with weird marks in it. I had never seen or heard of a chord symbol before, but he strummed some harmonies and showed me the corresponding hieroglyphics in his book. When I heard the chords I found I recognised them, 'E flat 7th? Oh that's what it's called, is it?' I said. He smiled benignly, 'Yeah, you've got it.' I got through the rehearsal and was determined to study chord symbols until I had them down.

That's how I joined my first band and that dixieland banjo player was the guy who set me on the road to learning jazz harmony and how chords were notated. I stayed with the group for quite a while and, although it was only a semi-pro band, it was pretty good and an excellent way to start my playing career. I seemed to be accepted as a fellow-musician after only playing for a few months. Mum and Dad were cautiously optimistic and I made almost as much on a Saturday night as I made all week at the DOS. I have a lot to thank my youth club mate for. If he hadn't dragged me along to the Swan that night, it might have been years before I played in public, if ever. The only problem was that we discovered my old clarinet was what they called 'high pitch', making it difficult to play in tune with the rest of the band. Brass bands used to play to a slightly sharper tuning than normal and the instrument was obviously made for that kind of work. It was also a simple system clarinet and most clarinettists at this time used the improved, but more complex, Boehm system.

I coped with the pitch problem by tweaking the tuning barrel a bit but I obviously needed a better horn. I soon saved enough to acquire a brand new Boehm system clarinet for about £25, the cheapest in the Boosey and Hawkes range.

While I was still at the DOS, I heard Bird - Charlie Parker - and was so bowled over by his electrifying music that I decided to take up the alto sax, as well as clarinet. One reason for getting the job had been to be able to buy equipment, like the new clarinet. My parents always did their best to help me and never asked me to contribute a penny towards my upkeep while I was living at home. I guess they decided to give me my head, for a while at least. I owe them so much. I would become an even greater burden on them in the years to come, but at least by the time they died they knew I had made some kind of success in music, even if it would never bring much financial reward.

I began hearing a lot of Bird on Willis Conover's *Jazz Hour* and couldn't wait to get hold of his records. The shop where I bought my first clarinet also sold a few secondhand 78s. It must have been fate because the only jazz record they had was a Charlie Parker disc. Not only that but, when I got it home and I put it on, the first side I heard was 'Night in Tunisia', with Bird's mesmerising four bar break. On the other side was 'Ornithology'. I couldn't have picked a better disc if I had tried. Even today, that four bar break in 'Night in Tunisia' remains one of the most awesome examples of musical bravura, mind-blowing in its speed and rhythmic and melodic complexity. I had heard it said by so-called experts that Bird played ugly, incomprehensible solos, filed with wrong notes. I never felt this. To me everything I heard him play was beautifully melodic and right. It was just that he played everything so damned fast.

I got hold of a copy of *Jazz, Its Evolution and Essence* by French musicologist André Hodier. Hodier was probably the first serious musician to write a proper analysis of the mechanics and aesthetics of jazz and his essays on Bird, Lester Young and Louis Armstrong are still among the finest I have read. Everything he wrote made sense to my young mind and, coupled with my study of recordings, it taught me things that are still valid to this day. The book included solo transcriptions that I studied avidly, stimulating me to transcribe many more Parker solos for myself. I owe a lot of my rapid progress at the time to my determination to spend as long as it took transcribing and learning to play dozens of great jazz solos. I would spend days on end struggling with the most difficult Bird solos and would not give up until I had figured them out, written them down in their entirety and learnt to play them. In those days you couldn't obtain sheet music copies of Bird's tunes, let alone transcriptions of his solos.

I met more and more musicians, some of whom invited me to the Bun Shop club in Surbiton, a baker's shop that turned into a jazz club in the evenings. I had managed to buy a terrible old

Besson alto saxophone and would play it there sometimes. At that club I got to meet people who became very close friends: Del Cooper, a good clarinettist; valve trombonist Johnny Sterckx; Eric Davis, a crazy fun-loving Scot who played drums and vibes; and trumpeter Gus Galbraith who eventually joined the Johnny Dankworth band with me. Gus came from a northern show business family and always impressed me with his confident manner onstage. He had a strong belief in his ability and seemed to relish the role of bandleader, something I always found painfully difficult. I also first met the precociously talented Dick Morrissey around this time. He was playing Johnny Dodds-style clarinet then, with rubber bands all over his instrument to replace broken springs. Some jazz purists back then considered that playing an old broken instrument helped you get that authentic New Orleans sound.

Dick had no interest in sartorial elegance and always dressed in what looked like a worn-out school uniform, complete with a tatty old school tie that was too short. The band at the Bun Shop was a strange ensemble to say the least. It was nominally a traditional jazz band, run by an over-zealous, jazz purist, trumpet player whose idol was Bunk Johnson. Del had a Dodds-influenced style, but a far more catholic taste in jazz. Johnny Sterckx was an oddball who played in a style that ranged from Kid Ory, through Jack Teagarden, to Bob Brookmeyer. Eric Davis, who played good drums and vibes, was more of a modernist and loved Milt Jackson. Imagine a group with Bunk Johnson, Johnny Dodds, Bob Brookmeyer and Milt Jackson, joined by someone trying to play Charlie Parker solos on 'Tiger Rag', and you will get the idea. It was certainly unique, but it kind of worked and the audience seemed to dig it. Fusion? Ha! We invented it!

Del, John, Eric and I began meeting socially almost every afternoon at the Cona Bar in Tolworth, one of the new coffee bars. These daily meetings became a kind of ritual and we talked for hours about music, art, science, sex and philosophy. John turned me onto the Russian philosopher Gurdjieff, who I began to read avidly. Del was a fine artist and I was crazy about bebop,

Bartók, philosophy, relativity theory and aeroplanes. Of course we all thought, with varying degrees of passion, we would soon discover the true 'meaning of life' and solve all its mysteries. Eric Davis provided the down-to-earth humorous counter-balance to our aesthetic debates. He just loved life, music and women and was always waking us up from our reveries to jump into his old Morris Minor 1000 and roar off somewhere for a laugh. He had a broad Glaswegian accent and when he had had enough of our philosophising, he would put on a big, rotting-teeth grin and say, 'Och! Come on guys! Let's away and go wenching.' He was a sales representative for the Creamola custard company and brilliant at his job. He never left a client until he had sold something. I'm sure they bought stuff in the end, just to get rid of him. He was always extolling the virtues of a new product called Creamola Foam, an obnoxious powder that made a foamy drink tasting like fruit-flavoured washing-up liquid. He almost convinced us of its wonderful taste, but not quite.

Del Cooper taught art and is a fine painter, having exhibited paintings at the Royal Academy. He had another great talent though: he was an amazing mimic. We all used to imitate the *Goon Show* characters but Del would have us in fits mimicking people he heard gossiping in shops or pubs, their voices and sub-urban mannerisms. It was a talent he later applied to many char-acters we met in the music business. He was great fun to have around. It was a wonderful period in our lives, full of energy and promise of great things to come. The only ominous side was my growing fascination with the seamier side of jazz and of Charlie Parker in particular. I was taking far too much interest in stories about heavy drug use in the jazz business. Later it would lead me to disaster but for the moment the use of hard drugs was merely a point of philosophical discussion in the coffee bar.

My main preoccupation was learning the alto and by mutual agreement I left Alan Rosewell's band. It was better for both of us as I was now bent on playing bebop, not dixieland. I began working with a new band, led by Gus Galbraith, the trumpeter

I had met at the Bun Shop. Gus put together an excellent group that played material from the swing era. He sounded a little like Buck Clayton and his band swung hard and sounded pretty professional. Dick Morrissey was on clarinet, Johnny Sterckx played valve trombone and I was on alto. We also had a guy called Alan Vale as a kind of manager. Alan got us a few gigs and ended up as MC at the Marquee Club. He arranged for us to do

Gus Galbraith Band, *ca.* 1958, including Johnny Sterckx (tbn), PK (alto), Galbraith (tpt) and Dick Morrissey (clar).

a demo record to promote the band and even managed to fix us a tour of Denmark. We were supposed to play several venues there but it didn't quite work out that way. I was excited to travel abroad for the first time but worried about the sea trip. I had begun suffering from a kind of agoraphobia, which manifested itself in a tendency to feel nauseous when I travelled. I had an aversion to throwing up, even as a child, but was now becoming quite paranoid about it. I was nervous of being away from home and scared of being seasick on the boat. The sea crossing to Esbjerg was rough and from there we had to take the train to Copenhagen.

In the railway station at Esbjerg, I had a weird and unsettling experience. I thought I was going to collapse, because my head started spinning and I found it difficult to keep my balance. It was just a case of 'land legs', a condition well known to sailors. Because I had got used to the motion of the boat, the railway platform felt like the deck of the ship and I had to adjust to walking on terra firma again. When we arrived in Copenhagen, we discovered that not only were we without accommodation but most of the gigs had been cancelled, or had never existed. Alan's plans turned out to be optimistic, to say the least. We were stranded for a whole week, with no money and only two gigs. I freaked out and wanted to go home. I even went to the British Embassy to see if they could help, much to the guy's amusement. There was no help from Her Majesty's Government, which was hardly surprising, but after we found some cheap digs, I relaxed a bit and made the most of it. To his credit, Alan had arranged for us to play the interval spot at the famous Montmartre Club in Copenhagen. I knew Bird had played there during his Scandinavian tour and was very excited just to stand in a place where Charlie Parker himself had actually played. The gigs went well enough and to my intense relief, we all got back safely; but my travel phobia was becoming a real problem and one that caused me grief for several years. In fact my fear of seasickness almost cost me my job with Johnny Dankworth's band a little later.

Things started moving quickly after the Danish fiasco. I worked with a band run by Bob Barter, and was beginning to get known locally as an up-and-coming alto player. Bob ran a commercial big band that played regularly for dances around the local area. Although I could read music, I was not a sight-reader and so was a little reluctant to join. Bob told me not to worry; the only way to learn was by actually doing it. I had been having saxophone lessons with Don Honeywell, an excellent baritone player who worked with Oscar Rabin's band, resident at the Lyceum Ballroom in the Strand. Don would bring some of Oscar's alto parts to my lessons, so I could practise sight-reading from real band parts. After a while, he told me there was nothing more he could teach me and that I just needed experience. This gave me the confidence to take the risk and join Bob's band.

Because Don played baritone, I went through a phase of wanting to play the big horn too. I had a passing passion for Gerry Mulligan and bought myself an old instrument. One day, as I was getting off the bus going to a lesson, some wag watching me struggle with the baritone in its case, yelled, 'What ya got in there, mate, a bleeding submarine?' I sold the thing a week later and bought my first cheap piano instead, a very wise move as I could now play chords on it and learn more about harmony.

Like many minor commercial bands, Bob Barter's played mostly stock Jimmy Lally arrangements. Lally had made a fortune arranging standards so they could be played by any number and combination of instruments. Unfortunately the very name, Jimmy Lally, was rather a joke among hipper musicians, as his arrangements were considered about as corny as you could get. Years later I was actually introduced to him in the Captain's Cabin, the pub we frequented when we did broadcasts from the old BBC Paris Studios in Regent Street. When someone asked, 'Pete, have you met Jimmy Lally?' it was all I could do to keep a straight face, but I found he was a charming, lively old man and an excellent musician. He knew all about the hilarity his writing caused and quite enjoyed his notoriety, I think. He told me how difficult it was to churn out the hundreds of charts he wrote and make them work with anything from just a piano to a full symphony orchestra. He did a good job and enabled hundreds of struggling dance bands to acquire libraries of music for very low cost.

Bob Barter helped me enormously by giving me good work and allowing me to learn to sight-read on the job. I played with that band many times, even much later in my career, especially when times got tough and there was not much work around. Bob has had some of the best guys working with him over the years and the music business is richer for his eccentric character. He really is an eccentric too. He would play Basie arrangements, conducting from the piano, and get up to cut the band off at the end, forgetting he had to play Basie's famous last 'Plink, Plink, Plink' on the piano. There would be two bars of silence, broken only by guffaws of laughter from the band, before the last chord, while Bob made a frantic dash across the stage back to the empty piano stool.

The Swan in Kingston, where I had played with Alan Rosewell on Saturdays, had a modern jazz night on Fridays. Ted Potter, a local drummer who owned a music shop, ran the club and featured many of the top modern jazz artists. This is where I first heard great players like Ronnie Scott, Tubby Hayes, Jimmy Deuchar, Joe Harriott, Derek Humble, Don Rendell and Phil Seamen. I began to meet some of these celebrated musicians at the all-night joints whenever I could get a lift into town. There was the Pad, run by Sam Widges, open nearly twenty-four hours a day. You could eat and drink in the daytime and it must have been the only cafe in London that had Bird and Billie Holiday on the juke box. Then there was the Mandrake Club in Meard Street. Musicians frequented these small dark places after hours, and would get together for impromptu sessions that often lasted until daylight. To a young musician from the suburbs it was exciting and a little frightening. Some pretty shady characters used to hang around, listening to the music. There were prostitutes, pimps, junkies, drug dealers and gangsters, but I soon got to know many of them and they rarely caused any trouble. One guy in particular seemed a permanent fixture at these joints. Always dressed in black, he was painfully thin, with a whitish-grey pallor to his haunted-looking face. His name was Denis Rose and he seemed to take a liking to me, encouraging me to get up and play. Denis played piano but other musicians told me he had originally been a trumpet player and was in fact quite a legend. He was the first British musician to figure out exactly what bebop was about. He understood the new harmonic and melodic ideas before anyone else and passed his knowledge on to the new generation of British musicians. Everyone had a high regard for Denis but he had become a shadowy Soho figure and never received the acclaim he deserved. He was very kind to me though, introducing me to people and helping me feel more at home in Soho's intimidating environment.

As my name got around I started getting asked to play at suburban clubs around the west of London, mostly back rooms in pubs. Venues like the White Hart in Acton and the Star and Garter in Putney would have regular gigs featuring a house rhythm section and sometimes a horn player, with a famous guest artist. I met Don Rendell early on. I also remember sitting in with Douggie Roberts, a fine trumpet player. I was very excited to play with him, as he was working with the widely acclaimed Johnny Dankworth Seven at the time. A semi-pro tenor player, Frank Noble, invited me to play at the Star and Garter and I first played there with Bobby Wellins, already one of Britain's most original voices on tenor.

At the White Hart, I met a host of star players. Week after week I played with a string of top names: Don Rendell, Jimmy Skidmore, Kathy Stobart, Bert Courtley, Harry Klein and others. I seemed to be able to hold my own and the word spread that there was a new young alto player on the scene. The first time I worked with Hank Shaw was a little difficult. Hank was with Joe Harriott's fabulous quintet. He was a great trumpeter with a prodigious and fluid technique. The first tune he called was Miles Davis' 'Tune Up'. I said I didn't know it but he just snapped back, 'It's easy, you'll hear it.' I asked him what key it was in and he said, 'It's in D.' Now this is B on alto, an unusually difficult key with five sharps. He could see I was flustered but simply grinned menacingly and called out the whole chord sequence. 'OK, Pete?' he asked and counted in the rhythm section. He forgot to tell me 'Tune Up' was also at a breakneck tempo of around 350 bars a minute. 'Christ!' I thought, 'This is it, the game's up.' But I did my best and after a couple of choruses I began to get the hang of it. I'd played fast tempos before, but not in five sharps. Hank was quite impressed and the rest of the evening went great. He gave me another roasting a year or two later, but only because he reckoned I was the only guy good enough to deputise for Joe Harriott one night, in Joe's own quintet when he was hospitalised with TB.

The most memorable day at the White Hart was when Tubby Hayes came to guest. If I could survive playing with Tubby, I could really consider I was doing OK. He was the supreme master of modern jazz tenor with a phenomenal technique and a hard-edged, 'take no prisoners' attitude on the bandstand. He seemed to accept my presence and didn't try to make things hard for me. I was very nervous but did my best not to show it. Funnily enough, although he didn't say much on the gig, I heard later that what impressed him most was how relaxed I was when I played. If he had only known! In fact he probably did know, but maybe liked the way I covered it up. In the macho world of modern jazz that was a sign you had what it took, provided you could play your butt off as well.

Another great thing at the White Hart was meeting Gordon Beck. He was only a semi-pro at the time, working as a drafts-man in the aircraft industry, but he had an exceptional talent. A little older than me, he would drive me home after the gigs and stay late chatting about music, in spite of having to drive back and get up early next morning to go to his day job. To me Gordon played as well, if not better, than any other pianist I had heard in Britain. His playing really moved me emotionally too. He had great technique, an exquisite touch, using the pedals far more than most jazz pianists I had heard, and he conveyed depth and sensitivity through the keyboard. He sent shivers down my spine, like when I heard Bud Powell play. I felt Gordon was wasted as a draftsman and I was right. I didn't know it then but I was soon to be partly instrumental in him quitting his job and turning professional.

Around this time I got to meet Kathy Stobart, a first class tenor player who is well loved and respected in a very male-dom-inated world. She liked my playing and introduced me to pianist and vibraphonist Bill Le Sage. Bill and Kathy were working with the Tony Kinsey Quintet and Kathy persuaded Tony to let me sit in one night with the group at the Flamingo Club in Wardour Street. The Flamingo was one of the premier modern jazz clubs then, so this was a great opportunity. Bill also gave me a lot of encouragement and I think he had a plan in mind for me. I played a couple of tunes and everyone in the band was very complimentary. Tony was about to reform his group and I guess Bill thought he should hear me with a view to booking me. I was a little disappointed to discover Tony had already booked Alan Branscombe on alto, but Bill told me he was sure it was only a matter of time before I stepped up to the limelight and, sure enough, my chance to work at a top venue was very close. That night at the Flamingo, I was introduced to the owner of the club, Sam Kruger. Sam was an intimidating man, typical of West End nightclub owners in those days, and his sons became very big in the burgeoning British blues and rock scene. During the evenings top modern jazz groups worked at the Flamingo but, after the evening session finished, the place was cleared and reopened for the all-night session, with mostly black customers from the West Indies, Africa, or the American armed services – there were many US bases in the UK in those days. The all-night sessions had an atmosphere of their own where both jazz and blues bands worked and hung out together, jamming and chatting to the early hours.

One night I popped into the Pad and Denis Rose was there chatting to Ronnie Scott. There was hardly anyone else in the joint as it was quite early. Denis asked if I wanted to play and I said I'd love to but there was no one around who played drums. He asked Ronnie, who he had just introduced me to for the first time, if he would play drums with us. We had a bass player but I had no idea that Ronnie ever played drums. 'OK,' said Ronnie. I remember we played just one tune, 'Now's the Time', and then Ronnie got up from the kit, mumbled something to Denis and walked out into the night. He probably had to go somewhere else but, being nervous about our first meeting, I took his actions to mean he wasn't impressed with what was going on and especially with me. He'd hardly spoken to me the whole time, after all. This was just after the news had broken that Ronnie, with his business partner Pete King, was about to open his own club. A week or two later I went to the Mandrake to sit in and was just getting my horn out of the case when I felt a hand on my shoulder. I turned round and there was Ronnie Scott. To my amazement and delight he asked, 'Pete, will you play at the opening of my new club?' It was an incredible moment for me, especially after my experience a week or so before, when he had seemed distinctly 'underwhelmed' at my presence. At last my big chance had come. I rushed home to tell my parents and all my friends and set myself to practise non-stop until the opening night, 30 October 1959.

Still suffering from my stupid travel phobia, I was dreading taking the train into town for the opening night. It was fine as long as someone was driving me, but travelling alone was a big problem and I didn't want it to ruin my big chance. Luckily my father offered to drive me and give me moral support. I had mixed feelings as, although I wanted him to see my gig, I wondered if it wasn't a bit un-cool to have your dad with you at a jazz club. The club was full to bursting on the opening night. Several groups were billed and the place was full of famous musicians. Tubby Hayes and Ronnie Scott were heavily featured and I went on half way through the evening for my one short set with pianist Eddie Thompson, Spike Heatley on bass and Jack Parnell on drums. (Ronnie's *Melody Maker* advert called it Jack's 'first appearance in a jazz club since the relief of Mafeking.') It all seemed a blur but, scared as I was in front of such illustrious company, I must have played OK because I got a warm reception both from the musicians and the audience. That was it – now I could relax and enjoy the rest of the night.

Dad told me how proud he was of me, which was wonderful to hear, and he beamed as everyone congratulated me. I tried to introduce him to the famous musicians I had told him about. Pete King, Ronnie, Tubby, Jack Parnell all shook his hand and said nice things about me. Then I spotted Phil Seamen. Phil was his usual crazy, larger-than-life self, shambling about and looking stoned, with his vaguely threatening aura. I had told my father all about Phil, his genius as a drummer and his drug addiction. I wanted to introduce him to Dad, but was nervous about how Phil would react. He didn't give a damn what people thought and might say or do anything. I didn't know him that well yet so, when I asked him to meet my father, I was delighted to see him turn round, make a huge effort to pull himself up to his full height, take a deep breath and shake Dad's hand. He seemed to sense he had to be on best behaviour and addressed my father with a dignified voice. His whole demeanour had changed and my father beamed when Phil told him how pleased he was to meet him and what a talented son he had. Once I got to know Phil I discovered how much he loved his own mom and dad and how he would always be on his best behaviour in their presence. Dad and I were in heaven and we drove home in the early hours after a night neither of us will forget. Mum was delighted the next day when we told her all about it. It seemed I had at last found a career I could be successful in.

Soon after the opening of Ronnie's club, Pete King asked me if I would get a quartet together and do a regular spot there. I said yes, of course, but it presented some problems. For a start I didn't know any good musicians well enough to ask them to work in my own band. The other thing was my continual phobia about travelling. I decided to seek help with the phobia later and deal with the immediate problem of getting a band together. In fact I never did fix myself a band – it was fixed for me by a guy called Dickie De Vere. Pete King was not happy about it because, although Dickie had been a great drummer, he was a shell of his former self due to heroin addiction. I had played with him several times at all-night joints and when he was on form, he was still brilliant, similar in some ways to Phil Seamen. I had also seen him so stoned he could hardly play. He happened to be there when Pete asked me to form the group and, before I could answer, Dickie just told Pete, 'I'll play drums and I've got a good bass player.' I was a difficult situation. Pete couldn't think of anyone else right then so I went along with Dickie and hoped he would keep straight enough to do the gig. The bass player was a young guy I had played with before, but who could I get on piano? I thought of Gordon Beck. He was the only pianist I knew well enough to ask and Pete seemed happy about it when I told him how good he was. Gordon was thrilled to do it, but there was a problem. The gigs at Ronnie's would not finish until about 3 a.m. and he still had to get up for his office job every morning. He finally agreed, saying he would just have to get by with very little sleep.

It worked out fine for a while until Dickie started to mess up. One night he was taking barbiturates by the handful, onstage while he was still playing, and the tempo got slower and slower. The funny thing was, he was so bombed out he looked up at me, as if it was the bass player's fault or something, and said in a despairing drawl, 'Hey Pete, what the hell's going on, man? If it gets any slower, it'll be going backwards!' It was all I could do to keep a straight face; Dickie had the same genius for words that Phil had. But things couldn't go on like this and we had to find another drummer. I had an unhealthy fascination about Dickie as he was the first guy I got to know well who was using heroin. I would ask him about it and how it felt. One day he took me to the big toilet in Piccadilly Circus, saying he needed a fix. I was scared, but went with him. He used to tip the attendant to let him use the washroom. In those days public conveniences often had special cubicles where you could lock the door and wash or shave. Once we were both safely locked inside, Dickie showed me the whole ritual of taking a fix. I had read about it in books but now I saw it for real: the heated spoon, the lighted matches, the cotton wool to filter the liquid, blood drawn up into the syringe, everything. It was quite a shock and I think he wanted to put me off any ideas I might have of touching the stuff myself. It did the trick, for a while at least.

I still had to sort out my phobias and my father got help through one of his work associates who knew a good psychiatrist. His name was Dr Gordon Ambrose and he was an eminent authority on the use of hypnosis in treating psychiatric problems. I have seen a few shrinks over the years but the only ones who did any good were those I could relate to on a human level, pretty much the way a good friend can help. Dr Ambrose and one child therapist were the only ones who ever helped me. Being basically neurotic, I have usually had better results treating myself. This is what happened eventually with my vomiting phobia. I felt nauseous whenever I travelled alone, even though I knew it was all in my mind. But as soon as I told myself I was just imagining it and was not going to throw up, the nausea took on a new and sinister form. I would find myself saying, 'It's different this time, I really am going to vomit.' I would keep telling myself, 'This is bullshit, you are not going to be sick,' but to no avail. One day, on a bus, I told myself for the umpteenth time: 'You are just imagining this crap.' Suddenly it worked. That damned phobia just disappeared. It was a huge relief. I still don't like feeling nauseous, but the phobia had gone. I guess it's just like learning an instrument. You have to keep repeating a difficult phrase over and over until it suddenly 'falls under the fingers'.

Just after Ronnie Scott's Club opened I was voted 'New Star' in the *Melody Maker* awards for 1959. This was a real honour, something I could give my parents to hang on the wall at home. One spin-off was my first BBC broadcast. It went well and I wasn't too nervous. With all these things under my belt, I could face the future with some degree of confidence that I had made the right decision when I decided to be a jazz musician. Maybe I could do something to make my brother proud of me and repay my parents for all the grief I had given them. Unfortunately there were terrible storms ahead but, for the moment, things were definitely looking up.

3

'What d'ya wanna play, Pete?'
Bud Powell

Playing at Ronnie's, my first BBC broadcast and winning the 1959 *Melody Maker* 'New Star' award, all helped to gain me some recognition as an up and coming alto player. I figured, now I was playing alongside some of my British jazz heroes, I would soon be making a good living as a professional jazz musician. That shows you how naive I was in those days. I thought stars like Tubby Hayes, Derek Humble and Don Rendell were touring the UK and Europe, playing jazz to packed houses between stints at the Flamingo Club and Ronnie's, and were all making a good living playing jazz. I soon began to realise most jazz musicians, even the best, were only making real money by doing commercial work of some kind, either in dance bands or in much sought-after session (film, broadcasting or recording studio) work, which was fairly plentiful in those days, if you ever managed to get on 'The List' as they called it. I found that I had to continue more or less as before, playing semi-regular gigs around the London area and backing that up with any commercial work I could get. At least I could sight-read fairly well now, thanks to playing all those Jimmy Lally arrangements with Bob Barter's band. I had dedicated my life to playing jazz and had made good progress so far, but I still needed to justify my parents' support by trying to make a reasonable living. Many of the musicians I met advised me to get any commercial work I could and to keep jazz as an enjoyable sideline. It's called 'paying your dues', I was told. I tried to follow their advice as I respected their wealth of experience in the business and wanted to become a good all-round musician. But my real aim was still to climb to the very top of the jazz ladder or bust, naively thinking that all it took was lots of practice and patience.

Having got this far, I wasn't about to settle for a lifetime of commercial work, with a few jazz gigs when I could get them. Surely that wasn't all I had to look forward to, after all my dedication so far? Maybe I should have stuck with aerodynamics, or even cartography, and just played jazz for fun, at weekends. As I was to discover, this depressing scenario is the stuff of most jazz musicians' lives anywhere in the world, even in New York. My frustration reached a climax one night in Guildford. I was working around the area with a small band, led by Dave James, a very fine pianist and a really nice guy. We played music for dancing, but with as much jazz as Dave could get away with. One Christmas we were playing at a Yuletide dance and Dave insisted on all the usual corny sing-along tunes to keep the punters happy. I towed the line but after the gig, in an uncharacteristic fit of youthful arrogance, I told him I didn't intend to play that corny shit ever again. Dave told me angrily that no matter how well I made it in jazz, I would still be playing Christmas party gigs in thirty years time, like he was, and I had better get used to the idea. That really stuck in my craw and I vowed, then and there, to prove him wrong and I told him so. Dave gave me a lot of help and I learned a lot from him. Of course, he was right, I was still playing Christmas and New Year's Eve party gigs for years after that, but I never forgot that night. In fact I guess I've spent the rest of my life trying to prove him wrong and, knowing Dave, that's what he would have wanted.

Although I was by this time feeling my feet in the music world and learning to deal with some pretty frightening characters, like Pete King, the manager of Ronnie Scott's Club, I was still a seething mass of pubescent complexes and wracked with feelings of insecurity. I was doing my best to hide it all, but it must have been a source of mirth among the older jazz fraternity. For a start I suffered from bad acne, which is not the kind of image you associate with being a hip jazz musician. Not only that, but the boils hurt like hell too. Thankfully I could still pour out my woes to my mum, and to some extent my dad, but it would have been naive to expect much sympathy from the hard nuts I was mixing with on the jazz scene in London, let alone, maybe, in New York one day. It went without saying that if you were ever to become recognised internationally, you could only do so by paying your dues in the Big Apple. I hadn't yet figured out how I was going to get there, but knew it was going to be essential one day. With my sheltered background and my phobias, I tried not to think about it too much. Thank God, I didn't know then it would be over twenty-five years before I even visited the Big Apple, let alone make it there, but that comes later in the book.

I had a few close friends I could confide in. There was Gordon Beck, who at that time ran me a close second in the emotional wreck department, and there was Del Cooper, who always cheered me up and made me laugh. Some time later, Del even painted my portrait, in oils on canvas. And I could always talk to Bill Le Sage, who had done so much to help me into the business. He was like a second father to me and remained so, even when I was at my lowest ebb, struggling with drug addiction. In retrospect, even hard nuts like Tubby and Jimmy Deuchar were pretty good to me, showed me the ropes and made me feel reasonably at home in the tough, cliquey world of British modern jazz.

Portrait by Del Cooper, mid-1960s.

One night in Ronnie's, Pete King said he had arranged my first out of town gigs as a solo guest artist. The thought of leaving London brought back my phobia of travelling. It may seem strange but the idea of getting on a train, on my own, to another city, was daunting in the extreme and I knew I had to overcome my irrational fear or I would never make it in jazz or anywhere else. The first gig was in the Midlands, and Pete, who knew I was scared of travelling, assured me that the local promoter, Harry, would take good care of me. I managed to cope with the train ride and do the gig and, to my great relief, Harry offered to drive me all the way back to London. The journey marked another minor milestone in my life. Harry was a loveable and extremely hip guy, and sympathetic about my nervousness. In the car on the way home he suggested a smoke of pot would relax me. Of course I had been itching to try it, but was always too scared. In those days, if you didn't smoke pot, you felt you were not really a member of the inner circle. Harry took me in hand and told me not to worry; he wouldn't let anything bad happen to me. He rolled one up and I had my first taste. I was apprehensive, so took only small puffs at first, but it started to feel good once the high kicked in and, after my initial fear had worn off, we talked and laughed our heads off all the way back to London.

I started to buy 'grass' myself after that but at first I would only smoke it at home, usually late at night after I had come back from a gig. I found it relaxing and listening to music became a completely different experience. I seemed to hear strange new dimensions in music I thought I knew well. It took a while, though, before I felt able to play in public after smoking a joint. You need to practise playing under the influence first and I found it gave practice a new dimension. This reminds me of when Zoot Sims was asked, one night when he was so drunk he could hardly stand up, how he could still play so great. Zoot's answer was, 'Because I practise when I'm drunk.' In those days nearly all the best players seemed to me to be hard drinkers and many smoked dope and used cocaine. I was pretty much teetotal and had never found booze much help as I didn't enjoy its effect. This worried me to some extent and may have been one of the factors that led me into using heavy drugs. It seems strange now but being able to drink heavily and still play seemed as important then as eating right, working out, not smoking cigarettes and knowing how to promote yourself do today. As I never got much out of alcohol, I deluded myself into thinking that taking other drugs might gain me extra 'street cred'. The sad and scary fact is that, when I became a heroin addict, I did get a little tighter with some British and certain well-known American musicians, Philly Joe Jones being a prime example.

The original Ronnie Scott's Club was a tiny, almost uncomfortably intimate place to work and to hear music. When the first American artists appeared there, we knew we were experiencing something special. It's difficult to convey the uniqueness of that time to those who weren't there. A few British musicians had worked day after day playing commercial music on the Atlantic passenger liners, purely for the chance to spend one or two nights in New York and hear Charlie Parker, Dizzy Gillespie and others, playing on 52nd Street. I missed out on this and never heard Bird but, at Ronnie's, we all had the chance at last to hear an endless stream of other jazz greats. Not only could we hear them play from just a few feet away but often there was the chance to hang out and even jam with them on occasion. Stan Tracey and the house trio accompanied them all, six nights a week. The beauty of it was that, in most cases, the Americans were just as happy to find such an admiring audience as we were to enjoy their music and their company. The story of those early days at Ronnie's has often been told but I have my own special memories. What I treasure above all is my good fortune in being there in this unique historical period. I learnt so much from the experience.

At this time I had heard American musicians only on recordings. Jazz education, as we now know it, didn't exist. There were no 'real books', no jazz courses, not even any decent jazz harmony books. We had to learn the same way the Americans did, by listening to the best players around, working out harmony on the piano and practising exercises we made up ourselves or picked up from other musicians. We certainly never had the chance to practise improvising at home with a backing CD. After playing alone in our back rooms, we just had to take a chance on when we were ready to sit in with the local semi-pro jazz group, if we got the opportunity, and hope to God we didn't make complete fools of ourselves. It was a tough, lonely university but, if you survived your first jam session, you had a chance to get to know and learn from your 'betters' and, if you had talent and worked your butt off, you moved on up the ladder. When the Americans came, even the top British guys renewed their education. They were far too streetwise to let it show, but they all knew the pressure was on them to prove themselves good enough for the 'Premier League'. As it turned out, they mostly did pretty well, at least as far as gaining the respect of the American musicians was concerned, even if they did not obtain public recognition or regular work.

Two of the first guys to play over here were Al Cohn and Zoot Sims. Ronnie Scott couldn't have booked two better people to start the ball rolling. Zoot and Al were pure jazz incarnate. They loved to play, respected Stan's trio and positively relished working with it, and enjoyed laughing, drinking, chatting, getting high and hanging out. They swung their asses off night after night and had a ball, falling in love with England, the admiring audiences and the excellent musicians they met here. This atmosphere of mutual respect and the musical revelations we witnessed week after week became almost routine, with one or two exceptions, as one star followed another into the old Gerard Street club.

I'll never forget the first time Ben Webster came to Ronnie's. We were all impatient to see and hear the man who produced one of the most beautiful, distinctive saxophone sounds in jazz and I was at the club long before he arrived for his first night. Pete King had met most of the Americans in the US before they ever played at the club but I'm not sure if he had heard Ben before, other than on record. As I came in, Pete came up to me and, in an uncharacteristically emotional tone of voice, described how he had strolled into the club before Ben's rehearsal was due to start and heard an indescribably beautiful sound coming from the dimly lit room. All he could see was the top of a big hat, behind the piano. Ben was on his own, playing a ballad. Pete was in raptures. To hear that unique tone he knew so well from recordings was just spine-tingling, the more so because Ben was using no microphone. It was hard to believe that his sound, so huge and warm on record, was even more magnificent in the flesh, with no artificial amplification. At the gig that night we all felt the same. He used the mike, but he really didn't need it. That was a great lesson for any saxophone player, right there!

It was the British saxophonists that had the best deal by far when it came to learning from the Americans. In the first couple of years, Ronnie, of course, made sure most of the star visitors were saxophonists and, usually, tenor players. It was a little unfair on other instrumentalists from the States but great for us reed players. I think the most important lessons we learned were not so much about technical proficiency – guys like Ronnie and Tubby already had that in abundance – but things like tone production, phrasing and most important of all, developing your own style. That is the hardest lesson to learn. Ben Webster had to learn that himself when, after slavishly copying Coleman Hawkins, one of his peers scolded him: 'Well Ben, now you sound exactly like Hawk. When are you going to sound like Ben Webster?'

To be honest, the weakest link in Britain in those days tended to be rhythm sections and, as Ronnie was only booking solo artists from the States, we had to wait a while to hear the top American rhythm sections at close quarters. Stan Tracey, the regular house pianist, always had a great understanding of comping (accompanying a soloist), but many British pianists, drummers and bass players still had a little to learn about the finer points. Stan has always been a special case, providing just the right backing, prodding soloists into new areas, inspiring them as well as laying down strong rhythmical harmonic punctuation. His debt to Monk is often exaggerated by critics and others, but I always felt his comping was influenced more by Duke Ellington. Stan always transcended his influences, producing a unique style, entirely his own. Add to that his large legacy of original tunes and his great bands and it is not surprising that Sonny Rollins and later Lalo Schifrin, in particular, considered Stan to be one of the world's great jazz talents. There were other pianists with prodigious techniques who were great soloists, but they often played too many notes, and in the wrong places, behind a soloist. Mind you, as far as comping goes, I also have to include Oscar Peterson and Art Tatum amongst the guilty. Great trio and solo pianists don't necessarily make good accompanists. On the other hand, Terry Shannon, who is now sadly all but forgotten, was a great accompanist. Terry himself never claimed to be a great soloist, but his comping was sublime and his solos were always models of taste and swing. It was for very good reason that Tubby Hayes used him on piano so much.

As time went by, I got to know most of the guys who came over to play either at Ronnie's or on concert tours (I often played the relief band spot or the last set or just hung out after maybe working the Flamingo). Musicians from the Ellington or Basie bands would often arrive, after their London concerts, to hang out at Ronnie's and maybe sit in. For instance, when Duke was in town, Paul Gonsalves, Ray Nance and Cat Anderson would sometimes drop in, and when Basie came, Frank Wess, Eddie 'Lockjaw' Davis and a very boyish looking Frank Foster would sometimes play for a bit too. Later, when I could drive, I would offer guys a lift to their hotel, often the White House in Albany Street. It was a way of getting them on their own, hopefully for a chat and just to be around them.

It was a while before the great Don Byas worked at Scott's. He was an incredible tenor saxophonist. He had one of the biggest sounds I have ever heard and his technique was legendary. Like Hawkins, Don was able to adjust to the harmonic advances of bebop. He was a little guy but known for his physical strength, about which he often bragged, often getting people to punch him hard in the stomach to show how well developed his abdominal muscles were. Like Ben and Lockjaw, he always carried a knife in case of trouble. One night I plucked up the courage to offer him a lift to his hotel, but he wasn't ready to go to sleep. Instead he said 'I'm not tired yet, Pete. Let's go tenpin bowling.' This was 3 a.m. and, thinking I knew Soho a little, I ventured that there was nowhere open at this time of night to play bowls. Don knew better and, sure enough, he took me to a bowling alley in a basement in Shaftesbury Avenue. It turned out to be open twenty-four hours a day and I never knew of its existence before. I had hoped to gain some slight insight into Don's ideas on music (we did talk a bit about mouthpieces), but instead he gave me my first and only lesson in tenpin bowling, in the middle of Soho at three in the morning. He beat the pants off me, of course.

When Sonny Stitt first came over I was really excited. This was the man Charlie Parker respected so much, reputedly once telling Stitt he was handing him 'the keys to the kingdom'. When he came to London he was playing mostly tenor sax and just a bit of alto. Sonny played the larger horn in a more relaxed but very distinctive style. He electrified us every night on both alto and tenor and Ronnie and Sonny began to have late night Saturday jam sessions where a few special guests would join in. Ronnie, Tubby and I played a couple of times together with Stitt and everyone had a ball. Sonny could be a little difficult sometimes, especially after too many scotches. He had a very competitive streak and would do his best to 'cut' anyone who dared to play saxophone on the same stage. I think he felt he had met his match with Tubby and Ronnie though. He certainly did his best to cut my ass at first. But by the time I got to play with him, I must have 'got my shit together', as they say, because, after a tune or two testing our mettle, he relaxed and just enjoyed jamming the night out. Many years later I discovered I made quite an impression on him, but more of that later.

A year or so after Ronnie's opened, Johnny Dankworth asked me to join a new big band he was forming. He also booked Gus Galbraith, the trumpet player whose mainstream band I had played with when I first made the switch from clarinet to alto. I felt honoured to have the chance to work with such a great band. I was still concerned about my sight-reading, but I could read a lot better than Gus. He had very little experience at all in that department, but improved very fast.

Dankworth had just finished a highly successful American tour, sharing the bill with the Duke Ellington Orchestra, and he wanted to start a fresh band composed entirely of top jazz soloists. In fact it was made up of a good two-thirds of the old band, including old hands like Danny Moss on tenor and Kenny Clare on drums. John had great players like trumpeter Kenny Wheeler and Art Ellefson, a Canadian like Kenny, on tenor. It was probably one of the finest bands he had had up to that point, with excellent arrangements and a plethora of top soloists. One new face in the band was Dudley Moore. Dudley would have us in stitches on the band bus with impromptu sketches and impersonations, but I had no idea he would end up a big star in comedy and films. To most of us he was just a damned good pianist and a fun guy to be with on the road.

At first I felt out of my depth, surrounded by so many hardened pros, but I soon adapted, and learned a hell of a lot. I still needed someone to turn to when my insecurities surfaced, but guys like Tony Russell, George Tyndale, Bobby Breen, Ron Snyder and Ed Harvey (known affectionately as Uncle Ed) were always good to have in your corner. Tony and Ed were in the trombone section and Tony was also the road manager. Ron Snyder played tuba and was a really nice guy with an impressive physique. He used to work out all the time and in those days that was considered odd for a musician. George Tyndale and Bobby Breen were West Indians by birth and I got particularly close to them. George was well known for his beautiful, Ben Webster-like tenor playing, but he had to play baritone with Dankworth. John bought him one and he soon developed a huge Harry Carney-like sound. He used to look after me like a surrogate father and I really grew to love and respect him.

Bobby was the vocalist in the band and everyone loved him, even though he drove us mad at times. He was always full of enthusiasm and a good singer, except maybe for one problem: he had a lisp. He was the butt of endless friendly ribbing, for both his lisp and his hilarious attempts at being super hip. He would have us in hysterics every time he sang 'Laura'. He sang it great but every time he got to the line 'You're the face in the misty light', it would always come out as 'You're the *faith* in the *mithty* light!' My eleven months with John's band were like a final year at university where I gained lots of experience in sight-reading, and section playing. We did dances, concerts, festivals and clubs, and a lot of studio work for television, films and recordings, including John's hit record, 'African Waltz'. The experience led to me getting session work of my own in the years that followed. Two gigs that stick in my mind were the Beaulieu Jazz Festival, which ended in a riot in which quite a few people got hurt, and the Essen Jazz Festival, about which more later.

The only time I had been in a recording studio before doing so with Dankworth, was to make a demo with Gus Galbraith's band. I was really thrown in at the deep end with John because the first recording we made was 'Ebony Concerto', the piece specially written for Woody Herman's band by Igor Stravinsky. It was a difficult work with a lot of clarinet in my part. Thank God, the tricky solo clarinet part was played by the great classical virtuoso Gervase de Peyer. In the event we ended up with a very good LP, which also included other large-scale works with full orchestra; quite a mountain to climb for your first recording. I remember poor George Tyndale had a tricky solo baritone entry on one piece. We were being conducted by a famous and very autocratic German-American conductor, William

Steinberg, who was in charge of the Pittsburgh Symphony at the time. After George made several attempts at getting his entry right, we were all fearful for him, confronted by this Furtwängler-like figure. But the Teutonic maestro defused the situation to our great surprise by telling George with a fatherly smile, 'Please. Ven I give you my finger, you vill enter.' The recording light went red and sure enough, when the dreaded moment arrived, Herr Steinberg suddenly looked over at George, held his finger up with a smile and, to everyone's great relief, George made his entry bang on cue.

In the main, the sojourn with Dankworth was enjoyable and rewarding, except for two minor hiccups. The first concerned the band's tour of Ireland. We were up in the North East of England on a gig and had to travel through the night to catch an early morning ferry to Ireland, from North Wales. This meant a long overnight drive in the bus and I was very apprehensive about what looked like being a rough sea crossing. Things weren't helped by something that happened on the gig that night. We were playing a fast Afro Cuban-type chart and I was playing the lead sax line with the correct, slight pushing ahead of the beat that I thought the style demanded. Now after their tour opposite Duke's orchestra, the guys were always going on about a great lesson they learned from such close proximity to Ellington. They figured British bands tended to push the beat whereas Duke's guys were leaning back on it, giving a more relaxed feel. The Americans did mostly have a more relaxed feel and I still think this is one of the secrets of great jazz. However, I felt John's band were over-emphasising this and losing some attack at times. This was most noticeable to me when we played some Afro Cuban arrangements. I was pushing the section a bit but I was nominally the lead horn, so I thought I was right to play it that way. Suddenly Danny Moss and Art Ellefson shot me dagger-like looks shouting 'Pete, you're rushing the beat like mad!' I was upset and suddenly very unsure of myself again. I was brooding about it on the bus and when I got to the port and saw how rough the sea was, my anxiety and fear of seasickness overpowered me. I got on the boat OK, but then started to freak out. I had to get off and, as the gangway had been hauled in, I just climbed over the side onto the quay and got on the next train to London.

By the time I reached my parents' house I was in a depressed state and convinced this would be the end of my career. Later that afternoon my father said Johnny Dankworth was on the phone and wanted to talk to me. I was expecting John to give me hell and fire me, but instead he told me everyone was worried about me, including Art and Danny and especially Bobby Breen and George Tyndale. They had all seen me board the boat but then went straight to the bar and never gave me another thought until they docked in Ireland and couldn't find me. In fact they called the port authorities who set up some kind of search, thinking I might have fallen overboard or something. Fighting back my embarrassment, I told John what happened and about my fear of seasickness. To my complete surprise and relief, he told me they wanted me back on the tour and suggested I have a day to recover; then he would arrange to fly me out to Ireland and back again at the end of the tour. Overjoyed with relief, I agreed and jumped on a plane the next day.

When I arrived in Dublin, Danny Moss and Art Ellefson assured me that they were sorry about upsetting me on the bandstand. They hadn't meant to; I was just being over-sensitive. After that I played the Afro tune the way they played it and thoroughly enjoyed the rest of the tour. There was a funny twist to the story, much later after I had left the band. I returned to substitute for someone one day and John rehearsed that old tune again. He suddenly stopped the band and asked us to play the head again. Then he said. 'Hey guys, I think you're dragging it a bit, can you push it a bit more.' I couldn't avoid ribbing Danny and Art saying, 'See, I was right after all!'

The other, more terminal 'blip' with the band caused me to hand in my resignation, but it was part of a change taking place in my own musical path. I was getting unhappy about the over-riding Parker influence on my alto playing and, like some others before me, I wanted to try tenor sax for that reason, to open up to other influences and, hopefully, develop a more original style. I bought a new Selmer Mark VI tenor and started practising it. John said I could play some of my solos on tenor if I liked. This was fine but I started to run into opposition, mostly from Danny Moss, who rightly considered himself one of the most important solo voices in the band. He didn't take kindly to me playing tenor solos. Spike Heatley also tried to dissuade me, say-ing I just sounded like an alto player, trying to play tenor. This was probably true at that stage, as it takes a while to find your-self on a new horn. Things came to a head one night at the Marquee Club. Danny had a go at me and John, about me play-ing tenor solos. I got mad at the whole thing and told John I was handing in two weeks notice. He made no attempt to persuade me to stay so, on the last gig of the two weeks notice, I said, 'John, I've worked off my two weeks and that was my last gig.' He seemed stunned and then told me he hadn't taken me seriously when I handed in my notice and had forgotten all about it. He said he was sorry to see me leave, but wished me well for the future, and that was it. I have played with him several times since, of course.

Dankworth was an amazing musician, a fact brought home to me one day at a recording session. He had written a long and dif-ficult soli passage for the saxes to play in unison, but suddenly decided he wanted it voiced out in harmony. He then did some-thing that stunned me. He came up to us, facing the sax stands, so he was seeing the music upside down, then spent ten minutes writing new parts, by ear, at the bottom of the page, in harmony and upside down. Not only this, but they were fully transposed into the correct keys for the different instruments. Any musician will tell you that this is no mean feat. My respect for John's musicianship was even higher after that.

For a while after leaving Dankworth, I found it hard getting work. I was determined to change to tenor for a time but, as people knew me as an alto man, some thought I was making a mistake changing horns. I continued to play alto, but was devoting all my time to the larger horn. I was still playing suburban clubs and Ronnie Scott's occasionally, but mostly on tenor. Two guys who went on to become big international stars occasionally worked with my quartet around this time. The first was drummer Ginger Baker. In those days Ginger would hang around the jazz clubs and had a reputation for being a big Phil Seamen fan, before going on to form the highly successful band Cream. He could almost have been Phil himself, because he adopted many of his weird mannerisms, tried to play like Phil and even looked a bit like him. He never attained Phil's ability as a jazz player but, when he became a big name in blues and rock, to his credit he continued to sing Phil's praises, even featuring him on one of his tours. For once Phil made decent money, if only for a few weeks.

Another guy who appeared on the scene and played a few gigs with me was Dave Holland. Everyone knew he was something special on bass and it was not long before Miles Davis snapped him up after hearing him one night in London. I never met Miles, but he was in Ronnie's one night when I was playing there. Like an eminence grise, he sat quietly on his own while the whole audience tried to steal furtive looks in his direction. I tried to ignore his presence but, after my set, I couldn't help seeing him as I walked past on the way to the band room. I guess I was hoping for some kind of reaction, but all I got was a long withering stare as his eyes followed my nervous walk to the back of the club. Someone asked me if he had said anything so I just told them about the stare and that I didn't think he was too impressed. But later I heard that he had apparently dug what was going down onstage. If it was true, you could have fooled me, but I guess that's Miles, inscrutable to the last. In any case I was shortly to have one of the greatest experiences of my musical life, sitting in with one of my all-time heroes. If Miles was intimidating, the clinically insane Bud Powell would surely be an even more terrifying prospect.

Back in the late-1950s, when I was a young jazz enthusiast, Bud was the pianist who made the biggest impact on me. His reputation among modern jazz cognoscenti was massive and I listened to every recording I could get hold of. I also avidly read about him and was deeply moved by the stories of his tragic life. He seemed to my young mind to be the archetypal tortured genius. Such artists have always fascinated me, probably to my disadvantage at times. I marvelled at his medium and up-tempo playing, but what really grabbed me was his interpretation of ballads. They seemed to be filled with enormous depth and sadness and he extracted a unique timbre from the keyboard when he played them. It was not so much the chord progressions and inversions he used, but rather the strange haunting quality with which he invested them. This effect is to do with his very personal handling of dynamics and the subtle placing of the chords in time. A wonderful example is the first few bars of 'Embraceable You'. The first chords are played in a simple quarter note rhythm in 4/4 time, but with miniscule variations in tempo, along with a subtle dynamic shading, that is quite unique to Powell. The effect is extraordinary in its emotional impact.

Another thing that was a revelation to me was how on ballads he would often play almost the same solo every time. It's sometimes said that the secret of great improvisation is never to repeat yourself, but this misses the point. Powell arrived at his final semi-static version of 'Embraceable You', for example, through a process of improvisation combined with an acute, almost classical awareness of formal structure. The result is not just deeply emotional and personal, but also a study in formal perfection. Masterpieces like this take on a life of their own, in the same way as, for example, Louis Armstrong's great 'West End Blues'. Charlie Parker also used his own familiar phrases over and over again, as do most improvisers. These characteristic phrases are in a sense like words from an artist's personal language, a language from which a multitude of stories may be told. It's not so much the 'licks' you use but the story you tell with them. What separates the greats from lesser players is the way they use their own 'dictionary' of 'words' to tell beautiful and personal stories. This to me is the essence of good style. Think of it – if you never repeat yourself, no one will ever be sure who you are. We only need to hear a bar of Charlie Parker to know we are listening to Bird. We recognise great musicians, from Bach to Coltrane and beyond, by their unique musical and emotional language.

We all hear music through the prism of our own emotions. I hear in Powell's music a strangely disturbing but beautiful world, tinged with elements of his courageous struggle against insanity. Others may feel differently but, having played with him and been in his company, I don't think this is too romantic a view. Before moving to Paris, Bud recorded an extraordinary piece called 'Glass Enclosure'. The title alone and the strange unsettling nature of the composition seemed to capture the nightmarish atmosphere of the asylum. Only Bud knew the real meaning behind that piece, but it was a strangely evocative title to say the least, especially considering it was recorded not long after one of his long confinements in an asylum. On a lighter note is this story about one of those periods in hospital. A musician friend who visited him described how Bud had drawn a whole piano keyboard on the wall of his hospital room. He suddenly jumped up, placed his hands purposefully on the virtual keyboard, as if playing a new chord, and said to his visitor, 'What do you think of this?' He expected the guy to see his fingers on the keys and hear the chord. Actually not so crazy, when you think about it, but the friend thought Bud was really spaced out.

Bud reminded me in some ways of one of my favourite painters, Vincent Van Gogh. He must have drawn that keyboard on the wall for the same reason that Vincent needed his paints in the asylum at Saint Rémy: to hold onto what little sanity he had in that awful place, by working and practising his art, however he could. Occasionally, Bud was allowed to play the piano while he was hospitalised, but only once a week. However, a unique event took place one Christmas at the Kingsboro Psychiatric Center in Brooklyn, when Bud was undergoing treatment there. Lester Young and blues singer Sonny Terry were also patients at the time. The doctors asked if there were any musicians in the hospital so Prez, Sonny and Bud volunteered their services and played at a Christmas concert. A recording of that odd trio would be something to hear!

I first heard Bud play live in 1961, at the Essen Jazz Festival, where I was playing with Dankworth's band. Essen's famous Grugahalle was filled to its huge eight thousand seat capacity. Bud's trio had Kenny Clarke on drums and Pierre Michelot on bass. I have never seen such a collection of legendary musicians together at one time. The Buck Clayton band was there, with Emmett Berry (trumpet), Vic Dickinson (trombone), Gene Ramey (bass), Buddy Tate (tenor) and Earle Warren, who borrowed my alto because his got lost in transit. Buck's band was virtually the nucleus of the old Basie band from the forties, but without Lester Young. Other musicians included Jackie McLean, and two guys we had never heard of before: Jimmy Witherspoon, whose fabulous blues singing was one of the highlights of the festival, and a young Roland Kirk. Roland practised his horns all day long, playing into the walls of the dressing room and the corridors, wearing sunglasses held together with sticky tape and bits of cork. We didn't even realise he was blind as it was by no means obvious. We just thought he was a bit crazy and wore the weird shades for effect.

I remember Buck's band going into a dressing room several times to rehearse. There wasn't a sheet of music anywhere in sight. Just as with Basie's band in the early days, they played all head arrangements. It's said that Basie had over three hundred tunes in the book when Prez was in the band but they were all head arrangements; even the harmony parts were worked out by ear and committed to memory. That night, I stepped into the bus going back to the hotel after the concert and it was like a who's who of jazz. In one row of seats alone I could see Jackie McLean, Kenny Clarke and Bud Powell with his wife, Buttercup – totally awe-inspiring for a nervous young kid from Surrey.

Back at the hotel, while I was chatting excitedly to some of the guys from Dankworth's band, Bud and Buttercup entered the hotel and Bud walked very slowly through the lobby and straight into the lift. He stared vacantly ahead of him as if in a deep trance. So slow was his solitary walk that Buttercup had time to collect the room key, put in a wake-up call and still arrive at the elevator, just as Bud reached it. We got in to go to our rooms too, and Bud stood motionless as the lift went up, staring straight ahead until he was led out and into his room. Could this be the same man who earlier had played with such sublime brilliance? When he wasn't playing, he seemed in a strange world of his own; even relaxing in the dressing room he seemed to be somewhere else. At the end of his set the audience was scream-ing for more, but he just stood in the wings looking dazed. Kenny Clarke had to lead him back onstage to play his encore, holding his hand like a little lost child. He played at his best all night but, every time the audience applauded, he looked stunned and stared at them with a lost look, rising from the piano trying to smile and bow to the sea of faces. It was as if he didn't even realise they were there until their applause disturbed his private world. It was a very moving experience and I really felt I was witnessing a genius at work, but a genius who lived in a nightmare world of sadness and insanity.

Witherspoon was in total awe of Bud. Jimmy was a big, tall, emotional, larger-than-life guy. The backstage area was full of musicians, stagehands and people who had blagged their way in. When Bud came offstage, 'Spoon tried to shake him by the hand and congratulate him. Bud just gave him a withering look, released his hand from Jimmy's powerful grip and walked off, laughing. But it was the most chilling laugh I've ever heard, starting softly, then rising to a loud insane guffaw, which echoed around the corridors leading to the dressing rooms. Like something from a horror movie, the sound seemed to reverberate around the whole building for ages. Witherspoon stood staring after him and then at us, speechless and shocked, with tears in his eyes and a look of horror, pity and profound sadness on his expressive face. There was a feeling of suspended animation that seemed to stop everyone in their tracks. It was a frightening experience, I can tell you. I've heard similar stories of Bud's reactions when people tried to congratulate him after a set. He would just stare at them, laughing as if *they* were mad. No wonder I was scared shitless when I eventually played with him.

When I saw Bud at the Blue Note in Paris a year later in 1962, I understood for the first time how totally insecure the jazz world was, even for our heroes from America. Bud was not playing with Kenny Clarke or even bassist Pierre Michelot. Instead, he was working with two run-of-the-mill French musicians who seemed to treat him with little respect. To my disgust, the drummer even made fun of Bud's odd demeanour, sticking one of his sticks under Powell's nose like it was a moustache, every time he adopted his characteristic head back posture while waiting to play. At first, Bud seemed to take no notice but, when the same thing happened at the beginning of the second set, he suddenly snapped and told the drummer to, 'Cut it out!' The most shocking thing, though, was that there were only between six and ten people in the club. How could this be? This was the famous Blue Note and this was the man who had received a standing ovation from eight thousand in Essen. Probably he got a good fee for the Essen concert, but I'll bet most of it went to pay off his medical debts from America. In Paris, he lived in Lester Young's old rooms in the Hotel La Louisiane, a terrible shit-hole of a place featured in the film *Round Midnight*. American musicians lived there only because it was very cheap and you could do your own cooking to save money.

My meeting with Bud came about through a change in my personal life. In 1961, I was, I'm ashamed to say, still a virgin at twenty-one. Suffering from bad acne probably didn't help. However, that all changed when I met Vicky, an attractive woman with a warm, caring personality. Slightly older than me, she was a fan and before long we became very close. She soon showed me the ropes in bed and was a tower of strength in other ways too. My acne improved no end! She gave me much more confidence in myself and, although we eventually went our separate ways, we still remain friends. She worked in the record business, knew Bud Powell and had been at some of his recording sessions in Paris. Vicky wanted to sing and became friends with Buttercup, who was herself a part-time vocalist. One day she told me all this and added, 'You must come over to Paris for a few days, meet Buttercup and sit in with Bud.' I was still nervous of travelling, especially abroad, so the idea of meeting Bud in Paris was thrilling but also daunting. But Vicky persuaded me Bud wouldn't bite and fixed the travel arrangements. It turned out to be a long weekend of firsts. My first night flight; my first flight in a jet too – one of Air France's new Caravelles. Travelling by jet was new in those days so, with my love of aircraft, this was bliss and after only forty-five minutes I was on the tarmac at Orly airport. By contrast, it took two and a half hours to fly back in a Lockheed Super Constellation. Only a few years before, these piston engine aircraft had been the pride of the Atlantic route.

When we had settled in our hotel, Vicky called Buttercup and arrangements were made to meet. The first night we went to the Blue Note, on the Rue d'Artois just off the Champs Élysées, and listened to a couple of Bud's sets. Next day, we went to the Hotel La Louisiane at around midday to be met by Buttercup. She was an over-large, friendly lady and full of life, but I was mortified to see the run-down suite of rooms that was their home after Lester Young left. There was a tatty bed in a kind of hallway. In the bed, fast asleep, was Bud's six-year-old son, snuggled up to a young black girl who was only about fourteen herself and apparently took care of the child. She may have been Bud's daughter but I don't remember her being introduced as such. After coffee and a chat, Buttercup took us in to see Bud, warning us he might not be too talkative, but not to worry. His bedroom was small, with bare floorboards and a small double bed. The only other furniture was an old chair and a plywood tea chest by the bed. A grubby tin lid served as an astray.

Bud was sitting up in bed wearing an old tee shirt and smoking a cigarette. He stared straight ahead at the wall and seemed unaware of our presence. Any kind of introduction was out of the question, so Buttercup did all the talking, She continually slapped Bud on the back as she punctuated her chatter with asides like, 'Didn't they, Bud, ha ha?' or, 'Ha ha, wasn't it, Bud?' Bud remained silent, staring into space, except for the odd disdainful grunt when she slapped his back and tried to get him involved in her chatty monologue.

After about twenty minutes we went back to the kitchen, leaving him to his lonely world. Buttercup's treatment of Bud has become a contentious issue but I saw nothing to make me doubt her caring nature towards him. We talked about him and the night to come, when I was supposed to sit in with him. She told us he would be fine at the Blue Note, explaining he had a daily routine that went like this: he would wake up late-morning and act quite normally, playing with his young son for a couple of hours; then he would drift into a semi-catatonic state for a while, going back to bed only to rise relatively normal again at about 9 p.m. He would travel by cab to the gig, which didn't start till about 10.30 p.m. When he went to work he was usually fine and would even hang out with his musicians after the gig, at a local tabac. He had to be constantly watched, though, and the musicians had strict instructions not to let him have alcohol. Buttercup was feeding him large amounts of Largactil, the drug used for keeping violent prisoners and lunatics quiet and noted for its terrible side effects.

Bud had been abused terribly in asylums, where they had forced him to have several courses of damaging electro-shock therapy. His schizophrenia and manic depression had been 'treated' with large amounts of Thorazine, a drug considered by many to be virtually a chemical lobotomy. Thorazine and Largactil have debilitating side effects and a lot of his strange behaviour could no doubt be attributed to these, combined with indiscriminating use of shock therapy. It's sad to think that, if he was alive today, his condition could probably be treated far more successfully, with modern medicines and techniques.

I had gained in confidence after working at Ronnie Scott's and then with Dankworth, but the thought of playing with Bud Powell was something else again. When Vicky and I arrived at the Blue Note that evening, Buttercup was not there; she rarely came to the club. I was introduced to Ben Benjamin, the large and intimidating ex-pat American proprietor. On hearing I might sit in with Bud he said, 'OK, if Bud agrees.' He then gave me a warning, 'Listen, Pete. Whatever you do, don't buy Bud a drink and make sure he doesn't steal yours.' Bud would steal people's drinks from right under their noses unless he was watched all the time. He was a Jekyll and Hyde and only needed one small drink to turn into a crazy and often angry drunk (a typical side effect of Largactil when mixed with alcohol). Finally, I was officially introduced to Bud. He was, as Buttercup had assured us, quite aware of his surroundings now but, after a brief attempt at a handshake, he sat down right opposite me and just stared fixedly straight into my eyes, with a disconcerting Buddha-like smile. I attempted to make embarrassed conversation but he just kept staring. Finally, after what seemed an eternity, he gave my alto case a long quizzical look and said, 'Is that your horn, Pete? Are you going to play?' At which, he got up and motioned me onto the bandstand.

I leave it to your imagination how I was feeling by this stage. I took my position and, conquering my fear, turned to face Bud. He was smiling at me from behind the piano and said in a friendly tone, 'What do you want to play, Pete?' 'Ornithology'? I ventured. He just kept smiling and repeated, 'What do you want to play, Pete?' This really threw me, but I suggested another tune and got the same response again. He showed no sign of irritation and kept smiling through the whole weird ceremony. After about three attempts to come up with something to play, he suddenly said in a decisive tone, 'Scrapple from the Apple', and started playing the tune, with no count in or introduction. I turned to face the front and joined in after a couple of bars. Musically it was a revelation. I had played that tune a thousand times before, but had never heard it sound the way he played it. Every phrase was filled with carefully-crafted subtleties and it was as if there were twice the normal amount of time between each note. The statement of the theme was a music lesson in itself but, when he started to comp behind my solo, it was like magic. I seemed to have so much time to think. It was like lying in a beautiful king-sized bed after struggling in a sleeping bag. Bud seemed to know more about what I was going to play than I did. He filled in all my phrase breaks, leading me into what appeared to be the only correct thing to play next. It was an extraordinary experience and my first exposure to that incredibly relaxed feel that seemed, in those days, an exclusive province of the American giants.

I was in a state of bliss, but tinged with abject terror. What would Bud do, now he had heard me play? I half-expected him to shout abuse at me, slam down the piano lid and storm off, or worse. After all, I knew the story about him doing something similar, to Bird of all people, in Birdland, saying, 'You ain't playing shit no more, Bird!' Well, I finished my solo, the small audience applauded and Bud went into his solo. When I got courage enough to turn round he was totally engrossed in his own playing, holding his head back and quietly 'singing' what sounded like drum fills, to accompany himself. It always looked as if his hands operated the keys by themselves, while his head alone was creating the music and even the backing to his own solo. His head and body were almost motionless when he played. There was absolutely no wasted movement. This was a lesson I also learnt from Lucky Thompson later. Most of the musicians from that generation knew the importance of using minimum physical effort with maximum concentration when they played. The tune finished and the first hurdle was over but what next? 'What next', turned out to be more of the, 'What d'ya wanna play, Pete?' routine. After the same two or three attempts at finding a tune we carried on, and so it continued, until the end of the set. I was in far too much of a daze to remember what else we played that night, but I think 'Confirmation' may have been in there somewhere. After the last number, Bud played two super-fast choruses of the classic bebop signature tune '52nd Street Theme' and then stood up. I turned to face him and to my great relief he was grinning broadly and, without saying a word, held out his hand to shake mine, then left the stage. It seemed I had passed the audition.

During the interval Bud came up to me at the bar and said with a grin, 'Hey Pete, you really like Charlie Parker?' I said, 'Oh yes, I love Bird,' But I wasn't sure if this was some kind of compliment or whether he was really telling me it was about time I started playing my own way. Maybe it was a bit of both. I discovered later that he talked for quite a while about the spotty-faced twenty-one-year-old from England who sounded like Bird. I was told Bud seemed to play better when I got on the stand. If that was true, I'm sure it was only because he needed another musician up there to relieve the boredom of playing night after night to an empty house with his mediocre trio companions.

Bud asked me back the next night to play but, when I did, I ran into opposition from Ben Benjamin. As I walked into the club he came up and said, 'Look, Pete, you play good, but people come here to listen to Bud. So just play a couple of tunes tonight and then let Bud play on his own with the trio.' I didn't want to cause trouble so I politely agreed. The thought also passed my mind that maybe Bud had something to do with Ben's remarks. I wasn't sure I could face another night of it anyway. After all, I had already achieved one of my life ambitions the night before and didn't want anything to spoil it. I tried to tell Bud, but he acted like he hadn't heard me, and asked me up to play again for the first set. We went through the same 'What d'ya wanna play, Pete?' routine again. I had gotten used to it by now, but this time it changed slightly. Vicky must have been talking to Bud because, when it came to the second tune, he said, 'Pete, "Loverman", for your wife.' For some silly reason I said 'She's not my wife, Bud. She's my girlfriend.' Bud, having none of this, repeated in more emphatic tones, '"Loverman", *for your wife.*' Not wanting to argue the point, I left it at that and we played the ballad. I had first learnt 'Loverman' from Parker's recording on which he played it in the unusual key of D-flat, rather than the regular F. To ask Bud what key he wanted to play it in would have probably led nowhere fast, so I just waited for his intro and sure enough, he played it in D-flat.

'Loverman' was the second tune of the set so, not wishing to blot my copybook with the boss of the Blue Note, I reminded Bud of Benjamin's orders and tried to excuse myself. His answer was silence, followed by another, 'What d'ya wanna play, Pete?' So I gave in and we played another tune. There then ensued a bizarre battle of wills between Bud and Benjamin, with me in the middle. Ben started, by yelling from the bar: 'That's enough, Pete. I told you to get off after two tunes!' Bud came back with yet another, rather stubborn, 'What d'ya wanna play, Pete?' He repeated it again, directed as much at Ben as at me. Very uneasy, not knowing what to do, I tried to make my apologies to Bud and left the stage, frightened and pissed off with Ben Benjamin, but not keen to argue with the boss.

The rest of the night was a letdown. Bud carried on with the trio but when he came off, after the second and third sets, he totally ignored me. I was despondent and figured I had let him down by not standing up to Ben's unreasonable demands. However, at the end of the night, he went over to the bar to get his overcoat, put his famous old black beret firmly on his head and started to leave the club. As he passed, he gave me a big smile and said, 'Goodnight, Pete.' You can imagine my relief. Vicky and I walked off into the Parisian night, happy as pigs in shit. I got to see the Eiffel Tower at four in the morning, but my most lasting impression of my first visit to Paris were the words, 'What d'ya wanna play, Pete?' A pretty innocuous question really, but one that stirs so many memories and emotions for me to this day.

4

'Peter, Peter, pumpkin eater, had a wife and couldn't keep her,'
Joy Marshall

On my return to London I carried on practising the tenor in the hope that I could make it my main instrument, for a while at least. I had become too reliant on my modest ability to emulate Bird on alto. But at least I was trying to capture the emotional aspects of Charlie Parker's playing, not just slavishly copying his phrases. I already realised that getting to the roots of Bird's style wasn't just a matter of playing loads of fast double tempo runs.

One of the great things about Bird was that he actually played far fewer notes than was at first apparent and used strong asymmetrical accents and silence to get his style across. Once you have acquired a fast technique, it's all too easy to overdo things and play too many notes. Bird created solos of absolute formal perfection. Due to his innate sense of tension and release, his genius for combining the two elements in exactly the right way was awesome. I was fascinated with how he would play a stunningly fast double tempo phrase but end it with a very simple three or four note climax. He would then leave a big silence before continuing. He understood instinctively how powerfully dramatic the effect of that silence was. It left you with time to enjoy the brilliance of what you had just heard. Every time I hear a Parker solo I am made aware of the endless variety he achieved using quite a limited number of his own characteristic phrases. Each solo is a string of stunning ideas, and each of these is a complete melody in its own right. There are very few passages where he simply strings notes together over the harmonies. This is what lesser players, like myself, tend to do a lot. Nearly every idea Bird plays stands up on its own as a complete, original melody. Classic examples are found in his various versions of 'Embracable You'. He creates a totally new melodic line over the first four bars every time, each line better than the original tune, each one worthy of being called a composition in its own right. The way he follows one great melodic idea with another throughout his solos, linking them together to make a perfect whole, is what places him way above most who try to follow his example.

Merely playing endless fast runs totally negates their effectiveness. After a while an audience gets used to hearing how fast you can play; it becomes immune to the effect and can end up just bored. Formal tension and release is a general law in aesthetics and applies to every artistic field. I would venture to say it's so basic it reflects a general law of nature itself. I am still struggling to play less notes. With the right rhythm section you can leave space, knowing they will fill in any gaps, then complement and inspire the forward flow of the music. The standard of rhythm sections has improved beyond recognition and up-and-coming musicians now have a vastly improved understanding of their role. However, on the now happily-rare occasions when I find myself working with a poor rhythm section, it is difficult to avoid playing far too many notes in an attempt to make up for their deficiencies. When guys don't listen to what you are playing, but are involved in just their own musical world, you have to shoulder alone the responsibility of making the music work and getting it over to the audience and this can lead you into filling in all your intended moments of repose with notes. The worst is when a pianist plays too many notes behind you and then takes a break, just when you are trying to leave room for him to fill the empty space. It shows he is not listening properly and it can be not only annoying but nerve wracking when it happens.

Parker's technical prowess became the main influence on a whole generation of musicians, but there were very few players able to learn other, more important, lessons from Bird's genius. Certainly the best British musicians following Bird acquired formidable technical brilliance, Tubby Hayes being the prime example. Players of Tubby's and Ronnie Scott's stature certainly developed their own styles to the point where you could immediately recognise them as individuals. They had their own voices, but I needed to develop my own individuality. My playing was becoming an amalgam of Bird and Tubby, a heady mix but it could lead down the road to predictability and even a musical dead end. Finding your own unique style is tough. Many alto players, including Americans, had encountered the same problem because Parker had such an all-pervading influence on the instrument.

Although I admired Bird with a passion, I also loved other musicians. As far as the new music was concerned there seemed to be just Bird on alto. There were other guys doing their own thing, like Lee Konitz, Paul Desmond, Cannonball Adderley, of course, and later the great Joe Harriott in Britain, but Parker was always there like a great sun, shining over his domain. I had to do something to break out from under his influence and felt switching to tenor might help. This at least opened me up to other influences and I hoped that the fact that there was a greater variety of tenor players to listen to might help me find a style. Since then I have never listened to alto players too closely, so as to avoid any more direct influences on the horn. Some people think I have been influenced by Phil Woods but this is not the case. If there is any similarity, it must simply be that we have both learned from Bird. Other than that, we have worked on our own styles independently. I began studying people like Stan Getz, Lucky Thompson, Coleman Hawkins, Ben Webster, Paul Gonsalves and, later, John Coltrane. I also listened a lot to other instrumentalists like Miles, Bud Powell and Bill Evans.

I was told Tubby thought I would make a good tenor player, once I 'stopped slipping in all that Ben Webster shit!' He was right, of course. Much as Tubby and I loved Ben, Getz and Lucky Thompson, trying to emulate them was not going to lead to a new modern style, whatever that might mean, In fact it was

Getz who ended up being one of my biggest influences and I'm still aware of it today. His influence was subtle. It was not so much his style, but his impeccable technical precision, his unerring melodic flow and his unrelenting swing. He is an object lesson to any saxophone player and it's not surprising that Coltrane once said of Getz, 'That's how we would all play if we could.'

While I was struggling with the tenor I was approached by Tony Kinsey. Tony was forming a new quintet in 1961 and asked me if I would join. I assumed he wanted me on alto but it turned out he wanted me to play tenor. This was very encouraging and I was pleased to accept the job. Tony always had a good group and plenty of work. His offer came at a perfect time. I could develop my tenor-playing while working with a top-line jazz combo. In fact, this was the first time I had the chance to perform regularly with a prestigious jazz quintet. In those days it was normal for a top ensemble to wear smart made-to-measure band suits and Tony paid for the five of us to be fitted out with them. They were really sharp, in silver grey mohair. The kind that shimmers in the stage lights! The original lineup was Tony on drums, myself on tenor, Gordon Beck on piano and Brian Brocklehurst on bass. Hank Shaw was supposed to be the trumpet player but he created a problem for Tony.

Hank was heavily into yoga and had even turned me on to a long postal course he was studying. When we arrived at the first rehearsal of the new band, Hank eulogised about yoga for an hour or more, telling us how he had been working on special exercises to train his memory to a very advanced state. Eventually we agreed to stop talking and get down to business. As we got our horns out, there was a cry of 'Oh shit!' from Hank. He had forgotten to bring his music. We fell about laughing as he tried to figure out how to get home and back again with the trumpet parts. Eventually we started rehearsing but, a day or so later, Tony called me to say Hank had suddenly decided to quit the band and go to Redcar, where he had been offered a residency with a well-paid local dance band. Poor Tony had laid out good money for all the band suits and we had rehearsed all the new charts, only to have Hank leave the band before we had done one gig. In the end, Tony managed to get Les Condon as replacement and he remained with us until the band broke up in 1964/5.

Les was to become a very close friend. He was a fine, original trumpet player and an excellent arranger and composer. Highly respected, both as a jazz improviser and as a first-call session musician, he worked regularly in the studios and also with the Tubby Hayes Big Band. Les took me under his wing and taught me a lot about coping with the music business and life in general. Tony helped me in many ways too and, although he became more and more involved in composing for films and television, he still plays drums occasionally with all his old fire. I will always be grateful for the experience of working with his quintet.

Les and I often co-wrote arrangements for the group. We would burn the midnight oil, brainstorming and trading ideas. On one particular night, when we were writing a new chart for the band, I came up with what I thought was a good idea and banged out some chords on the piano to show him. Les listened and then said, in his often rather caustic way, 'Yeah Pete, but what has it got to do with the rest of the arrangement?' It was a lesson I never forgot. In my youthful enthusiasm I had concentrated solely on the one idea and had not figured out how it related to the big picture. Les would often snap at me if he thought I was wrong, but he was usually right and always, within a second or two, it would all be forgotten and we would be laughing and coming up with a new and better idea. We worked well together and had a ball. Les always had a great understanding of what 'works' musically, but he never got the credit he deserved. On the sadly rare occasions when we met, in the years before his death in 2008, there remained a close bond of love, respect and understanding between us. His abrasive enthusiasm and musical intelligence were always there, digging, provoking, and shining a spotlight on any bullshit, just like the old days.

With guys like Tony, Gordon and Les, the quintet was bound to be a great band. We did a load of work, regularly touring round Britain, plus the usual London West End clubs, radio broadcasts and some television work. One of our regular gigs was the Cavern Club in Liverpool. It was a shit-hole of a place that stank of disinfectant. There was a big problem with rats and you could smell the Dettol halfway down the street. Soon we had our own problem with the Cavern when some young kids with guitars started taking over the place. Eventually, thanks to the Beatles, we never worked there again. In fact, come to think of it, we never worked a lot of places after that because of those damned kids!

We soon lost the Marquee Club to the Rolling Stones as well. I have to admit to being prejudiced against the Beatles because of the disastrous effect they (and the pop scene in general) had on those struggling to keep the jazz scene alive. I don't want to alienate Beatles fans and have nothing against them personally, but I cannot go along with those academics and music historians who consider them revolutionary musical geniuses.

One seemingly erudite musicologist who expresses this opinion goes on to say that contemporary straight music has been influenced by the Beatles, citing minimalist composers such as Steve Reich and Philip Glass. He may be right in saying that minimalism was an attempt to reject the over-intellectualised music of the total serialists, like Pierre Boulez, and to regain an audience that had dwindled to just a few cognoscenti. The Beatles may have influenced certain contemporary composers but, for my taste, minimalism has degenerated into an aesthetically bland ideology. It could even be accused of 'dumbing down' classical music. This is never more evident than in the repetitive and simplistic minimalist clichés used behind so many television films and documentaries these days. I'm heartily sick of hearing that same succession of major and minor thirds repeated endlessly in straight eighth notes that sounds like a police siren, De – Da - De – Da – De – Do - De – Do - . I love harmony and this abandonment of all but the most rudimentary harmonic language is anathema to me.

We are going through a very depressing period in the arts. Art has to progress to survive and should reflect its own time, but many of the signs are not good. For example, in the visual arts we are confronted with endless 'installations', with claims by their creators they are statements about the meaning of art, rather than works of aesthetic power and beauty. Back in 1917, Marcel Duchamp's infamous display of a public urinal as a work of art was intended to be anti-art, or Dada (an annihilation of all preconceived artistic dogma). But Duchamp's urinal was merely intended to shock, not to be admired as a work of art in itself. Dada's artistic anarchy led to a new period of great creativity in painting and sculpture. But when are we going to see a new blossoming of real artistic genius again? Most conceptual artists now seem preoccupied with making ever more outrageous and predictable statements about art, in the hope they get taken up by the Saatchi Gallery, win a Turner Prize and make loads of money.

Having got that off my chest, back to Tony Kinsey. He had good connections, so the quintet also worked occasionally on the Continent. One particularly memorable concert was at the Comblain la Tour Festival in Belgium in August 1962. Our set was just before the main attraction, Cannonball Adderley's sextet. Cannonball had his brother Nat on cornet and Yusef Lateef on tenor, flute and oboe. I knew Yusef from when he played Ronnie's. He was a lovely giant of a man with a huge sound on oboe. Ronnie used to call him 'You've lost – Your teeth' (but my favourite Scott announcement was: 'Ladies and gentlemen, next week we are presenting a great new quintet at the club, featuring Stan Getz and Stuff Smith - the Get Stuffed Quintet!') At Comblain la Tour we were surprised to see Cannonball using a white, Austrian guy on piano. It was young Joe Zawinul. He had only just joined the band. Years later I discovered that Cannonball's concert had been recorded and the result became a classic live album.

Around this time Lucky Thompson appeared at Ronnie Scott's. He had been one of my early discoveries on record, when I was first encountering jazz. After finding that first Parker 78 rpm record in the secondhand shop, I had asked the local record store if they had any jazz albums. The only one found was a 45 rpm EP of Lucky Thompson, recorded in Paris with Martial Solal on piano. I again struck lucky, because it was a revelation. Lucky had a tone reminiscent of Coleman Hawkins but with a modern harmonic approach. I first heard him on Bird's recording of 'A Night in Tunisia', but his playing on this French recording was a far more stunning display of his brilliance. When I got my own tenor I dug out the old EP and set myself to transcribing and playing all four solos from the record. By the time he played at Ronnie's, Lucky had changed his sound considerably and had also taken up soprano, on which he had developed a new and very original approach. His tone on tenor was now much lighter, perhaps influenced by his discovery of the soprano. Unfortunately, Lucky and Stan Tracey's resident trio didn't see eye to eye and there was considerable tension during his three weeks at the club. However, everyone was amazed by his playing. Thompson had a stunning technique. He would weave the most original melodic lines through the harmonies; always the unexpected and always with relaxed perfection, even at the fastest tempos.

I got friendly with him and asked if he would give me a lesson. I had heard he did a lot of teaching in Paris, where he had taken up residence. He had heard me play and told me he didn't think he could teach me anything as I had my shit together pretty well already. But he said I was welcome to come over to the hotel, hang out, and bring my horn too. When I went to see him, he wanted to talk about the problems with the rhythm section, as he was upset at the bad publicity he was getting because of the situation. Lucky seemed a really nice, sensitive soul to me, although Stan Tracey told me he had been very nasty to the guys. It doesn't excuse his behaviour to Stan, but I did get Lucky's side of the story. He told me he couldn't understand why the musicians got so upset. According to him, he only asked them to change a few things when they played behind him. He said he was not trying to put anyone down and respected their abilities as individuals. He just thought they weren't working together in the way he wanted. Then he told me an interesting story to make his point. He asked me which I thought was the worst rhythm section he had ever worked with. I didn't know so he told me. 'Thelonious Monk, Art Blakey and Charlie Mingus'! As he pointed out, they were all great players but, as a rhythm section, a nightmare. Three giant individualists but, according to Lucky, when they played together, a disaster.

He seemed to have a knack of rubbing some people up the wrong way. He told me he had had big problems with the US musicians' union because he stood up against some of their bad practices and wouldn't tow the line, causing him to lose work and alienating him from some of the other musicians. I don't know the truth of this, but I had no reason to doubt him. He was a perfectionist and backed it up with his own high standard of musicianship. Lucky was an above average sight-reader and I had the impression he kept a little aloof from some of his fellow-musicians. To me he came across as a sensitive man, whose search for perfection in himself and others was probably mistaken for obsessive arrogance.

After a while, he suggested I get my horn out and play so he could see how I held the instrument. One of the most startling things to see in his playing was his absolute minimum use of effort. Like Bird, it was hard to see his fingers move at all. He showed me how he had achieved this, explaining it was vital, in order to obtain a good technique on the horn. Lucky had perfected this to the highest degree I have ever seen. The secret is to use as little finger movement as possible, thereby saving physical and mental energy for the music itself. He stood behind me while I held the horn and gently manoeuvred my wrists until he found a position for me where all the keys could be operated with hardly any movement of the fingers or wrists. He explained I might find this awkward at first but it would pay dividends if I could persevere with it. He showed me some very simple exercises, designed to keep both my wrists locked in position. Then he showed me how to practise with my fingers always touching the keys, instead of lifting them off. This is difficult to do but he was a master at it and, because his fingers were always so close to the keys, they seemed not to be moving at all, even at the breakneck tempos he often used. I did persevere and, also applying some things I had been reading about the mental aspects of practising, I began to expand my technique in a new way. I had also been working on developing the ability to translate what I heard in my ear straight onto the horn. Lucky's short lesson was a kind of catalyst and everything started to come together into a unified whole.

One of my practice techniques was to sing a note in my head and attempt to hit it straight off, on the horn. I don't have perfect pitch but I could do it sometimes, especially if I was tired and very relaxed. I would then use that note, whatever it was, as the first note of a tune and play the melody by ear, starting on that note. The idea was to play the whole thing without knowing what key I was in. That way the sounds you hear are translated directly into finger movements, without any reference to written notes or keys. After a while I was able to play most of the tunes I knew in any key. This gave me more confidence to play whatever I heard and this freed me to concentrate on creating melodic lines, without the constant hang-up of wondering if they would come out on the horn right. I had always been aware that Bird practised in all the keys and assumed it was a standard requirement if you wanted to be any good. George Coleman, who was notorious for playing tunes in every key, told me years later that when he started you had to be able to do this if you ever hoped to play with the top guys in New York. If you tried to sit in with them, they would often play in some remote and difficult key, just to frighten you off. It wasn't just to give you a hard time. They were working on new important ideas and couldn't afford to have their limited after-hours sessions spoiled by people who couldn't contribute something meaningful. It was a tough school in those days.

When I was with the Dankworth band I used to practise a lot of French classical saxophone music and obtained a recording by Marcel Mule. He was, without doubt, the greatest classical saxophone soloist of the time. He was a virtuoso and had a beautiful rich sound on alto, quite unlike the bland tone normally associated with the instrument in a classical setting. The 'French saxophone school' uses a warm vibrato and Marcel's tone, in the middle and low registers, had the richness of a cello. He was professor of saxophone at the Paris Conservatoire and edited many books of studies, some of which Bird used for practice. I was fascinated to learn that Lucky often met Professor Mule at Selmer's in Paris, where they would try out the latest saxophones and practise together. Once, when I told Art Ellefson I was working on classical studies, he threw me by saying he thought it was better to practise what you were going to play, rather than working on that kind of thing. He was making a good point but I couldn't understand how to practise like that, since you never knew what you were going to play until you started soloing. His words stuck in my mind, though, and it took quite a while before I figured out how to put his advice into practice. Eventually I realised that if you just improvise on your own, you can always stop and work on things that give you trouble. You can even turn the ideas into exercises. The point is that you will often find yourself going for those same phrases on a gig. They are part of your growing stylistic language and singling them out while you are practising does improve your playing. This is what Art meant, I guess.

Soon after I met Lucky, I got friendly with Ben Webster. Ben was a wonderful man but could be a bit of a handful when he had been drinking, which was most of the time. He used to have problems with taxi drivers in particular and sometimes got into trouble, pulling his knife out if he thought they were ripping him off. When he had had a few his voice would get louder, with a strong Texan twang. He would be drinking in the downstairs bar at Ronnie's and you would start to hear his voice all the way upstairs. In fact, Ben was just very lonely and loved to talk and hang out. I often took him to his hotel, the White House in Albany Street, where the staff all adored him, in spite of the odd difficulties. One New Year's Eve he got the entire night staff pissed by the time the day shift came on. I was with him one night when he talked and talked. By about 8 a.m. I was getting tired and told him I had to go. He wasn't having it and threatened to pull out his knife if I tried to leave. 'OK,' I said, 'I'll stay for another hour, then I gotta split.' He called room service and this West Indian came up. He wouldn't let him leave either, but I managed to convince him that the poor guy had to collect all the garbage from the rooms by 9 a.m. Ben let him go, but not before I could stop him giving the guy a ridiculously large tip which he couldn't afford. He was generous to a fault.

Ben would spend any money he had left from booze on hugely expensive transatlantic phone calls. He would call Jim and Andy's Bar in New York and talk for hours to the proprietor and anyone else who happened to be in the joint at the time. He insisted that I should talk to them as well, raving to them about London, me and my playing. If you were a jazz anorak, which I'm not, Ben was your man. He would tell endless stories about when he was with Duke Ellington. Till the end of his life he was in awe of the Duke and told me a lovely anecdote about what a great psychologist he was. When they recorded 'Cottontail', the famous Webster feature and a minor hit, Ben thought it was a good time to ask for a raise in salary. He went into Duke's dressing room and approached his boss. Duke looked over from tying his bow tie and told Ben, who was a heavy gambler, 'I ain't going to give you a raise, Ben, because, if I do, you're just going to get "that old rich feeling".' Ben loved him for it and said the Duke was only trying to save him from himself. If he had given him a raise, he would have just gambled it all away. Duke understood his musicians very well and rewarded them in odd ways sometimes. I heard he once put a deposit down on a house for Paul Gonsalves, rather than give him money that he would have spent on his heroin habit.

Speaking of Gonsalves, I remember Tubby and me jamming with him one night in Soho's Downbeat Club. Paul was a bit drunk but still playing his ass off. He suddenly turned to Tubby and me and said with obvious concern, 'Hey man, there's something wrong with my horn!' Tubby and I had a look and one of the pads was about an 1/8 of an inch above the tone hole. It should have been a tight fit and neither Tubby nor I could get a note out of the thing. We quickly fixed it and told him to try it. Paul was ecstatic and, with tears in his eyes, said 'Oh man! Oh thanks, it's wonderful!' He had somehow been playing a totally unplayable horn for over half an hour. It really was a case of complete mind over matter. For the rest of the session Paul was just over the moon and played like there was no tomorrow.

Ben Webster would occasionally play me one of his own records, but not out of any desire to boast. It was an album he made with Art Tatum. He was so proud of it because he worshipped Art. He would sit in raptures saying, 'Oh, Pete, listen to what Art plays here.' Ben paid me a big compliment once when I brought along a tape of myself playing 'Body and Soul' on tenor. It took a while to pluck up the courage to play it to him, knowing how he respected Coleman Hawkins, who had made the classic recording of the song. But he insisted, and he loved it. He said, 'Man, they've got to release this on record.' He thought it was so good it would become a new classic. Mind you, he had downed a few scotches at the time. They say you shouldn't mix your drinks but Ben never paid any mind to that. I used to watch in amazement as he swigged from three bottles, one after the other: gin, brandy and scotch.

I got so relaxed around Ben that I invited him to have dinner with my parents. He was really touched at the offer and we fixed a date, so Mum could get a good old English roast for him. The day arrived and we drove to Tolworth. I don't think a black guy had ever been seen in that part of suburban London in those days, let alone a jazz giant like Ben. Mum and Dad were nervous and I was worried in case Ben got drunk and caused problems, although I felt I could handle him by then. In the event I needn't have worried. He was on his best behaviour and very respectful. My father got on great with him. He loved Mum's cooking too and enjoyed every minute of the evening. I think it was a rare experience for him to just meet a regular, nice English family, to be made welcome and to get his first taste of a traditional roast beef dinner, complete with Yorkshire pudding. It was a wonderful night.

* * *

Jazz has developed into a very wide spectrum of music these days, encompassing many international styles. Probably some of the most successful British musicians have been those who became involved in what is sometimes called 'European jazz'. Great artists like Kenny Wheeler, John Taylor and John Surman achieved truly international fame using the whole of Europe as their base. Record companies like ECM did a lot to develop both European and American artists like Jan Garbarek and Keith Jarrett. Their music encompassed many new influences, from the European classical tradition to the folk music of many countries, as well as the African-American roots of jazz.

I have always been driven to play jazz firmly rooted in the Black American tradition. As a white boy from the London suburbs I chose a difficult route. I had an obsessive desire to play and even think like an African American. In the sixties, especially, I felt a need to be accepted as one of them, so to speak. After all, I loved their music so much and had become steeped in it. This could be seen as a negation of my own British culture but the African-American lifestyle seemed to fit better with my psychological make up. I also have a great admiration for European culture and its music but I find it difficult to combine or reconcile the two musical worlds. When I play jazz I think more like a black American, whereas European music inspires me to compose European music. However, because I had had no formal training, it was many years before I was able even to contemplate writing in a more classical manner.

Back in the sixties, I wanted to soak up everything I could about Black American culture. This rather deluded aim led to serious problems, the worst of which was probably my first marriage. I found myself becoming very attracted to black women. John Dankworth was, of course, married to Cleo Laine and his staff arranger, Dave Lindup, was also married to a beautiful black woman. They knew about my predilections and used to say, jokingly, 'We must fix Pete up with a nice black wife.' I was taking my obsession with jazz a bit far, looking back on it, but it took a few years to come to my senses. In fact, that reminds me of a story about Hank Shaw. He wanted so much to be black when he first started playing that he got conned by some West Indian guy who sold him some expensive pills that he claimed would turn him black. Poor Hank fell for it!

Tony Kinsey's quintet had a booking at the Flamingo one night with a guest singer. Her name was Joy Marshall. Joy was a black American with half-Cuban blood who was trying to get work in the UK. She had gained quite a reputation at a nightclub called the Purple Onion in San Francisco, where she lived. An agent in London, Beatrice Bram, managed to set up some work for her over here. Although she was about seven years older than I was, Joy seemed to take a liking to me and we started going out together. She was a tough customer and more a cabaret artist than a pure jazz singer. I was rather intimidated by her and one night, while I was at her flat, she told me she was worried about continuing the relationship because she would end up wanting to get married. Actually the main reason things moved in that direction was pressure from her damned agent. 'Bee' Bram, as she was known, was on to her all the time about getting an English husband so she could work in the UK without the hassle of renewing her work permit every few weeks. I was aware of this but so infatuated with the idea of going out with a black woman that I decided to go ahead with the marriage. I felt the challenge would either 'make a man of me' or destroy me completely. I guess it nearly did both in the end.

We were together for two hellish years in which she did her best to humiliate me. She worked a lot at the Blue Angel Club, an upmarket cabaret joint in Mayfair, and was earning far better money than I was. Many famous people frequented and worked at the club, including the young David Frost, who had been in the Cambridge Footlights Revue and was then working in cabaret as a satirical comedian. The main attraction, though, was Leslie Hutchinson. 'Hutch', as he was known, was a West Indian singer and pianist who had been encouraged by Cole Porter to work in cabaret. He took London by storm before the Second World War, selling over a million records. His work, at expensive clubs like the Café de Paris and Quaglinos, made him the toast of the town, a friend of royalty and a darling of the rich nightclub set. But by the sixties his fame had dwindled and his main gig was at the Blue Angel.

Wedding with singer Joy Marshall, 1962.

We had our wedding reception at the club and many celebrities showed up, including the brilliant Irish comedian, Dave Allen who was just beginning to make a name for himself. Like Lenny Bruce in America, he was pretty outrageous and took delight in making fun of his fellow-Irishmen, using his brilliant sense of comedy to expose all kinds of hypocrisy, especially some of the aberrations of Irish Catholicism. He was a great favourite with musicians.

Bee Bram caused all kinds of problems at the wedding itself, putting my mother and sister into a taxi and sending them off on a frantic trip across London with instructions to get hold of papers necessary to legalise Joy's marriage status. They even had to pay for their own taxi when they rushed back with the papers. Now Joy was officially married to a UK resident, Bee could make her considerable commission from her future bookings with no further hassle.

Joy wound me up big time and was always taunting me about my English suburban background and the fact she earned more than I did. She took great delight in quoting an American limerick at me, 'Peter, Peter, pumpkin eater, had a wife and couldn't keep her.' Boy, that hurt! I tried to put up with it, but one day she pushed me too far. Seeing my sudden, uncharacteristically angry reaction, she must have thought she had finally pressed my 'fight' button because, the next thing I knew, she pulled a carving knife out of the kitchen drawer and threatened me with it, saying, 'If you lay a finger on me I'll kill you!' Realising I had finally stood up to her and got her attention, I gave her a cold, withering look, snatched the knife from her and without taking my eyes off her, calmly placed it back in the drawer, saying icily, 'Don't ever try that shit on me again, bitch!' I was angry and scared but it did the trick. She skulked off and never tried that again.

Things didn't get any better, though. Joy just made my life, and probably hers, a misery. Around this time she joined the Dankworth band. Cleo hadn't worked regularly with John since before I was with the band and he had decided he needed a singer again. I was paranoid that Joy was having affairs behind my back and one night, when she was late coming back from a gig with John, it came to a head. I knew John would be giving her a lift back to our home in Claygate and I went out in my old Wolseley 6/90 looking for them. I found them parked in a lay-by in a country lane near our flat. In fact, I think, they were only talking but, looking back on it, what followed was hilarious. They spotted me as I did a rally-style 360 degree handbrake turn. John and I were both fast drivers, and there followed a mad car chase through the winding country lanes. I never saw Joy leap out of a car as quick as when she arrived home that night. By the time I had screeched to a halt, she had dived into the flat and John had put his foot to the metal and screamed off in a cloud of tyre smoke. Next morning, Joy had gone out and a very sheepish-looking John Dankworth knocked on the front door and explained how nothing had happened the night before. It was quite surreal to have my old boss driving about fifty miles just to apologise and explain that he and Joy had only stopped for a chat in his car.

John and I laughed the whole affair off in the end. The incident that finally drove me almost to suicide came later. Joy had been asked to take over the leading role in a touring musical, starting in Manchester. It could have been a big break for her but, for reasons I never quite understood, she messed it up. I got a sad, tearful phone call saying she had been sacked and would I please drive all the way to Manchester, pick her up and bring her home. She sounded so unhappy and said she really needed me. I thought she had finally realised she had a damned good husband after all. These feelings grew when I arrived in her hotel room and found her giving an interview to a newspaper. She was telling a journalist that all she wanted to do now was to spend time with her husband and start a family. It turned out to be total bullshit just for the newspapers and her image, which she was trying to salvage after getting fired. As soon as the reporter had gone, she turned on me and abruptly ordered me to get the car and drive her back to London, *tout de suite*. I had arrived only an hour before. The two hundred mile drive back was a nightmare. I guess she felt badly humiliated about getting fired and took it out on me, now she had got her ride home. Some time after that, Joy became pregnant but her gynaecologist advised an expensive termination after a short stay in the exclusive London Clinic. I never really knew for sure whether it had been a problem pregnancy or whether she had in fact simply had an abortion without telling me. In fact, to this day I don't even know if the unborn child was mine. I had, long before, given up believing much of what she told me. By now the whole marriage was a nasty humiliating mess, but I hung on as best I could in spite of being suicidal at times.

At least things were going from strength to strength with Tony Kinsey's band. Annie Ross, the amazingly talented British singer with the famous Lambert, Hendricks and Ross vocal group, left LHR and moved back to England. Touring the world non-stop for years had taken its toll and she needed a change. Tony was a good friend of Annie's and we started working with her a lot. Annie was multi-talented, came from a show business family and had been virtually 'born in a suitcase'. She was a child star in Hollywood and lived and worked in the States most of her life. She hung out with Bird and Dizzy and all the 52nd Street guys in the fifties. Now back in England, it wasn't long before she started working again with us accompanying her. She was a real show business person and we did some great shows.

Tony wrote the music for a new revue called *Wham Bam Thank You Ma'am*. The book was written by script writer and comedian Marty Feldman. Marty was a big deal then and an incredibly funny guy. He had a terrible eye impediment. I guess you would say he was seriously boss-eyed but it gave him an hilarious appearance that he used to great comic effect. Although he was weird as hell in appearance, he was married to a stunningly beautiful and sexy woman. They were deeply in love and were a wonderfully warm and happy couple. We used to call them 'Beauty and the Beast'.

On the opening night, Annie was supposed to sing one number sitting sedately on a flying trapeze. The damned thing got hung up somewhere in the flies and poor Annie, great trouper that she was, sang the whole thing hanging by one leg, upside down. She never blinked an eye, but we all fell about laughing and could hardly play. The show was a great success, with some fine old music hall stars in it, like the legendary Fred Emney and the Irish actor, Dermot Kelly. Marty Feldman's sketches were wonderfully surreal. This was a great time for satire and *That Was The Week That Was* started a new era in television comedy.

Wham Bam Thank You Ma'am was soon followed by an even crazier revue, put together by Dan Farson and full of more old music hall acts. One that particularly sticks in my mind was a guy with the stage name of Bob Tray. His act would end with him singing a mad song in which he accompanied himself by banging his head violently with a metal beer tray in time to the music. He bashed himself almost unconscious every performance. He showed us his head once. Under his hair, his cranium was covered in huge, ugly, red and purple wheals. He was completely mad. Those guys always had to have some kind of gimmick to get work but, shit, what a way to earn a living!

One of the most interesting projects we worked on was a play by Frank Norman, *A Kayf Up West*, directed by Joan Littlewood at the legendary Theatre Royal, Stratford East. Frank also wrote the better-known hit, *Fings Ain't What They Used t'Be*. Joan was a real Cockney from London's East End, with a great reputation as a cutting edge film and theatre director. Way ahead of her time, she used a lot of improvisation and other new techniques, and actors loved to work with her. She directed all Brendan Behan's plays, the best known of which was probably *The Borstal Boy*. Behan, a notoriously wild Irishman whose drunken exploits were always in the papers, unfortunately died of alcoholism during our run and Annie, Joan and several of the cast flew out to Dublin for his funeral, getting back just in time to do the show that night. The quintet not only played onstage but we all had bit parts as well. I only had a few lines but it was my first tentative experience of acting. The play was based on real events and characters from the Harmony Inn, a cafe in Soho's Archer Street where musicians used to hang out.

Joan was fascinating to work with. She was so inventive and, although she swore like a trooper at the cast when things weren't going right, everyone loved her as much as she loved her actors. One night the word went around that Marlene Dietrich was coming to see the performance. She must have had a high regard for Joan Littlewood to bother coming to the tiny theatre and she seemed to enjoy the play. After the performance she stayed awhile, drinking and talking to us in the bar. There I was, hanging out with this legendary diva! She had an incredible aura about her and I was impressed with her formidable intellect and her knowledge of the theatre and art in general. I was over-awed by her reputation but she seemed quite approachable and relaxed in this intimate theatre setting.

Around this time Tubby Hayes asked me to join a new big band he was forming and I was thrilled to accept. I could usually fit the gigs into my regular schedule with Tony Kinsey's quintet and Les Condon was also going to be in the new band. Tubby's big band was without doubt the greatest Britain had ever produced up to that time. It was full of the very best guys and, with Tubby's writing, a shining beacon of perfection as a jazz orchestra. You only have to hear some of the old television and radio recordings to realise that band has never been surpassed when it comes to hard-edged, hard-swinging brilliance. There have been other great British bands since, but Tubby's has withstood the test of time and is now a legend. The spirit in the band was phenomenal. Everyone would pull out all the stops if we had a gig with Tubby, no matter how stoned we were and, boy, did we get high in those days! It was a matter of honour and respect, for Tubby and for our fellow-musicians in the band. We were the best and we intended to stay that way. Originally I played tenor, but later took over the lead alto chair. I continued to work with it right up to Tubby's untimely death in 1973. In spite of the fact that he precipitated one of the lowest points in my life while I was in his band, Tubby and I remained close friends.

One night, Joy told me the shattering news that she had slept with Tubby after one of his quartet gigs and intended to carry on doing so. I was not surprised she had two-timed me, but that she had done it with Tubby was a bombshell. I had to carry on working with the band and everyone soon knew what was going on. I asked friends like Les Condon and bassist Phil Bates what I should do. Phil said I should do the macho thing and kick Tubby's ass. Les was more pragmatic and, in the end, I followed that approach. I knew the marriage was over and the best thing was to leave Joy. I decided not to get violent. Tubby was only short but built like a brick shit-house and would probably have kicked my ass instead. I arranged to meet him in my car to talk the thing through. It was the only way, as neither of us wanted me to leave the band. I decided the music was more important than trying to get heavy and fall out with Tubby, especially as both Tubby and I reckoned the affair with Joy would never last anyway. I packed my bags and left Joy but Les Condon told me that, although I had made the right decision, I must get my head together and get a lawyer. He warned me that, because I had left Joy, she could get real nasty and claim I was the guilty party in any messy divorce suit. I didn't think she would be that mean but Les was right: I couldn't take that chance.

I went to a lawyer and to my horror he told me I had to get a detective and catch Joy and Tubby in the act if I wanted to cover myself and show I wasn't the guilty party in the divorce. Bear in mind I was totally crushed and humiliated by the whole thing and the last thing I wanted to do was spy on them sleeping together. There was no way out, the detective insisted: he and I must go round to the flat at 6 a.m. and catch them at it. There followed a nightmare that I never want to live through again, although looking back it did have its funny side. The official procedure was to creep up to my own front door or to the windows of the flat, trying to get visual and audible proof that Tubby and Joy were there in *flagrante delicto*. We heard their voices and the deal was to wait until 8 a.m. and then bang on the door and confront them. Funnily enough, they were already starting to argue and fight. Tubby was not going to find his relationship with her much better than mine had been. We knocked on the door and announced, from outside, who we were. But Tubby told us to 'fuck off!' and continued arguing with Joy. In fact, he was getting ready to leave for the airport as he had a gig in Germany that day. What I didn't know was that some of the guys on the gig had arranged to meet him so they could travel to the airport together. Suddenly a cab pulled up and Jimmy Deuchar, Harry South and a couple of other close friends of mine arrived at the door to see me and the detective peering in through the letterbox trying to get 'the evidence'! I've never been so embarrassed in my life. They stared at the scene, saying 'What the fuck's going on, Pete?' As I tried to explain, Tubby answered the door, let them in and slammed the door on me and Sherlock Holmes. We could hear them all laughing their heads off inside although, other than Tubby, I think the guys were as embarrassed as me.

The detective decided we had enough evidence, so we crept away like stupid cat burglars, and all that was left for me was to lick my wounds. In spite of this I kept working with the band, but it was a humiliating nightmare. There is an old BBC television *Jazz 625* show of the band that captures this time and still gives me the creeps when I see it. I am sitting on the end of the sax section, staring straight ahead with a look of thunder and every so often the camera pans to the audience, where you can see Joy right in the front row, her black face smirking right at the camera. Check it out next time you watch it. It's like something out of *East Enders*. People say I know how to play the blues. If nothing else, that experience gave me hands-on knowledge. After that, playing the blues became second nature to me!

I was soon able to bury myself in new work when Annie Ross opened her own club, Annie's Room, in Covent Garden. Tony's quintet became the resident band at the plush new venue and we played jazz there six nights a week and accompanied a procession of great jazz singers. They would do two weeks at a time and this was usually accompanied by at least one well-paid television show for which we provided backing. We got good exposure and my reputation as a tenor player came on in leaps and bounds as I played with all the artists. The word even spread back to America. Annie would be featured regularly, of course, as the star singer, but we also did regular stints with Jon Hendricks, Joe Williams, Ernestine Anderson, Dakota Staton, Blossom Dearie, violinist Stuff Smith and many others.

Jon Hendricks and Dakota Staton stayed over in Britain and I often worked with them on gigs and tours outside of the club. Jon was amazing. On the first rehearsal he had only rhythm section parts and was doing all the Lambert, Hendricks and Ross vocal arrangements of the Basie band book. LHR had between them written hip lyrics to every note in the Basie arrangements, including all the solos, and Jon expected me to play all the ensemble parts with him, by ear and by memory. He would just sing and teach me the whole arrangement, then sing my harmony parts. I had to memorise the lot in just one rehearsal. I did my best and got maybe a third of it right on the first night. By the third night I had them all nailed, to Jon's delight. The great thing was that learning music by ear under pressure like that really gives you invaluable training. The music soaked into my brain so deep that, when Jon came back a few months later, I could still remember the whole damned show. Unlike most scat singers, Jon never used the usual clichés. He just improvised like a horn player. This was tough because, when we swapped eight bar sections, he would immediately grab hold of anything I played and top it with his next eight bars. He had an unfair advantage because he didn't have to finger a horn but just sing and, with his ears, it was hard to keep up with him. It was great, though. Just like working with a top-line horn player. I am not a fan of most scat singing and very few can take it to that level of inventive perfection.

Dakota Staton was another great singer with a powerful voice and personality. She had some beautiful arrangements, many of which had been written for her by Benny Carter. The only problem was the guy she had with her who acted as her agent, musical director and manager. Alhajj Talib Ahmad Dawud, alias Hajji, was a trumpet player who had worked with the Dizzy Gillespie big band. In fact, I believe that great tune 'Dahoud' was named after him. About five-foot nothing, with a massive ego, he tried to take over and gave everyone a hard time. He was funny, though. They were like the 'odd couple'. Dakota was a large, fat lady, much bigger than Hajji and he would look up at her and call out, 'Hey, Beautiful!' That was his nickname for her.

The tempos were never right and Dakota was always glaring at Hajji, who counted the numbers in, trying to conduct the quintet all the time like some black midget Leopold Stokowski. In turn, Hajji would yell at the band: 'Too fast', or, 'Too slow, pick the tempo up, man!' He was a real pain in the ass but Dakota sang her socks off every night. One night, when I was backing her with my own quartet, Hajji was sick and Dakota asked me to count in the band. I was not too keen as she was always bitching about the tempos. If Hajji couldn't get it right, how was I going to do it? She told me not to worry and I did the honours. Her opening tune was always a very up-tempo 'Cherokee' in the key of G and I had to count the band in and then play a fast and furious solo tenor intro for eight bars. To my amazement, the whole night went great and Dakota came up and said it was the best gig she had done in years. The tempos were all fine and I realised it was Hajji who was causing all the trouble. Without him there she could relax and enjoy herself. Later on they split up and I did many gigs backing Dakota with my own quartet. We had a ball every time and became really good friends. She used to wear very tight dresses and the only way she could get her considerable frame into them was to get me to zip her up. To get enough of a purchase on her zip, I used a small pair of pliers that I carried around in my sax repair kit. I still have those pliers in my case. Every night I would hear a voice booming out of her dressing room, calling, 'Hey, Peter, have you got your pliers?' That was my cue. I would go in, then she would breath out as far as she could and say, 'OK. Now, Pete!' That way, we managed to shoe-horn her into her dress. It became a great joke between us and had everyone mystified, wondering what the hell we were up to on our own in her dressing room every night, with this mysterious pair of pliers.

I was beginning to cope with my grief over my broken marriage but to do it I started using a lot of cocaine. I now had easy access to the drug and to heroin, although I was scared of trying that at first. For some strange reason, my association with Joy plus my higher profile at Annie's Room seemed to make me more appealing to women. Don't ask me why, but I began to find girls approaching me more often. I guess they mistakenly thought if someone like Joy found me attractive enough to marry maybe I had something going in that department. They may also have felt sorry for me when my marriage broke up; who knows? Anyway I started having quite a few flirtations, had a ball and began to regain my confidence.

About this time, Ernestine Anderson came to work at the club. Ernestine was a beautiful singer. She had a lovely soulful way of interpreting a lyric, swung like mad and had a great blues feeling. She reminded me a little of the great Dinah Washington. In fact Ernestine was a big fan of Dinah's, but had her own unique style. I had always loved her singing and also found her very attractive. I was thrilled she was coming to the club, but had no idea she would show more than a passing interest in me too. From the first rehearsal I was madly in love. Too nervous to approach her, especially after what I had just been through with Joy, I waited for Ernestine to say something. One night she asked if I fancied hanging out somewhere after the gig. We got in my car and drove around talking. She had been a friend of Joy's and knew about my marriage problems. She was so understanding as I poured out my story to her. I was now living in a flat with Hank Shaw in Streatham and bucked up courage to invite her back. She said she would love to and we spent the rest of the night together, talking and laughing. It seemed she was immediately attracted to me when she saw me wearing dark glasses at our first rehearsal and thought Joy had treated me very badly. Ernestine was a tough cookie but, unlike Joy, she had a very warm and loving personality and a heart of gold. For the rest of her stint at the club we were very close and she did wonders for my self-esteem. I think, in truth, that I had just been infatuated with Joy, but I was really deeply in love with Ernestine and will never forget the wonderful but sadly brief time we spent together.

One night, shortly before I worked with 'Steen', as Ben Webster used to call her, I was at a friend's house snorting cocaine. When I ran out my friend gave me a taste of his but I didn't realise, until he blurted it out two weeks later, that he had mixed heroin with it without telling me. When you snort a lot of cocaine your nerve endings get a bit frayed, especially as it wears off. When I got home that night, the nervousness just wasn't there. I had a great night's sleep, woke up feeling fine and forgot all about it. I was scared of heroin for obvious reasons, but also because it can make you vomit and I always hated that. If my friend had only kept his secret my life may have been different, but when I discovered I had already taken it and felt fine, my fear disappeared. I started trying it, mixed with cocaine. You get all the same rush from the cocaine but the heroin tempers the nervousness and you can control the overall effect, by getting the balance right between the two. It would prove a terrible mistake but for a while I kept things under control and spaced out my heroin use so as not to get hooked. It takes up to a week or more of daily use before you get addicted.

While I was with Ernestine I took heroin for several days and felt the first signs of mild withdrawals one day when I ran out. I now had to use it regularly, but in relatively small amounts. Before she returned to the States, Ernestine warned me I needed to be careful or I could end up in serious trouble. We promised to stay in touch while she was away. In fact I didn't hear from her until a few days before she returned for another gig at Annie's Room, a few months later. She was upset and very disappointed to find I was now well hooked, just as she had warned me. She couldn't bear to see me going downhill that way and I either had to straighten up or jeopardise our relationship. I let her and myself down badly. Things had gone too far so the brief relationship ended. Maybe it wouldn't have worked out in the end anyway, but I had not helped matters and I was grief-stricken to lose someone I was so deeply in love with. Fortunately there was no animosity between us and one night, a few years later, Ernestine came with a new partner to a show I was working in. I had by then married again and I introduced my wife Linda to Ernestine. Linda knew all about my earlier relationship with Ernestine and it was nice to see them hit it off OK. I think Steen was glad to see I was happily married at last, to someone who she could see was very special to me.

One fortnight, Nina Simone worked at the club, but she used her own band. We just played between her sets. Nina was a strange woman, hugely talented, but with the reputation of being very difficult and unpredictable. She was aloof, but very courteous to us. She always said hello when she had to go through our band room to get to her own dressing room. She was accompanied by an imposing-looking white guy who was said to be an ex-police chief. He reminded me of Rod Steiger in *The Heat of the Night*. I believe he was also her manager and you wouldn't have wanted to mess with him, so I guess he took good care of Nina's business. He never said much but seemed a nice guy. It was rather bizarre to see Nina Simone, the great black singer and civil rights activist, with this white ex-cop!

My habit got worse by the day and I spent all my wages on drugs. I could just about keep myself supplied on a regular basis although I was forced to return home, as I couldn't afford to pay rent any more. One Sunday, when my parents were away, I ran out of heroin and couldn't get any until the following day, if then. I experienced full blown heroin withdrawal for the first time. It was terrifying, I felt so ill I had to lie down. But every time I did, all my nerve endings were on fire and I had to get up again. I writhed on the floor in torment, unable to get up and throwing myself about like a rag doll. I was so scared I called an ambulance, naively hoping they would realise I needed heroin and do something to help. I was carted off to casualty but then brought home again with no treatment, having been told there was nothing wrong with me and not to waste their time. The withdrawals got even worse so I called the ambulance again. This time they laid me on a hospital trolley and left me, but because I was thrashing about with my nerve endings screaming, I fell off the trolley and crashed to the stone floor. Doctors rushed in and gave me an injection. I hoped it was heroin or morphine and I felt myself drifting into a deep sleep.

Heroin withdrawals affect people different ways but, to someone who has not experienced them, it's impossible to convey the terrible effects on body and mind. I vaguely remember being in another ambulance, but when I awoke it was 3 p.m. the following day and I found, to my horror, I was in a mental hospital. The ward was full of lunatics; a real mad house! I pleaded with the doctors that all I needed was some heroin, but they insisted I was insane. When my parents arrived in the evening, having found out where I was, I told them I had to get out of there, right away. The doctors couldn't force me to stay as I had apparently signed myself in before they sedated me the night before, but they warned Mum and Dad that, if I were released, I would be back for sure inside a week, and under a restraining order. After more examinations and pleas from me and my parents, I was allowed to return home. I should have been playing with Tubby's band that night, but I never made it. The next day I managed to score heroin and things carried on as before. Tubby overlooked my missed gig and I continued working as best I could, but I could no longer escape the fact I had become totally dependent on heroin and needed help.

5

'I don't give a fuck if you're Lawrence of Arabia,'
Tony Kinsey

The residency continued at Annie's Room, but I was also working elsewhere with Jon Hendricks and Dakota Staton and sometimes with blues singer Jimmy Witherspoon. Jimmy knocked me out when I heard him at the Essen Jazz Festival in 1961, where I first saw Bud Powell play, but it was at Annie's club that we first worked together and we hit it off right away. He was a big man but he loved to squeeze himself into my MG Midget when I would give him a ride. It turned out he was a big fan of this very British sports car and had a fancy white one at home in the States. I learnt so much accompanying 'Spoon. He had tremendous charisma and playing with him was like having a conversation. He would sing the first line of a blues and put so much feeling and innuendo into it that I would try to almost speak through my horn, answering his phrase. I would attempt to convey the meaning of actual words and he would usually get what I meant and beam all over his face. It was just as if we were talking to each other, rather than him singing and me playing the tenor. That's real storytelling in music.

You have to know how to leave singers space and complement their words when they breathe. Hajji told me at Dakota's first rehearsal, 'Don't you be playing when she's singing, man. Come in when she's taking a breath.' I never forgot that lesson and by the time I worked with 'Spoon I was getting quite a reputation for accompanying singers. It's an art in itself and very rewarding, provided you are playing with a good artist who really knows how to express a lyric. You have to know when to hold back and let them set the musical agenda. I got spoilt working with great singers like Ernestine, Witherspoon, Dakota, Joe Williams,

Mark Murphy and, later, Ray Charles and Tony Bennett. But it can be a drag with people who don't have their kind of deep feeling for lyrics, story telling and soul. I tend to avoid working with vocalists these days because those guys are hard acts to follow. For me there has to be a special empathy with a singer, or it becomes frustrating and I feel like I'm wearing a bit of a straight jacket and just can't play well.

Dakota and Hajji were well aware of my addiction problems but tolerated them because I always did my job well onstage. One day they decided to take me in hand and try to get me off junk themselves. They arranged for me to stay in their flat for a few days so they could look after me, while I tried to go cold turkey. Hajji insisted I eat as much as I could, as he said this was vital while taking 'the cure'. Of course you can't face eating anything while you are trying to kick heroin. Although withdrawals didn't affect me this way, many addicts throw up violently. Hajji knew this and gave me instructions to go down to the cafe below the flat and come back with two large malted milk shakes. He then broke several eggs, mixed them into the shakes and stood over me while I tried to force them down. He was very insistent they should be malted shakes and said, with the eggs added, they would make a high protein drink that I could hopefully keep down while I couldn't stomach anything else. He told me he had helped other guys in a similar way in the States. After this strange meal I was put to bed while Dakota read me verses from the Koran. Both Hajji and Dakota had long before converted to the Muslim faith, like many other African Americans at the time. None of this did any good, unfortunately, but they were really kind to me and I was moved at their almost parental concern for my well-being. They did their best to help but, when I said I just couldn't take any more, they let me out to go and score some heroin. In fact they were very understanding and stuck by me. They did their best to keep me on an even keel at least. They really were taking on the role of surrogate parents and I owe them a lot for that.

Annie Ross was very well connected with show business people and often had famous guests drop in at the club. One night I was aware of a strange excited murmuring going around the audience. Suddenly a guy came up and asked politely if he could sing a number with us. It was Tony Bennett. He sang 'I Lost my Heart in San Francisco', to rapturous applause. He was really sweet and, surprisingly, quite shy. He thanked us and said how much he loved the band. In fact he gave me a nice mention in a newspaper interview he did at the time. I worked with him briefly again several years later and played a couple of alto solos on a CD, *The Art of Excellence*, he made in Britain in the late eighties.

Early one evening, the pianist and composer Lalo Schifrin, who had not long left Dizzy's band, also came and sat in. Another night, during the making of the movie *Lawrence of Arabia*, Annie arrived with a whole team from the studio. Everyone was getting drunk and Peter O'Toole took it into his head to stagger over to the bandstand. He picked up a drum stick and began hitting one of Tony Kinsey's cymbals, right in the middle of a number. Tony was furious, stood up and yelled at him to piss off. O'Toole arose to his full height, faced Tony, and boomed out with his best, though rather drunken, Shakespearean voice, 'Don't you know who I am? I'm Peter O'Toole!' Tony, with a sudden stroke of comic brilliance, yelled right back at him, 'I don't care if you're Lawrence of Arabia, get the fuck off my drum kit!' Everyone cracked up, including O'Toole and he didn't bother us again.

The guest artists at the club were almost exclusively singers and we sure had some great ones there. Joe Williams did two weeks. It was the first time I had heard him outside the Basie band environment. He was a superb cabaret artist. For the first set he would sing good commercial standards and ballads while guests were dining. The second set he would sing more jazz-orientated things and for the last set he was the Joe Williams we all knew, singing nothing but blues. Joe was a great artist but he

The Tony Kinsey Quintet, early 1960s. *Left to right*: PK, Kinsey, Gordon Beck, Les Condon, Jeff Clyne.

had a penchant for the good life. He was well connected with the British upper class set and, like Jon Hendricks who had similar social aspirations, flaunted his friendship with lords and ladies and some of the minor royals. I usually got to play plenty of long solos behind the artists but Joe only gave me about eight bars during the whole first night. I wasn't bothered but someone must have got onto him about it because the next night he made a kind of apology. He told me that when he first joined Basie, the Count would only let him sing one tune a night until he had established himself. Joe was checking me out the same way but gave me more and more to play each night after that.

The one exception to the 'all singers' regime was violinist Stuff Smith. That was a wonderful couple of weeks. Stuff had gained a lot of respect from the modern jazz guys after he made a great recording with Dizzy Gillespie, so we were looking forward to working with him. Stuff was a great player, a real original and a lovely guy, if a little eccentric. He had us enthralled every night, especially when he played 'Body and Soul'. He played it differently every time and with a surprisingly modern approach, the way he had on the record with Dizzy.

Blossom Dearie was always a big success at the club. We would often hang out and talk, especially about Bill Evans, whom she knew well. Blossom played good piano and told me she learnt a lot from Bill. However we had a bit of trouble in the club one night while she was there. The main room was separated from the bar by a glass partition. I was sitting in the bandroom while Blossom was singing in her quiet inimitable way and playing piano. All of a sudden, one of the waiters came into our room. He had removed his shirt and was covered in blood from a head injury. Apparently some Covent Garden porters had decided to start a riot in the bar. There was a terrible fight, with broken bottles, broken chair legs and God knows what else. It was total mayhem but Blossom, who could see the whole bloodthirsty scene through the glass partition, carried on singing as if nothing was happening. She was a real pro and just kept working as the chairs, bottles and blood-stained bodies flew around, crashing into the toughened glass partition. Eventually the police arrived; a couple of people were carted off to hospital for repairs and the evening carried on as if nothing had happened.

* * *

I was still spending most of my wages on drugs, often driving at high speed to the East End and back, between sets, to score. Things were getting severely out of hand. Phil Seamen once told me if he ever found me taking heroin he would kill me but, if I did, I was to go straight to him for help. Now was the time to turn to him and he advised me to become a registered addict. In those days it was possible to register with the Home Office and get your supply from a doctor, if you could find one to take you on. Phil had been registered for many years with the top addiction specialist in the UK, Dr Isabella Frankau. Lady Frankau, as she was known, was the wife of Sir Claude Frankau, consulting surgeon at St George's Hospital, and had an illustrious career.

During the Second World War she had been a top psychiatrist for the RAF and part of her job was finding ways to keep our pilots awake during their long dangerous sorties. There was not much she didn't know about drugs. We couldn't have kept those pilots in the air, with hardly any sleep, without resorting to various kinds of amphetamines. She once gave me an envelope filled with pure nicotinamide tablets she had had made up specially, instead of giving me extra cocaine. She had discovered during the war that it kept pilots awake and nicotinamide was far less dangerous than stuff like Dexedrine. It was only natural she would become a leading authority on drug addiction after the war.

Frankau had a private practice just off Harley Street and her patients included people like Stan Getz and Bill Evans when they were in London. She was also a friend of William Burroughs, the outrageous author of *The Naked Lunch* and a one-time heroin addict. I shared the waiting room with him once, when he came to see Lady Frankau on a social visit. Most addicts were reluctant to get registered as this put you on the Home Office list as an official addict, with all the restrictions that could imply. Phil persuaded Lady Frankau to take me on as a private patient and, knowing I was broke, she never charged me consultation fees. The morning I got registered, she gave me a script for a small amount of heroin and cocaine, asking me to return later that evening so she could assess me properly. It so happens that I was recording at the EMI studios on Abbey Road with Dakota Staton that afternoon. The recording turned out well and Dakota told me, many years later, she thought it was one of her best albums. Phil met me at the end of the session and we returned to Lady Frankau's about 6 p.m. After further consultation she agreed to give me more than enough heroin and cocaine to supply my needs on a regular basis. Starting from that night, I became a legally registered heroin and cocaine addict, one of less than a thousand in the entire United Kingdom.

At first it was as if a huge weight had been lifted, but it soon became clear there was a sting in the tail. When I started using heroin, I would snort it into my nose, but now I was injecting, first into a muscle in my backside but, very soon, mainlining it straight into a vein. My real taste was for cocaine but, when you mainline that, you get a massive and instant rush that wears off very quickly. You then have to have another fix, maybe as little as fifteen minutes later. I was now mixing cocaine with heroin, in a speedball, as they called it. It's a lethal cocktail, which results in a rapid and uncontrollable increase in your heroin use. What had at first been a perfectly adequate supply was soon no longer enough. I was using all my script long before the next one was due and constantly had to pester Lady Frankau for more. I had made friends with a local chemist who lived over the shop and I began to call Frankau at her country estate in Cambridge on Sundays. I learned to dread Christmas, bank holidays and Sundays as I had always run out after a couple of days. She had said it was alright to call her there in an emergency, but it became a bizarre ritual, every damned Sunday. Sir Claude would always answer the phone saying, 'Oh no, you again!' and pass me on to Lady Frankau. After giving me the usual mild ticking off, she would phone my chemist, who would open the shop specially and dispense my extra supply. Even that was not enough. By early Monday morning I'd be sick again and would call my GP at 8 a.m. He would then leave me a small script in the box, so I could pick it up before he opened the surgery. By 9 a.m. I had returned with my supply from the chemist and straightened myself out enough to travel up to the West End to see Lady Frankau and start the same weekly ritual all over again. It was ridiculous. The more I took, the more I needed.

I once had to work a few days in the North East with Dakota. We were doing cabaret spots in two different towns every night and I soon ran out of stuff. In the end I got my father to call Frankau and arrange to get more drugs which he delivered to the airport, from where they were sent by regular flight to

Newcastle, where we were based. My whole week's wages went on the plane fare. I crawled out of bed, getting a taxi to Newcastle Airport in time to collect my tiny package from this damned big airliner. The airport staff must have thought I was totally mad. But I made all the gigs.

Somehow I continued to play all right when I did work, but my life was now totally occupied keeping myself supplied with drugs. I was playing on automatic pilot, with periods of violent withdrawal and pleas for extra scripts from Lady Frankau. Life was a complete nightmare. If I hadn't been registered, I would never have been able to afford what had become a huge habit. Frankau eventually reduced my script in stages to a more modest amount, but I was also buying extra as well. My health was deteriorating badly and one night I woke up with severe chest pains. I was rushed to Kingston Hospital, where I had originally come into the world. Now I was nearly to die there.

It turned out that I was suffering from severe pneumonia and pleurisy. One lung had collapsed completely and they were fearful for my life. I wasn't worried about dying: that would have been a bloody relief. I just wanted the pain in my chest to go and to make sure I got my heroin in hospital. That could have been very difficult but, thanks to my understanding GP who had administered a double shot of morphine at home, arrangements were made for me to get my official heroin doses in hospital. Cocaine, however, was totally out of the question. Taking it can be lethal if you have any kind of infection, as it badly weakens your immune system. In fact, apart from tiredness, depression and a certain mental craving, the withdrawals from cocaine pale into insignificance once you have experienced heroin deprivation. After a couple of days the pain in my chest caused by the pleurisy had subsided, I got just enough heroin to alleviate withdrawals and I settled fairly happily into resting and recovering from the pneumonia. It took several weeks and various combinations of antibiotics before the pneumonia cleared up but I felt better than I had for a long time and I still had a small cocaine script to look forward to when I got home.

Altogether I spent six weeks in hospital but, sometime in the fourth week, I had a shock. After having received what I thought were my heroin injections, three times a day, I was suddenly informed by a very happy chief consultant that I had received no heroin at all for the last ten days. He proudly announced that, therefore, I was cured of my addiction. He thought I would be pleased but, idiot that I was, I was furious. What happened next shows how far addiction can be a state of mind. I started having violent phantom withdrawal symptoms, couldn't sleep a wink and went into a blind panic. The nurses apparently had been having a right old time trying to substitute vials of distilled water for my heroin. I had given them a big problem because I always insisted on seeing the vials for myself, to check they had 'Diamorphine Hydrochloride' clearly marked on them. They had shown me heroin vials but then switched them behind my back for water. Apparently Lady Frankau, my parents and the doctors had all been involved in the conspiracy. I knew Frankau had done this before to one of her patients and because of that I had kept a keen eye on the situation in case she was trying to pull the same stunt on me. What made it worse was that my parents had, on instructions from Lady Frankau, thrown my small cocaine script away too. The doctors prescribed a nightly sleeping tablet that helped a bit, but I decided to score some stuff as soon as I got out of there. I wasn't ready to be cured yet and it's very true that you can't get rid of an addiction until you make up your own mind to kick it.

As long as they could keep me fooled, it wasn't hard to taper me off gradually, as I was not getting strong enough injections to do more than just keep me from getting withdrawals. One of the nurses was a pretty young black girl and we ended up laughing about the tricks they resorted to. She told me she was from Kikuyu stock and she took a fancy to me. One night she came very close to me when the other patients were asleep and we fell into a passionate embrace. That did more to help my rehabilitation than all the antibiotics. After I left hospital we went out together a couple of times but when she realised I was back on heroin, I never saw her again. Lady Frankau reluctantly took me back on her books rather than see me score on the black market, but she gave me much smaller scripts.

* * *

One day there was some kind of problem with one of the artists at Annie's Room which led to the Tony Kinsey Quintet falling out with the management of the club. Our residency came to an abrupt end and I was out of work. Shortly after that, however, I was approached by the club bosses who wanted me to come back with a quartet of my own. This put me in a difficult position. Les Condon and Tony Kinsey were well established on the London session scene, so were able to make a reasonable living without the club residency. But I was getting hardly any studio work, partly because saxophonists were expected to double on flute and piccolo, which I didn't play. I was forced to take the gig at the club, but this didn't go down too well at first with Tony or Les Condon, who thought I was acting in an underhand manner, considering we had lost the gig because Tony refused to accompany one of the artists with just a trio when she decided she didn't want Les and me on the gig. She had been told she was working with a quintet but had brought all the wrong horn parts with her and got mad because we made her look a bit of a fool when she pulled some prima donna shit with us. I felt bad about going back to the club after that, but I reasoned that if I could get re-established there with my own quartet, I could maybe get Les and Tony back into the gig later. I had very little alternative and started working again with my own quartet.

We worked with many of the same artists as before but eventually Annie managed to get Anita O'Day to do a two-week stint, Anita had become a big star again after her appearance in the film *Jazz on a Summer's Day*. I was worried about working with her as she had a reputation for being difficult. The first time I saw her was at the Marquee Club with John Dankworth's orchestra, long after I had left it. She was singing the Woody Herman arrangement of 'Four Brothers' and got very animated when the band got to the rather tricky coda, yelling at them to stop and play it again, and get it right. This didn't go down at all well with the guys, all of whom were doing an excellent job. You could have cut the atmosphere with a knife. Anita always travelled with her own drummer, John Poole, a crazy American and a bit of a loose cannon. He was also her manager and probably her lover too. More importantly, he kept her supplied with heroin. Anita told me he could find it in any country in the world, within a few hours! When she worked at Annie's Room she had given 'The Doctor', as she called him, the sack and used my regular drummer Benny Goodman. In the event we all got on fine with her and Anita and I got quite close, once she realised not only that I could play, but that I was also a fellow-addict.

The last Sunday of Anita's stint we did a television show, live from the club. Being a Sunday she and I were both out of heroin and sick as dogs. After the show we went to a party in the hopes of scoring. The cupboard was bare so Anita tried to ply me with whisky instead and, like Hajji before, tried to get me to eat to help relieve the withdrawals. She was pretty tough and able to cope well with being strung out, killing the pain with whisky. That never worked for me; booze just made me feel worse. Anita cleaned up not long after that and went on to have a healthy life and a successful career. I spent the rest of that night driving round London trying unsuccessfully to score. I don't know how I got through that television show. In the lobby of Ronnie Scott's Club there is still an old photo of us taken at the show. In it, Anita looks fine behind her dark glasses but I look like death warmed up. Now, every time I play at Ronnie's, it still gives me the creeps when I see it.

Eventually things started to go sour at Annie's Room again. I think business began to drop off. One week we didn't get our wages and I tried to get heavy with the manager, demanding he pay me. I should have known better as he was well-connected with the London underworld. The next thing I knew he had me up against the wall by the collar. I thought he was going to beat the shit out of me but he didn't. Later he paid me, apologised and said he was uptight because he was having serious financial difficulties himself. The writing was on the wall, though, and the musical policy at the club soon changed for the worse. Eventually we got two weeks notice and I was out of a regular job for the first time in quite a while. In the end that great club, which had started so well, fell by the wayside and closed its doors.

* * *

I had always been very fond of fast cars. My first had been an old Wolseley 6/90, but later I had a red MG Midget sports car. I was a big motor racing fan and through a friend, Roger Simon, who was an assistant film director, I got the chance to drive a racing car round Brands Hatch. Roger was the 'unit director' on the John Frankenheimer movie, *Grand Prix*, and in charge of hiring all the stunt drivers. *Grand Prix* is probably the most authentic film about the sport ever made and the stunt drivers were all top Grand Prix guys, like Graham Hill and Chris Amon. Roger had good connections with the racing school at Brands Hatch and managed to get me a chance to try my hand there for five laps in

PK sitting in a 1970 vintage Palliser Formula Ford owned and raced by his friend Keith Norman, Spa, Belgium, *ca.* 2003.
Photo Vince Maiolini.

a Formula Junior single-seater, very similar to today's Formula Ford class. I was put first behind the wheel of a TVR sports car, with an instructor. I had to drive the car normally while he made notes and gave me a mark, B+, which wasn't bad as I was not told anything about racing technique. Then there was a briefing with a top racing driver and instructor. We novices had to learn basic flag signals and rules of the track. Then we were given helmets and waited our turn to get in a Formula Junior. I really wanted to learn as much as I could from the experience so started quite slowly, steadily building up my speed each lap and leaving my braking later and later as I got used to the car.

The first thing you notice in an open-wheeled racing car is how difficult it is to see the track properly as you are seated so low and the wheels block your view. It is especially difficult to see the apexes of the corners, which is vital when you are racing. You soon get used to it, though, and by the fifth lap I was going almost flat out down the main straight, towards the infamous Paddock Hill Bend. Paddock is unsighted at first, as it drops downhill away from you. It's as if you're speeding towards a cliff top; then, when you finally see the track below, it is way off to your right down a steep incline. If you haven't already spun off, the track starts to tighten up on you. If that doesn't catch you out, the adverse camber regularly will. Even the best drivers come unstuck there at Paddock. To get through it fast you need skill and a load of courage. On my last lap I thought I had left my breaking late until one of the professional racers shot past me, breaking about seventy metres later than I did! It was an eye-opener. Anyone who fancies himself as a bit of a boy racer should realise he is in for a shock if he thinks he can drive fast against the 'real deal' guys. But by the fifth lap I was having a ball and, on accelerating out of what used to be called Bottom Bend, I was pushing hard enough for the rear end to step out. It took me by surprise, as I didn't think I was going fast enough to get close to the limit. This was a real racing car, though, and handled beautifully. I just applied a touch of opposite lock and the Formula Junior reacted immediately and straightened up. The five laps were over in a flash. I would love to have taken a proper course of lessons but you needed serious money for that.

* * *

Around the time I first got registered, I rented a room in Glebe Road, in Barnes, south London. Phil Seamen also had a room there and it was handy for doing gigs at the Bull's Head, where I often worked. The rooms were depressing but cheap and other musicians would often drop in. However, this was eventually the scene of one of the lowest points in my life, when I realised I was spraying my blood over the walls, trying to find a vein to inject into. I was finally thrown out on my ear, owing back rent and leaving most of my belongings and my record collection there to pay the debt.

I had reached the point where it was taking me up to an hour to find a vein that still functioned before I could inject the 'speed ball' of heroin and cocaine, relieve my terrible withdrawal symptoms and feel human enough to start the day. When you have to make many attempts to find a vein, you repeatedly have to remove the blood filled syringe before trying another vein. After a while the blood starts to clot in the syringe. This means that the next time you press the plunger of the syringe, the congealed blood blocks the needle. The result is that the syringe and the needle part company violently under the pressure, then a mixture of blood and drugs spurts out, spattering your shirt and face. What I hadn't realised was it was spurting out so fast it ended up on the walls themselves.

The truth is that the only thing on your mind when this happens is you have wasted more of your valuable drug supply. After all, you can easily clean up the mess later, once the drugs have turned you from a gibbering aching wreck into what you imagine is a normal human being again. One of the crazy ironies of the situation is that once you start mainlining heroin straight into your blood stream, you are stupidly prepared to go through the long agonising ritual of finding a vein to get that powerful, rapid relief, rather than simply pop the stuff straight into a muscle in your backside or thigh. When you inject straight into a vein, the full effect of the drug takes as little as three seconds. Doing it the easy way, into a muscle, it takes three minutes or more and the hit is not as powerful. Three minutes seems far too long to wait and yet, after ten minutes or so, the relief is just the same.

I never really got the wonderful buzz described by many heroin addicts. In any case, after a very short time the only high is the ability to change from a sick shadow of yourself to what appears to be healthy normality. Believe me, in the end this Jekyll and Hyde transformation is itself the only real turn on. It's that feeling of instant control over your physical and mental state that becomes the real addiction. You feel like some kind of Lazarus, raised from the dead, except you are the one performing the apparent miracle. The physical pain of sticking a needle in your arm becomes a part of the whole experience. Many addicts were actually terrified of needles before getting hooked, me included. I used to feel that pain was a kind of penance that justified, in my mind, the relief that followed. The whole thing becomes a ritual described by doctors treating addicts as 'needle addiction'.

Les Condon gave me shelter for a while but I was soon homeless, bumming around, sleeping whenever someone would give me a room for the night. Finally I was forced to live at home again, becoming a terrible burden on my long-suffering parents. Even my father kicked me out for a while, but relented and let me come home again. Life was such a surreal nightmare during this time that I find it hard to remember what happened and when. I have vague memories of certain events but they merge into a horrible blur, and their exact chronology eludes me.

Music was my only means of scraping a living and was ceasing to bring me any joy. Playing had become nerve-wracking and just damned hard work. But I did my best to play well, especially if I was working with Tubby Hayes' band. I also made an album with Zoot Sims and Al Cohn, produced by Jack Sharpe. *Zoot and Al in London* was recorded at Lansdowne Studios in Holland Park and I was asked to write two original compositions for the date. As usual, I left it to the last minute and ended up writing non-stop for a whole day and night. I was still copying parts in the studio, on the session. I never even got around to giving the tunes titles. When the record was finally released, Jack Sharpe had named them 'Pete's Tune One' and 'Pete's Tune Two'. I was using masses of cocaine with the heroin, to keep myself awake, and had a gig in Richmond after we finished the record session. Somehow I struggled to keep awake through the gig, then jumped into my MG Midget and set off to Jack's house in Finchley, where he was giving a party for all the guys on the session. Dog-tired from lack of sleep, I stopped at traffic lights on the North Circular Road, near Hanger Lane. The lights went green, I set off and the next thing I remember was a loud bang. After only a few yards I had fallen asleep and driven straight into a large tree. The MG was a wreck and I was bleeding from a minor cut on my head, but at least I was now suddenly very wide awake. As I had nowhere to stay I had to get to Jack's house and a kindly motorist, who had stopped to help, gave me a lift. I arrived at the party with my head still bleeding slightly, and feeling like a total idiot. Al and Zoot were there, wondering what the hell had happened, but on top of this who should arrive right after me but my estranged wife Joy. That was all I needed! I didn't expect any sympathy from her and she didn't give me any, the bitch!

While I was living in Glebe Road, Bill Le Sage had asked me to play a television show in Hamburg, with a band he had put together for the event. Bill was still prepared to employ me; he was always a good friend through thick and thin. We rehearsed in London and then caught the plane. I spent nearly the whole flight shooting up in the WC, but we arrived safely at the Norddeutscher Rundfunk studios in Hamburg. After the first day of rehearsals there, I ran out of drugs and had to get Jackie, a girl I knew, to fly out from London with a fresh supply from Lady Frankau. I missed one of the rehearsals, suffering bad withdrawals in the hotel room until Jackie arrived. By then, the whole studio knew I had a big drug problem and even Bill was worried whether I could make the gig. On the day of the show I was summoned early to the studio after the make-up people decided I desperately needed a haircut, of all things; my damned coiffure was the last thing on my mind. While the rest of the band were getting ready to play, there was yours truly, sat in a chair in the middle of the huge studio, having his bloody hair cut. I had saved just enough medication to get me through the concert and, according to Bill, I played fine. In fact, he told me I was the least of his problems. A lot of the rest of the band had got drunk and Bill was far more concerned they were going to wreck the gig. Strange as it seems, as long as I had my medication, I could always play my horn and take care of business. Booze, on the other hand can really mess your playing up!

Other humiliating things happened while I was in this sorry state. For instance, Pete King barred me from Ronnie Scott's for a short while because a punter told him that someone had been in the WC cubicle for over an hour and he was worried in case they were ill or something. Pete knew immediately it was me, fixing in there. He banged on the door, read me the Riot Act and banished me from the very club where I had had my first big break! I was totally gutted and couldn't help thinking about when Charlie Parker was banned from Birdland. I began to realise how Bird must have felt; not that my pathetic experience was in any way comparable. Another time, when I was even too broke to pay for my prescription, I waited outside a West End recording studio, hoping someone I knew would come out and lend me a fiver to cash my script. I think Allan Ganley, who had been playing drums on a session there, helped me out that time, but the humiliation was intense. If I had not reached such a low state I might have been recording in that studio, myself, instead of bumming money off fellow-musicians just to get a fix.

Sensing I was coming to the end of my rope, I made a couple of attempts to cut down and then to get off heroin altogether. One time, Lady Frankau, reducing my script more and more, arranged for me to stay with my sister Brenda under twenty-four hour supervision. I was only on a small amount of heroin but still using quite a bit of cocaine. Brenda and her husband Alan were living in a police flat and this must have increased my cocaine-induced paranoia. Alan found me hiding in the wardrobe one day. I was hallucinating that the police were surrounding the place and watching me through the bedroom windows and I was trying to get away, through the bloody wardrobe. It's hilarious to think about it now, but it wasn't funny at the time. My ever-present, overpowering feelings of guilt convinced me that I could hear the police talking about me on their radios and that they were about to raid the flat and arrest me, even though I was doing nothing illegal.

Alan was a good cop, and he got me out of quite a few scrapes. On one occasion, he clocked on and was told they had an arrest warrant out for me. He arranged to handle it himself and knocked on my door with the warrant, accompanied by another copper. I had been caught speeding and, having not shown up in front of the judge, was to be arrested for contempt of court. Alan sorted it all out and arranged for me to go the following morning instead. He duly picked me at 10 a.m. sharp and we went to the local nick. As we had to wait, I told him I badly needed a fix before facing the judge. 'OK, no problem,' he said. 'There's a toilet over there, but don't take all bloody day like you usually do.' We set off to the court in a police car with Alan and the two officers who had nicked me. They were all mates and we had a good chat on the way. Under oath, one of the traffic cops explained, with obvious embarrassment, that I had broken three different speed limits and driven through a red light before they caught up with me. He realised it sounded bad for me, so he took great pains to point out to the judge that it had been three in the morning, the road was empty, I had been driving faultlessly and had in fact stopped at the red light and looked both ways before going through it. He really did his best to get me off and the judge let me go with a very short driving ban and a small fine. The contempt of court charge was simply dropped.

Eventually Frankau weaned me off drugs altogether. Just before she finally got me off, I had arranged to go to my brother's house in Buckinghamshire for a rest. My sister Brenda was there too, as my brother was ill with jaundice. On the Sunday I was out of heroin and called Frankau, who arranged a meeting in a garage forecourt on the A1. Brenda and my sister-in-law Mary took me by car to meet Lady Frankau. There followed a bizarre scene in which I begged on bended knees for just one last fix. I knew Frankau always carried a massive supply of heroin. She finally relented in disgust and gave me one intravenous tablet from one of the dozen or more full bottles in her bag. I was utterly humiliated that Brenda and Mary had seen my total lack of moral fibre. Heroin addiction can so easily destroy every last vestige of self-respect. Confronting and then trying to haul yourself out of such total destruction of your self-esteem can take many years and you never shake off the mental scars completely. Eventually I got off heroin and cocaine but I still felt awful. Things reached rock bottom and the only thing left was to try to climb out of the hole I had dug for myself.

You are supposed to get over the physical effects of heroin withdrawal in about a week to ten days, but the mental torment goes on forever. I couldn't sleep and was exhausted, with absolutely no self-confidence. Then, one day, someone gave me an ampoule of Methedrine (methamphetamine), a powerful stimulant. In theory this was the last thing to use to replace the calming effect of heroin, but it made me feel so much better. I bought some more and it helped me get myself together. It gave me a boost, like cocaine, but didn't make me as nervous. It also lasted for hours and, when I didn't have any, I just felt tired and depressed but it was nothing like the agonies of heroin withdrawal. I told my GP who said he would be happy to prescribe as much as I wanted, if it kept me off heroin. I was soon taking massive doses straight into my veins but was able to function normally. I seemed to have renewed mental and physical vigour and looked forward to the future for the first time in years.

But I was using more of the drug, and after a while my GP decided he couldn't go on prescribing Methedrine in the amounts I needed, so he arranged for me to see a doctor I shall refer to as Dr Smith (not his real name), who had a drug clinic attached to a large mental hospital. Smith seemed at first to be a pretty good guy. He had a policy of letting addicts dictate their own regime, as long as they didn't take liberties. He gave me all the Methedrine I could handle and that was a huge amount. Settled into a semi-controlled environment, I was able to build my life a bit and began studying classical music in my spare time. I buried myself in scores and books, mostly about Béla Bartók, whose music I adored. At the same time I also got interested in the visual arts and took up painting and drawing. From child-hood I had a talent for drawing, having won a prize at the age of eight on a vacation with my parents at Butlin's Holiday camp in Skegness. I had drawn a picture of a Spitfire fighter plane and walked away with first prize. While we were there, Dad had also taken me to see the resident dance band, which happened to be the Ivy Benson Band that year. It was an all-ladies band and I was thrilled with their music. Thinking back, this

PK's pencil drawing after a photograph of Cézanne

experience must have played a big part in my future love of jazz. Ivy had some great soloists and these were heavily featured at their weekly Sunday concert in the camp theatre. The rest of the week they played for dancing but Sunday was their concert night.

I set myself to learning all I could about art, and particularly admired the work of Cézanne, Van Gogh and the Impressionists. I pored over books on painting and drawing technique, colour and form, as well as art history, and set about putting my knowledge to work. I had lost much of my enthusiasm for playing jazz and was looking towards selling some paintings one day, to boost my income from music. Soon I could produce fairly good, if rather photographic pictures, but I realised there was a lot more to painting than making good copies from photos. At least I was beginning to understand what makes a good work of art and what painstaking work it took to produce art of any real value. Like music this would be a steep learning curve, but I was determined to give it all I had. I made as many drawings as I could from life, in pencil and charcoal, and used pastel chalks and occasionally oils to make colour sketches. I soon found out that sketching from life is a vital foundation, much the same as learning your scales and chords in music, and had to become second nature before you tackled more advanced work.

I had something new to take my mind off drugs, but it was going to be a long, painful road to full recovery. There were many more crises to come and I had not shaken off my addiction problems by a long way. But I had made a start and would at least manage to rebuild my reputation and carry out my work commitments with more enthusiasm and reliability. Fortunately I was about to meet someone who would play a huge part in my salvation, who would return my love and stick by me through thick and thin.

6

'I can take him away from you any time I like.'
Philly Joe Jones

One Sunday night I was doing a one-off gig with Tubby Hayes'
big band at Ronnie Scott's Club. Apart from the usual excitement of a gig with Tubby, the night was memorable for two
other reasons. Firstly, Philly Joe Jones sat in on drums for a
couple of numbers. He had just taken up residence in London,
ostensibly to teach, as he was not officially allowed to work as a
musician here, being an American citizen. Everyone was excited
to play with him, but one of the tunes went a bit awry when
Philly played the whole chart with a kind of 12/8 feel whereas the
tune was in a fast 4/4. Somehow we got through the arrangement and I doubt the audience noticed anything was wrong, but
the guys in the band were rather amazed that Philly didn't figure
out what was happening and slot into the correct feel. Maybe he
was either spaced out or he reckoned the chart sounded better
his way.

The second reason for the night being memorable for me
was a more personal one. After the gig two ladies came up and
started chatting to me. One was a rather heavily-built woman
called Jean (not her real name), who I knew slightly. I usually
tried to avoid her, but this night she had a friend with her who
seemed much more attractive. In fact I had met her once before
when she was living with trumpet player Douggie Roberts who
had played in the Dankworth Seven. Jean introduced me to her
friend and suggested we all go back to her place for a coffee. I
wouldn't have accepted but I wanted to know more about her
friend Linda Froud, a tall slim girl with a warm friendly
demeanour and an air of mystery. She wore cute little glasses and
was dressed elegantly but with a modesty that hid her shapely

body. Something about her excited me and it had been a while since I had had any relationships with women.

The night was bizarre at first. Jean suggested we stay at her tiny one room flat, as it was late, so I suddenly found myself sharing a bed with both of them. I was wondering what the two ladies had in mind and was torn between excitement at what might be about to happen and my own shyness. Jean was soon asleep leaving Linda and me talking quietly. It soon became obvious that we were both sexually aroused and wanted to be alone together. I had forgotten any fantasies I had had about 'threesomes' and just wanted to make love to Linda. The situation was impossible, as Jean might have woken up at any moment. We decided to make coffee but there was no milk so, at four in the morning, we strolled down Knightsbridge to look for some. By the time we had found a milk machine and returned to the basement flat in Beaufort Gardens, we had told each other our life's stories and figured out a way to meet again, somewhere where we could make love all we wanted.

Linda was a receptionist at a Birmingham motel and the only place to be together was in her tiny room there. She shared it with another girl on the staff but when Linda was on the night shift we could have the room to ourselves for a few hours. We had the most fantastic sex and were obviously falling in love. I drove to Birmingham several times a week to be with her. She was forty-two years old when we met in 1967, fifteen years older than me but when she undressed she looked like a beautiful, slender twenty-year-old.

Because of the age difference between us, while I was a mere baby in 1940 Linda was already a pubescent fifteen-year-old and full of youthful vigour, took the war in her stride like most teenagers in those days, and worked in a Birmingham factory, making protractors for RAF navigators. She had to pick her way through rubble and body parts after each night's bombing, wondering if the factory would still be standing when she got there. It was something you just got used to and anyway, she was now becoming interested in boys and the latest dance music from America.

Linda spent one of her summer vacations at a relative's house in Cornwall, on the perimeter of St Eval Air base. While my childhood dreams of being a Spitfire pilot were still taking shape, she had already developed an eye for the handsome young fighter pilots at the base. We often talked about our very different memories of the war. OK, so some off-course Luftwaffe bomber pilot missed his target and dumped a bomb close enough to our old Anderson shelter to cover me in dirt and make my mom furious, but down at St. Eval one day a solitary Luftwaffe fighter singled Linda out for a more 'personal' attack. Well she took it personally anyway! She was taking a baby for a walk in its pram along the perimeter fence when a guard rushed out of a pillbox, grabbed her, the baby and the pram, threw them into a ditch and lay on top of them. The next thing she knew there was a horrendous noise and dust flying up all around, inches from her face. A lone Messerschmitt was strafing the airfield and bullets were hitting the sides of the ditch. That was the day Linda personally took on the Luftwaffe and survived!

In time her childhood love of music led her to become a dancer and singer and in the fifties she became a Bluebell Girl. Bluebell dancers, considered the best hoofers in the business, had to be six feet tall and good-looking, and Linda fitted the bill perfectly. Madame Bluebell was notorious for chaperoning her girls, even locking them in their hotel rooms after shows. Whereas I used to be rather shy and timid, Linda was the opposite. One night she and a roommate climbed out of their hotel window using a rope made of sheets and went out on the town, managing to get back without being caught.

She had a natural singing ability and the warmth and sincerity of her voice, coupled with impeccable intonation and the way she could communicate the meaning of a lyric, led to her singing at the best places in the Birmingham area and later at the

Spanish Gardens, an exclusive nightclub in London's West End. She worked with the excellent Sonny Rose band in Birmingham's top dancehall, the West End Ballroom, where Nat King Cole made a guest appearance on one occasion. He was there with his wife and child and heard Linda sing. After telling her how much he liked her vocal style he asked if she would look after his kid, so his wife could join the audience to hear his show. That's how Linda ended up with a cute little baby, Natalie Cole, sitting on her lap while Nat performed onstage.

Her singing talent never reached the wide audience it deserved. She had an illegitimate son, Stephen, and in those days that was a terrible disgrace, especially in the suburbs of Birmingham. It's hard to imagine now but she had to endure neighbours' remarks like, 'There goes that harlot with the bastard child,' and shit like that. At one stage she was working all day in a factory, singing half the night and trying to bring up her son. The strain of that, and a later relationship with an alcoholic musician who regularly beat her up, took a toll on her health and she became ill with a burst ulcer while singing at the West End Ballroom. She tried to work again too soon after a big operation and was horrified at the weakness in her voice. Eventually she ended up performing with terrible musicians in working men's clubs in the Manchester area, often with just organ and drums. In some of the worst venues she sang between wrestling bouts. So she quit singing professionally. By the time we met she sang only when she felt like it and, although I tried to encourage her to restart her career, she insisted she had had enough. It's a tragedy that her wonderful vocal talent was wasted.

When I met her in 1967 I was back living with my parents and struggling to get enough work. My mum took an instant liking to her and told her a lot about my problems and background. Very quickly, Linda decided, with Mum's blessing, that I must get somewhere of my own to live. She took everything in hand and found a cold water bedsit off the Edgware Road. It was an awful place but cheap. We decided to live together but at first she kept her job on in Birmingham so at least one of us was earning a regular wage. This wasn't ideal so she took the initiative again and, scanning the London papers, found an ad for a couple to act as janitors at a house in Knightsbridge, in Beaufort Gardens. I wasn't keen but Linda insisted we take a look as, although it paid only a minimal wage, we could live together with a roof over our heads for free. When we got there we realised, to our astonishment, it was the very same place where we had spent that first night together. Apparently Jean, who had been the janitor, had a history of mental illness. She had tried to attack a resident with a knife and lost her job. Linda convinced the owner, Mrs H., that we were perfect for the position, so we moved in almost immediately. We would be responsible for letting all nineteen rooms and collecting and banking all the rents, but the hardest part was that Linda had to clean all the rooms every day.

The only thing that worried us at first was that three of the rooms were let to high class prostitutes. Mrs. H. assured us this was legal, but said that she would collect their rents herself. Obviously there was some special arrangement between her and these ladies of the night. We stopped worrying about it and became friendly with all the girls, who were good fun to be around, telling us hilarious stories about their clients, some of them in quite high positions. The girls told us, 'If you ever recognise any of the men coming and going, don't breathe a word to anyone.' Linda swore she once recognised the voice of a high ranking member of the Cabinet. Don't forget this was not long after the Profumo affair, when Christine Keeler and others were making a fortune servicing the sexual fantasies of several public and political figures.

Years later, I met Christine Keeler when she paid a visit to the Bull's Head jazz pub in Barnes one Sunday, and I became friendly with a West Indian guy who had been in all the papers at the time of the Profumo affair for taking a pot shot at Christine. He was her ex-boyfriend and merely shot in her general direction to frighten her, in a fit of jealousy. Unfortunately, because of the scandals going on and the fact that he was black, they threw the book at the poor guy and sent him to jail for several years. He told me after he got out that he had aimed to miss, never intending to hurt her, and I believe him. I got to know him well after he had done his time. He started driving Tubby's quartet and sometimes my own group to gigs.

As we settled down together, Linda began the long process of getting me back on my feet again but I was using vast amounts of methamphetamine and scoring a little heroin when I could get it. One ampoule of meth was considered a large dose and only used professionally, under strict supervision, to induce abreaction. But I was injecting five ampoules from a large ten millilitre syringe. Then, leaving the needle in my arm, I would detach the chamber and quickly replace it with a smaller one containing two ampoules. Seven ampoules in all. I was doing this up to five or six times throughout the day and night, hardly ever sleeping. Absolutely crazy! It would take years and many set-backs to get finally straight, but at last I had a place of my own, a wonderful woman in my corner and had clawed back a little of my self-respect.

As it was part of our job to let out rooms, we could rent some to musicians from time to time. Canadian trumpeter Maynard Ferguson came from the US to live in England in 1968 and started a big band based in Manchester. Later he moved to London and offered me a job in the band. We got on real well so after a while he asked if he could take two rooms, for him and his whole family. We fixed them up and Maynard, his wife Flo and his children were soon happily living with us in Beaufort Gardens. He told us that one reason he had had to leave the US was that his beautiful house in upstate New York had burned down and that had left them broke and homeless. His insurance had expired and I guess he was virtually bankrupt. Maynard and his family were well into the sixties hippie movement, so being poor didn't seem to worry them unduly at the time. I was about to trade my old car in for another one but Maynard decided it would be just the thing for him and his family and bought it. They drove around in it happily like a band of gypsies. We had great times together for the next couple of years. The band was fantastic and we did a load of work in the UK and several festivals in Europe. We also made a few albums including *MF Horn* in 1970 and *MF Horn Two* in 1972.

Maynard was a trumpet phenomenon. When he first came to the UK, he took a while to get his chops together and his high notes back again after a long layoff but, by the time I played with him, he was in fantastic shape again. He not only had amazing range in the high register but also a huge sound all over the horn and he was a good soloist as well, although he never considered himself to be a real jazz improviser. His energy was phenomenal. When we had out of town gigs he would often drive the whole band in an old minibus. He'd drive us up to Manchester, for example, do the gig, blow his butt off and then drive us all the way back to London again and he would be talking and laughing the whole way. I remember when we went to Italy on tour. On that occasion, Maynard drove down from Manchester and picked the rest of us up in London. Without stopping we drove to Dover, crossed the Channel and then carried on pretty much non-stop until we reached the northwest coast of Italy about six the following evening! To be fair, someone did take over the driving for a few hours but I don't think Maynard ever actually went to sleep. I eventually lay down on Linda's lap and nodded off, but then woke up suddenly with a scream. I was having a nightmare in which I was falling down an icy slope surrounded by snow drifts. I had gone to sleep at night somewhere in Germany. But when I awoke, dawn had broken and we were high in the snowy wastes of the Alps. Christ! For a minute or two I thought it was a continuation of my damned nightmare, until I heard Maynard, still cracking jokes with the guys. The Italian tour went well and I bumped into Lucky Thompson at a festival there. It was good to see him again and we managed to have a brief chat before we went our separate ways. Not long after that he gave up playing for good and I never saw him again.

Around this time, in 1967, I heard through the junkie grapevine that Lady Frankau had died of cancer. Although I was no longer a patient of hers, my mind went back to one day when I was in her surgery. As usual I was bugging her for an extra script. She let me have one but suddenly blurted out rather angrily that she had just been diagnosed with cancer and added, 'I don't know what the hell all you people are going to do when I'm gone!' She then explained how, as the only member of the House of Lords who knew anything about drug addiction, she had used her considerable reputation as an expert in the subject to fight our case in the House for years, against a mounting political clamour to toughen up the Dangerous Drugs laws. I felt terrible because, although I tried to express my genuine shock and sadness at the terrible news she had received, she was dismissive, knowing only too well that most of her patients would be more concerned about where they were going to get their drugs if she died, than about her well being. I had left the surgery feeling sick with myself and about the moral depths to which many addicts fall. By the time I heard the news of her death I had regained some of my dignity and felt I had to at least try to make amends a bit by calling her husband, Sir Claude. I bucked up courage and made the call, expressing my deepest sympathy. He was gruff as usual but reluctantly accepted my attempts at commiseration, adding the rider that he reckoned the continual strain of dealing with her patients had worn her out and probably accelerated her illness and subsequent death. I sometimes wish I had never made that call.

She had been right about the drug laws. Soon after her death the government pushed through a raft of new legislation. You could no longer get hard drugs from a doctor but had to be registered at one of the new addiction clinics, where they soon refused to prescribe heroin and cocaine and brought in the use of methadone as a substitute. Very soon, unable to face the ever tightening regimes in the clinics, addicts turned to the new black market. The old so-called 'pushers' could no longer sell some of their spare supply, as no one was prescribed these drugs any more. So the field was opened up to the criminal fraternity and for the first time in Britain addicts turned to dangerous foreign imported drugs (heroin from China and cocaine from Columbia, etc). There was even a rumour at the time that the Mafia had a secret meeting in a London hotel to decide whether it was economically viable to distribute drugs in the UK. I heard they decided against it but we all know what has happened since, without any Mafia involvement.

Forty-odd years on, the situation has deteriorated to a point where, notwithstanding a few moves to bring back the old system, I doubt we can ever successfully get back to the sane drug policy that Lady Frankau fought so long and hard for. She warned governments what would happen if they changed the law and she predicted exactly the situation that exists today. Up until her death the British government at least listened because they knew she was the top authority on the treatment of alcohol and drug abuse. She was often accused of over-prescribing, but she thought it was far better to have a few registered addicts selling on some of their spare supply of pure medicinal heroin and cocaine to non-registered addicts, than have them all turn to illegal supplies of impure drugs from criminal gangs and cartels. In Frankau's day, although cannabis came mostly from abroad, just as it does now, organised crime bosses thought there was no real demand for heroin and cocaine in the UK and, as they say in this modern world of globalised capitalism, 'No demand. No supply!'

As he was now resident in London, it was only a matter of time before I met Philly Joe Jones. I forget exactly how we met, but Philly was already well aware who I was. He always made it his business to sus out other addicts wherever he was in the world, especially if they were good musicians too. There was a

very practical reason for this, as Philly explained. The more
addicts you knew, the better chance you had of obtaining drugs
if you ran out. I was disturbed to discover that, among certain
American musicians, my reputation as an addict seemed to be as
well-known, if not more so, than my credentials as a musician.
The first time I ever met Dizzy Gillespie, he made a beeline for
me and asked if I had any cocaine to spare. When I told him I
was only carrying heroin he declined abruptly, muttering, 'No
thanks, man, I never touch that stuff!' I think he was shocked
and although I met him many times over the years, I could never
get close to him the way all the other British guys did.
Whenever Dizzy was in town he would give everyone a big bear
hug and chew the fat, laugh and joke. I had been introduced to
him many times but he hardly ever spoke more than a few words
to me. This changed a bit when I did a week opposite his band
at Ronnie's one time. He was more friendly then but, a while
later, when I saw him at a festival somewhere and several of the
regular faces were chatting to him, he blanked me out again. I
just thought, 'Oh, to hell with him. It's his problem,' until someone suddenly asked me if I had met Dizzy. I looked right at him
and said in a loud voice, 'Oh, sure, we've known each other for
years, but Dizzy never seems to remember.' It did the trick
because he looked rather embarrassed and blurted out, 'Oh, hi
Pete! How ya doing, man?', as friendly as you like. I guess I made
my point at last. I've often wondered, though, if he had some
kind of gripe against me from that first meeting years before.
Probably my imagination, and I never discussed it with him.

I had no such problems with Philly Joe. We soon started hanging out together like old mates. I would go to his flat and he
would come to ours. We would talk about music and a hundred
and one other things, including dope, of course. I was getting
my regular supply of Methedrine and Philly was using the same
drug, mixed with heroin. The two, used together, work like a
speedball but better because, unlike cocaine, Methedrine gives a
much longer-lasting high. Philly Joe soon had me messing with

'H' again and whenever I needed a fix he would say, 'OK, Pete, come over in an hour.' I would often have to drive him to his 'connection' and then wait outside in the car, while he had a fix and collected the stuff. I'd drive him home and we would hang out and talk. Philly had a very tough constitution and was one of those rare people who could control his addiction to some extent. I never saw him get desperate for the stuff, even when he was sick, and he told me he would often go without for a day or two just to make sure his body was still in good health. Apparently the first time he went to Japan with Miles he had to go 'cold turkey' as there was no way you could get stuff out there. He did the whole tour like that and told me he couldn't understand why he always seemed to have loads of dollars in his pocket despite spending money like water in a constant buying spree. Only then did it come home to him just how much he had been spending on drugs before. He had a load of money to show for the tour for once, but probably got high again as soon as he got back to the States. Whereas I would be incapable of functioning at all when I was sick, it seemed Philly's only symptom was a tendency to throw up. One day I saw him when he was sick. He chatted away as if there was nothing wrong but had a big bucket of water by his side. Every so often he would retch into the bucket and then carry on chatting. He told me that if he was sick on a gig he would be constantly running off the bandstand, and back, to throw up in the toilet.

Philly Joe had a real humorous fascination with vampires and Count Dracula. He had made an album featuring, among others, Johnny Griffin and himself doing a hip take-off of the famous Boris Karloff role. We would fall about laughing as he relived his 'bebop vampire' routine again with lines like, 'Children of the night, ve vill make beautiful music together.' Or, 'Drink up your blood before it clots and bite your momma goodnight.' He was a friend of Karloff's and told me that Boris was a very funny guy and a lifelong morphine addict. He used to have big parties at his Hollywood mansion where, instead of sitting in chairs, the guests would relax in luxurious open coffins that he had propped up against the walls all around the house. Philly had a little touch of evil himself and when he would say in jest, 'I am ze bebop wampire', it had a comic but strangely sinister ring of truth about it and Linda was always warning me to be careful when I was with him. She knew we would both be getting high and, although she admired Philly's drumming, she never trusted him and tried her best to keep me in check. It would have been so easy to fall into the abyss again while he was around.

Philly knew only too well Linda was watching us and he would always be onto me saying, 'Pete, you're getting henpecked, man. Don't let the bitch tell you what to do.' I wasn't stupid and would argue with him about it. I didn't like him saying things like that, even though I was sometimes torn between the two of them. It came to a head one day when he was at our flat. He was trying to wind me up about it in front of Linda and she got real mad at him. Linda hated needles and I always took care of my cravings in private. Suddenly he pulled out his syringe and started to prepare a fix in front of her. We both had a go at him but he gave Linda a hard look, waived the syringe at her, pointed at me and said, 'Baby, I can take him away from you any time I like!' Linda flipped completely and went for him. She swore at him like a trooper and almost physically threw him out of the flat screaming, 'Get out of our home and never show your evil face in here ever again, you asshole!' Philly was stunned at Linda's fury and slunk out of the flat. He had met his match and although it meant I never got my free shot of heroin, I had to back her up. It was quite a moment and a turning point in what could have been a ruinous relationship for me.

The next day there was a knock on the door and Philly was standing there with a sheepish look on his face and a big bunch of flowers. He apologised profusely to Linda, asking for her forgiveness. She let him in, thanked him for the flowers, and then laid out her ground rules to him. 'Number one, don't ever try to tell Peter he's henpecked again . . . I know only too well he needs a little heroin to calm his nerves sometimes . . . We respect you and your music but I will fight to the death for Peter's health and career. Number two, Peter never allows me to see him taking a fix and neither will you, or you're out of here. We love you, Philly, but I will not have you messing our

Philly Joe Jones' *Mo' Joe* CD.

lives up. I've said my piece. Now, if you're going to do what you have to do, do it in the bathroom.' After that Philly was very polite and respectful to Linda and told me what a great woman I had. I knew that only too well but he was used to women who just towed the line and idolised him. He could see Linda was no fool and would kill to protect her husband and he admired her for it. Maybe he wished he had met someone who could have kept him in line like that.

With the air cleared, things got more productive between Philly and myself. Because he hadn't got a British work permit yet, he didn't play much. This meant we hardly ever got a chance to work together on the bandstand. He mainly taught drums and was supposedly writing a drum tutor book. He would often talk about this but it seemed to me he was not actually doing much writing and I figured it would never see the light of day. In fact, he did complete the book eventually and I hear it's a seminal work in the sphere. One day he asked me to come round and talk about a new recording project. He wanted me on the sessions and also to help him with some of the writing. The record was *Trailways Express*, later re-released as *Mo' Joe*, the title of one of Philly's originals on the album.

I was surprised to discover that he could play the piano quite well and had an excellent grasp of harmony. I had manuscript and pencil ready and Philly started by playing about four bars from one of his compositions, complete with interesting harmonic voicings. He looked up and said 'Have you written that down, Pete?' Now, neither I nor Philly can hear, analyse and remember music after one playing, so I asked him to play it again, slowly. He did but played something different this time. I told him and he objected saying, 'It wasn't different. It was the same thing. Here, listen.' He played it a third time and it was another new version. We argued a little and in the end I told him the only way this would work was if he gave me the melody line and the basic harmonic progression. Then I could work it out back at home and do the arrangement. In the end I think I did this on one of the two originals and Philly arranged the other one himself. The other chart I did was 'Gone, Gone, Gone'. Philly wanted to incorporate in it the arrangement of Gil Evans' 'Gone' from Miles' *Porgy and Bess* album, but scaled down for just the three horns we were using on the session. Although in his sleeve notes Brian Priestley wrongly attributed the work to Philly Joe, I did the new orchestration and had Harold McNair play the original flute line on the intro, with myself and Kenny Wheeler on alto and trumpet respectively.

We cut the album over two days in October 1968 at Trident Studios. Twenty minutes or so before the end of the last session, the producer, Alan Bates, told Philly we needed another couple of tunes. After about five and a half hours spread over two days we had just twenty odd minutes left to record two more! Philly turned to the guys in the band for ideas and someone suggested 'Here's that Rainy Day'. We just put the red recording light on and did it in one take with no rehearsal. Still needing one more, I suggested 'Baubles, Bangles and Beads', a tune I often played at a nice slow medium tempo in 3/4. I figured we needed just one tune at a more leisurely pace, as all the others were medium-fast to up. Philly agreed and said, 'Yes let's do it.' As soon as the light went on he launched into a drum intro about twice as fast as I had in mind. We got through the thing but I was never comfortable with the tempo. Listening to it again after nearly forty years, it doesn't sound so bad after all, but I notice that nearly every tune is a little too fast, even 'Gone, Gone, Gone'. But then again, Philly and I were pretty 'speedy' ourselves at that time, which explains it, if you get my drift.

Talking of making records fast reminds me of an album I recorded with Jimmy Witherspoon. We did the whole thing in one morning. I was playing tenor and Hal Singer, who was also on 'Spoon's record, had to make an album of his own that afternoon in the same studio. Hal was a blues tenor man who had made some kind of minor hit record in the States. Neither of us had met or heard of each other before. But he liked the way I played and asked me to join him on his album. We roared through that too, in three hours, right after lunch. Two twelve-inch LP's in one day, with time to do a gig in the evening, Both albums turned out great too. *Trailways Express* took a bit longer because Philly spent more time working at getting what he wanted. Philly had a thing about where solos should start and end. He had already talked to me about it but wanted the guys on the session to get it too. He didn't like the soloists to start and finish right on the beginning and end of the chorus every time. He liked you to carry your solo over into the next chorus or finish a little short, so it was not too clear-cut and obvious. I think he maybe learned that from Miles. It sounds much more fluid and interesting when one soloist takes over from another like that and I have always remembered that little trick, one of many things I picked up from Philly Joe.

Phil Seamen and Philly were great friends. They used to hang out together a lot and were always winding each other up. Not long before he died, Elvin Jones told me that he and Philly, and a lot of other great American drummers, used to talk about Phil in reverential tones. He told me they would always say, 'That's the way we'd all play if we could.' I doubt many in Britain realise just how great a drummer Phil was. I knew Philly Joe had agreat respect for him, but what he told me was a revelation. Phil was at a party once with Philly. He kept staring at him and then said, 'Hey Philly, you know that record you did with Miles, *Porgy and Bess?*' 'Yeah,' said Philly. 'Well you know that track on it, "Gone, Gone, Gone"?' 'Yeah, What about it?' said Philly. Then, to everyone's horror, Phil looked at him with a glint in his eye and yelled: 'Well, you fucked the ending up, didn't yer!' Everyone expected Philly Joe to get mad, but he just gave Phil a knowing look like a naughty boy who'd been found out. He knew he had messed up the ending on the record, but no one had noticed before, until Phil spotted it.

* * *

I was becoming more and more interested in painting and was also getting heavily into studying classical music. I spent less and less time practising my horn and threw myself into drawing and painting, and into studying all the books I could get hold of: in particular, books about Béla Bartók, my favourite composer. I poured over his scores and tried to learn as much as I could about his compositional methods. I took Linda, who had developed the same interest, to as many Bartók concerts as I could and began a long road of discovery that continues to this day. It would be many years before I was able to fulfil my dream of writing a classical composition, but the die had been cast and all those long hours of study are now just beginning to bear fruit.

I started showing my artwork to friends and when ex-Coltrane bassist Jimmy Garrison came to Ronnie Scott's with Archie Shepp's band, we became friendly and I soon got around to showing him some of my paintings. He was so impressed that he asked me if I could do a portrait from a small photo of him proudly holding his new baby. It was a tiny snapshot but I said I could do it. I took the photo and commenced work on a large pastel. It came out quite well, and after mounting it in a nice frame, I took it round to his hotel. He was thrilled to bits with it and took it back to the States. Jimmy died and I don't really know what happened to it, but a few years ago I was working in France with American ex-pat drummer George Brown, who had been a close friend of Garrison's and, when I mentioned the portrait, he told me he remembered seeing a picture just like it on the wall of Jimmy's flat in New York. So maybe it still exists somewhere in the Garrison estate. Who knows?

I stopped painting sometime after I met an amazing old man called Mr Pac. One day I was waiting for Linda outside a grocer's shop, when she came out chatting to a couple she had met inside. They were Polish, both in their eighties, and looked Bohemian. He wore a shabby old coat and had egg stains on his shirt. To my astonishment, Linda had discovered that Mr Pac was a professor of art and his wife a professor of geography. We gave them a lift to their house which turned out to be an amazing place. It contained a huge artist's studio with an enormous north-facing window from floor to ceiling covered in adjustable white blinds. Apparently the house had once been owned by the famous painter, Walter Sickert. The studio was filled with wonderful works painted by Mr Pac in an original post-impressionist style. They were a lovely old couple, still obviously in love and very warm and friendly. He had been a cavalry officer, and he told us how, when the Poles were fighting the Russians some time early in the century, his father had turned his big mansion, right on the front line, into a field hospital and insisted on having wounded Polish and Russian soldiers arranged in alternate beds, while Russian and Polish shells were flying in both directions, right over the house. It was his father's way of trying to bring understanding between the opposing armies. Mr Pac asked us to visit again and to bring some of my paintings. On seeing them he said I had talent but he could show me things to help me improve. His favourite painter was Matisse, whom he called the greatest colourist ever.

The Hayward Gallery had just opened and Mr Pac suggested we all go to see the first show, which just happened to be a Matisse exhibition. We spent an incredible couple of hours there while he gave me a painting lesson, using Matisse as his guide. I learned more about colour and colour perspective in those two hours than you could learn in two years at art college. His quiet critique of Matisse's genius was so fascinating we ended up with a line of people following us round with ears straining to catch his words. Then, suddenly he stopped in front of a view from Matisse's Paris studio and said quietly to his wife, 'Oh look, do you remember, we took that studio over from Matisse when he moved out.' Linda and I were stunned. This wonderful old man was not just a brilliant painter and teacher but had known many of the Impressionists personally and lived in one of Matisse's old Paris studios.

He advised me to work more from nature than from photos, because painting from photos was very difficult to do well. Of all my drawings the one he liked best was a very free, almost abstract, chalk drawing of Charlie Parker. I had worked from a photo but had made a real effort to put my own expression into it. He advised me to continue in this manner and to get away from too literal an interpretation of my subject matter. I had already realised that, just as in jazz, you have to find your own way to express yourself. When I showed him a portrait I had done of Linda he said something that had a profound effect on me. Linda was naked with a lovely suntan and I had posed her

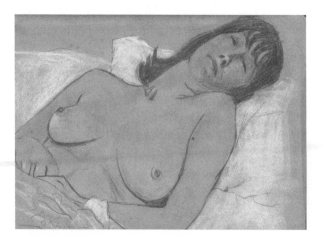

Opposite: Linda King drawn by PK (*black and white chalk on grey paper*).

Right: Charlie Parker by PK (*pencil drawing*).

on a mattress on the floor and painted what I saw. He explained that the bright pink mattress jarred with the warm brown of Linda's body. The mattress should be a much colder colour to make the colour harmony work properly. When I pointed out that these were the real colours he said, 'Yes, but it's a painting, you can change the colour!' I knew the pink looked wrong but thought it should be possible, by subtle means, to make it work as it was. The simple and obvious idea of altering nature had not occurred to me. But I now had a clearer idea of what I had been doing wrong. I realised that, if I was going to becoming a 'real' artist, I would have to work long and hard at it, the same as I had done with music. One day I intend to return to the struggle but I knew it would be impossible to put in the time without compromising my music. I didn't want to be what old artists used to refer to as a 'dauber', so I eventually decided to put my artistic aspirations on hold, rather than become another dilettante.

7

'Pete said the gig pays four pound . . .'
Maynard Ferguson

One afternoon there was a knock on the door and on opening it I was confronted by a uniformed police officer. 'Are you Mr King?' he asked. 'Yes,' I said. 'Are you the husband of Joy Marshall?' he continued. This completely threw me for a second as, although we were still legally married, I had had almost no contact with her for two years. I told the officer I was indeed married to Joy at which he said, in that special tone reserved for next of kin, 'Mr King, I'm afraid I have some bad news for you. I'm sorry to have to tell you your wife has been found dead in her flat.'

My policeman brother-in-law once told me that this is the job police hate more than any other. The officer must have been a little stunned by the lack of immediate grief on my part. I noticed a look of relief on his face when, after I had explained our marital situation, he realised I was not about to break into floods of tears. It was a weird feeling though. Linda had always felt I was still in love with Joy despite, or maybe because of, my angry protestations that I wasn't. The news of Joy's death and my lack of any normal reaction to losing her finally proved to both of us that I really was no longer in love with her, but with Linda.

In fact my immediate concern was breaking the news to Tubby. Although they were no longer together, I knew he would be pretty upset and I felt I should tell him right away, rather than him learning the news through the newspapers or worse. He was shaken up but we decided to put on a united front, especially in dealing with Joy's parents in the States, as her death was initially surrounded in mystery. For one thing, she died while in bed with a young guitarist whom she had taken back to her flat. Apparently she had been drinking heavily and had also taken a load of barbiturates. The poor kid awoke to find Joy stone cold dead beside him. He called the police and ambulance but, by the time the emergency services had arrived, he had taken fright and disappeared, which looked more than a little suspicious to the police. There was also a malicious rumour going around that she had been having an affair with a young married doctor who prescribed her sleeping pills and that she may have been blackmailing him to get extra prescriptions. Tubby and I did our best to keep all this away from her mother, who came over from San Francisco for the funeral.

The day after the news of Joy's death, while I was out playing a lunchtime gig at the Bull's Head in Barnes, Linda had a strange call from a young guy. He asked for me but, when he found I wasn't there, started to hang up the phone. Linda sensed he may have been the person who had been with Joy and managed to keep him on the line. He was in quite a state and admitted he was with her when she died and that he had fled the scene before the police arrived and didn't know what to do. Linda calmed him down and persuaded him to come over and talk to both of us. He arrived shortly after I got home. The poor kid who was only about eighteen, I think, poured out his story to us. We managed to persuade him to tell the police the truth about how he had panicked at the thought of a grilling by them, on top of the shock of waking to find Joy dead. He went to the police and straightened the matter out to their satisfaction. Nevertheless, the odd circumstances of Joy's death meant there had to be an inquest and we all had to be present. At the inquest the doctor said death was caused by a combination of barbiturate and alcohol poisoning, but that it was unlikely that Joy knew what she was doing because of the large amount of alcohol she had consumed.

The coroner brought in a verdict of 'death by misadventure'. I was amazed to discover only very recently that Joy's death had been reported in America in the December 1968 edition of *Jet*, one of the most influential African American magazines. The report, under the lurid headline 'Alcohol, Pills Kill American Singer in London', carried a wedding photo of Joy and me, and even quoted my words in court. To my shame I had completely forgotten Joy's full name until I saw it in the magazine article. Her married name was Joan Pipkins King.

Right underneath the report of Joy's death was an item about Stokely Carmichael, known as the Prime Minister of the Black Panthers, accusing the record industry of 'a boycott against his wife, South African singer Miriam Makeba'. He claimed this was because of fears that he would use her royalties to buy guns.

Linda, myself and a couple of Joy's friends had to go round to the flat and clean it up before her mother arrived from the States. It was in an uncharacteristic mess and in one room we found a full length dressing mirror smashed to pieces with a huge axe lying close by. The young guitarist had told us of the turbulent events on the night of Joy's death. She was drunk and in a highly charged emotional state. At one point she had lashed out at the mirror, as if hitting out at her own reflection. It was unlike Joy to entice some young kid musician, who she hardly knew, back to her flat. It seemed to Linda and me that she must have been pretty lonely and going down hill fast, emotionally. The young guy told us she had screamed out for me several times in her drunken stupor. Tubby knew as well as I did that, for all her evil streak, Joy had a very sad side to her personality. She had told me many times she was convinced she would die a premature and violent death: a scary premonition or a self-fulfilling prophesy? We'll never know. One of Tubby's compositions, 'Song for a Sad Lady', was dedicated to her. I played it many times with his big band, both before and after her death.

After the stress and upheaval of the inquest and the sub-sequent funeral, things returned to normal and, as I was now technically a widower, I was free to ask Linda to marry me without the horror of trying to get a divorce from Joy. Linda accepted immediately and we planned to have a simple wedding in Kensington Registry Office as soon as possible. One of the things that convinced me to take the plunge again was something Dakota Staton had told me, before I ever met Linda. Knowing all about my disastrous first marriage and my predilection for black women, Dakota gave me some advice. She was very keen on astrology and when she discovered I was a Leo and Joy was a Scorpio, she told me I couldn't have picked a worse person to form a relationship with; a Scorpio and a Leo together was a disaster waiting to happen. Then she added, 'Peter, you should stop getting hung up about all those black chicks and look out for a nice Sagittarian girl . . . Leos and Sagittarians always make good partners.'

I didn't believe in astrology but knew Linda happened to be a Sagittarian. Of course, I took her to meet Dakota. She fell in love with Linda straightaway and was pleased I had found what she considered to be my perfect partner. My mother also was relieved and happy that we were to get married, in spite of our age difference. Many in the business thought I was jumping out of the frying pan into the fire, marrying a woman fifteen years older than me, but we were together for forty years until she died peacefully in my arms, after a long illness, so I guess we proved them all wrong.

We planned the wedding for 27th February 1969 but one afternoon, a couple of months before that, I got a call from Ronnie Scott's office, asking me to get my ass to the television studios immediately. It turned out Ray Charles was just starting a mini tour of the UK and was short of a tenor player. The word was that their regular tenor man had been busted for drugs at the airport, but I never found out for sure. Anyway, I couldn't miss an opportunity like that. The only problem was I had a £4 gig that night at a local London pub. Luckily Maynard Ferguson happened to be in his room upstairs in our house, so I told him my predicament. He said I had to take the offer with Ray and, as for the pub gig, he would deputise for me. When I explained my little gig was only worth four quid he said, 'Don't worry about that, Pete . . . Get to the studio and leave that to me.' So, I told him where the gig was, jumped in the car and shot off to White City, arriving in time to run through one number with the band before the end of the last camera rehearsal. Of course, I adored Ray Charles and was elated, but at the same time terrified. It was an all black band at that time and I felt like a bottle of milk in a crate of cokes. Another thing made me nervous. Les Condon had worked with Ray's band a couple of years before and had told me about the atmosphere there at the time. He said the guys in the band were all great to him but, when he was offered the gig on a permanent basis, he overheard one of the band managers saying, 'Ray, I don't think it's a good idea to have no "pale face" in the band, It's gonna cause trouble back in the US.' Les turned down the gig, partly because of what he overheard.

I put this out of my mind for the time being as I concentrated on sight-reading the whole damned Ray Charles book, which I would have to do right there on television that night with no rehearsal. I grabbed the tenor pad and looked through it. The other guys were helpful and showed me a couple of the harder parts I might want to check out. And to my relief the book didn't look too difficult. After a while, some of the musicians started quizzing me about whether I was going to join the band permanently. This rather worried me, although they all sounded friendly. I said I had no idea. At that stage all I knew was I had to do the television show. I was soon asked if I could make the rest of the UK tour, which was only about four dates. Then an old character, who turned out to be the band wardrobe man, came up and started measuring me up for a band jacket. 'Hey Pete, try this. It's a little big but it's all we can find . . . Is it OK?' I proudly put on my jacket and a freshly pressed band shirt and continued studying the music.

Just before we went on to do the show, someone told me to leave all the solo bits out; the other tenor player would take care of them. I was disappointed but said 'Sure, of course.' Running on pure adrenaline, I got through the show without mishap. It was a fantastic experience to sit in the middle of the band and hear Ray and the Raylettes singing from just a few feet way. It was truly awesome and I had goose bumps the whole time. Regarding the band itself, two things struck me. One was how so much energy and passion was achieved with so little volume. The music was so relaxed, yet the energy was mesmerizing. The bass guitar in particular was real quiet, but grooved like mad. The other thing that struck me was how wonderful it felt to play the many repeated ad lib riffs. I had gotten sick of play-ing 'repeat till fade' sections at the end of many studio takes. They just get boring after a few times. But with Ray, those long repeated sections took on a life of their own. The individual phrases seemed to sound different every time we repeated them, never boring; and their urgency was exhilarating in the extreme. I had played similar figures time and again but everything sounded different in Ray's band. It's difficult to fathom out what makes those figures feel and sound so different, but I've come to realise that, as well as not over-blowing them, it has a lot to do with the tempo. More often than not, Ray's tempos were just a little slower than you had imagined they would be.

Tempo is so important and very subtle as well. The slightest change can make the music come alive and Ray always knew exactly what the tempo of any tune should be. I first realised this about tempo when I played with Bud Powell. He took tunes like 'Scrapple from the Apple' a tad slower than I had been used to, allowing the full beauty of the melody and rhythms to come out and giving so much space to play in. Tempo, a relaxed feel and subtle dynamic levels are all vital. I remember being amazed, when I heard the Basie and Ellington bands live onstage, at how quiet they played. Big bands in particular have a tendency to play far too loud. Even Maynard's band was often guilty of getting carried away when he hit those high notes. However he had a wonderful big fat tone all over the trumpet and never sounded shrill. Duke's band, on the other hand, would play very quiet and this gave the individual horns the ability to produce a wonderful warm, rich timbre. When they turned up the heat, they never played really loud and yet they sounded like they were raising the roof right off the theatre. They didn't need to bust a gut; their full, rich tones and relaxed but exciting swing made the loud passages truly awesome.

The next day, when I saw Maynard, he told me he had a ball playing at my pub gig. Despite the fact that I had warned the promoter Maynard would be subbing for me, they seemed to think that he had just dropped in to jam with the band for fun. They couldn't believe that I had actually booked Maynard as an official bona fide dep. They must have thought paying him my measly four quid would have been an insult. After waiting awhile, he finally went up to the promoter and said, 'Hey man, Pete told me the gig was worth £4. Can I have my money, please?' He got his fee and we had a great laugh about the promoter's embarrassment when he realised his mistake.

I played another three concerts with Ray Charles' band and they let me play one, and then two or three solos during the band's warm up sets, before Ray came onstage. After each gig, the old wardrobe man took my jacket and told me just to throw my band shirt on a heap on the floor. Then every night he would give me a newly pressed jacket and a freshly washed, ironed and starched shirt. He took real good care of all that stuff and always with a smile. Guys were still coming up and asking me whether I was going to stay on, but I had no idea, as no one had said a word about it. Finally, on the last gig, in Wolverhampton, I was asked to play a solo whilst Ray himself was onstage.

At the end of the first set one of the minders told me Ray wanted to see me. I was ushered to his dressing room and Linda, who was with me this time, came too. The minder said, 'I'm sorry but I'm afraid she will have to stay outside,' but Ray overheard and called out, 'Hey, that's OK. Let the lady come in too.' Suddenly the door shut behind us and Linda and I were alone with the great man. I introduced her to Ray and then he asked me if I would join the band permanently. The problem was they were leaving the UK very early the following morning for an extended European tour and would then return directly to the States for more concerts. This would have meant cancelling our wedding and I would not be back in London until the annual band holiday the following spring. Ray told me he could pay me $200 a week which would increase to $300. He offered to fly me back to London in the spring and then, if I wanted to stay with the band, back to the States again after their break. He also told me he had heard I wrote music as well and said he wanted me to do some arrangements for the band. He was really sweet to us both and made me and Linda feel very at home. I would have loved to have worked with Ray but our forthcoming marriage, and worries about four to five months on the road all over the world, made me think twice. I told Ray about the marriage, but not the other stuff of course, and was torn between taking the gig and missing a good opportunity. Ray finally said, 'Pete, we would love you to join the band but I understand your problem. Let's leave it like this – if you want to make the gig, be at the airport tomorrow morning at 6.30 a.m. If you're not there, that's OK. I'll just pick up another guy on the Continent . . . I really hope we see you in the morning.'

We drove home and I needed someone to talk to. Maynard was away so I called Philly Joe and we got to his place about two in the morning. He was strung out and had been throwing up in a bucket all day. We talked about the Ray Charles offer and he advised against it. Reluctantly, Linda and I made up our minds that I should not take up the offer, so I never showed up at the airport. If I had not been so concerned about my drug problem, Linda would probably have let us delay the wedding until the spring. This was the first time I had to turn down a great opportunity to work abroad with top American musicians. It was not the last, unfortunately. Philly, and later Maynard, told me I had made the right decision, as the pay was not very good and I would have just been buried away in another big band. In fact, not long after this I read a report that the Raylettes had walked out of a concert when they got back to the States, as a result of an argument about pay and conditions. Basie alumnus Henry Coker was playing trombone in the band and his daughter was singing with the Raylettes. Chatting to Linda on one of my gigs, she told her she was pretty pissed off because she had just married and had had to leave on the road right after her wedding, without even a honeymoon. Ray had a strict rule that no wives or husbands could travel with the band at any time. I felt better about the missed opportunity after that. I was working quite a lot anyway, playing many gigs with Maynard and doing some session work and my own guest appearances, and now we had a wedding to look forward to. However, I still wonder what my future might have been if I had faced up to the difficulties and taken Ray's offer.

Our wedding was small-scale but wonderful. The reception was at our tiny flat and our prostitute friends at Beaufort Gardens did a lot of the planning for the reception. They helped with the catering and one of them lent Linda a beautiful mink coat for the day. Linda's mum spent the night before the wedding in our flat, while we were out at a gig. We had a switchboard, through which all calls to the rooms went, and Linda's mum acted as switchboard operator for the night. The girl who lent Linda the coat received the usual volley of business calls and when we got back Linda's mum said, 'Ooh, that young girl you introduced me to is ever so popular. She had loads of men friends calling her, all night.' We burst out laughing at her delightful naiveté.

We were also friendly with Ossie Clark, one of the very top dress designers of the 'swinging sixties'. He designed and made a beautiful, original, gold trouser suite, just for Linda. It would have cost a fortune if we had had to buy it. As for a honeymoon, that was out of the question until later. We couldn't afford it. In fact, when the reception was over we were both so tired we went to bed and read a book. After all, we had been lovers for two years already. Years later, we had a weird experience with Ossie. He visited us one day with a young foreign boy who he was having a relationship with. We didn't really like the guy and he was a bit on the wild side and messed up on drugs. A few weeks after

Wedding day with Linda, 27 February 1969.

that, Ossie was brutally murdered in his flat. The same kid who had been sitting in our front room had killed him in a vicious attack. I believe there were over twenty stab wounds.

After a few months we managed to find a little time and money for a kind of honeymoon on the east coast of Italy. Then sea, the sun, and Linda's love soon helped me feel better than I had for years. I returned free of drugs and healthy with a sun tan, and things were looking up. Within hours of arriving back in London, I had to leave again for Stockholm to begin a three-week tour of Sweden with Maynard Ferguson's band. The other guys were there the night before so the band bus picked me up from the airport and, instead of getting some rest in an hotel, I faced a six-hour coach ride to the first gig. For the trip, Maynard had booked Cecil Payne on baritone and we became close friends during the tour. Cecil had recently left Woody Herman and told me he was worn out by the experience. Travelling literally 365 days a year had taken its toll and Cecil had ended up having to kick a heroin habit. Now he was trying to wean himself off a dependence on alcohol. He was a lovely, kind man, and a hell of a good soloist with an original style, but had a rather sensitive nature that made him vulnerable at times. I liked him a lot and we hit it off straight away, pouring out our life stories to each other and having a damned good laugh too.

In fact the laughing started as soon as we set off on the bus. Cecil had figured out where you could buy liquor and that was not easy in Sweden in the sixties. Although they had relaxed the laws a little by then, you could only buy drink in an hotel at enormous expense, or at a store owned by a state monopoly, the Systembolaget. These were hard-to-find establishments that looked for all the world like grey, stone-fronted post offices from the outside. You would never have known these places sold liquor because there was no shop window and nothing on display. Cecil had checked it all out as soon as he arrived and tipped the driver to stop at the first systembolaget he came to. After a couple of weeks we realised you could always spot them on a Friday afternoon after around 4.30 p.m., because there would be long queues of well-dressed guys with brief cases, lined up outside them. That was when office workers and businessmen could stock up for the weekends, when everyone in Sweden seemed to get crazy drunk.

Cecil never seemed inebriated, but had to have a small amount of whisky, in milk, to keep himself straight. The milk hid the whisky from disdainful eyes and also protected his stomach, which had given him trouble. Cecil and I spent a lot of time together on the road and we helped each other quite a bit. By the end the tour, he had pretty much weaned himself off booze and he spent a happy night at home with Linda and me before he returned to the States. We kept in touch with him as much as we could and next saw him when he came over with Dizzy Gillespie's big band, where he was given far more solo space than Maynard ever gave him. I don't know why, but Maynard seemed to treat Cecil with less respect than he deserved. It upset Cecil and the rest of the guys who all admired and liked him. It was good to see him in Dizzy's band, happy again and playing great.

* * *

Sadly, death was soon to pay another visit. This time it was my mother, who had suffered for years with heart trouble. My father had just retired and they decided to sell the house in Tolworth and move to Olney in Buckinghamshire, where my brother was living. While they were temporarily staying with my sister, Mum was admitted to hospital and I got the dreaded call soon after, to come to the ward as she was not expected to last more than a few hours. It was a big shock, and I know my struggles with drugs had not helped her illness. On rare occasions, when I was causing my parents extra grief, my father would blurt out, 'Son, you're killing your poor mother, you know she's not well!' Strangely enough, when she was rushed to hospital in a critical condition, the guilt which I had tortured myself with for years seemed to disappear, leaving just great sadness that she was about to leave us all. I arrived about midday and took turns round the bed with my father and a few relatives. Mum was unconscious and on oxygen. After a couple of hours my father, who knew I had a gig that night, told me there was nothing more I could do at the hospital and that I should return home and try to prepare for the gig. He knew how badly I needed the money. I drove home but the ordeal had left me shaken up so, with feelings of guilt returning, I phoned Philly Joe to see if I could score some heroin to get me through the next few hours. The answer was yes, so after talking it through with Linda and struggling again with my conscience I made my way to Philly Joe's place. My plan was to get a fix, grab a sandwich, rush back to the hospital and, depending on the situation, decide then whether to make the gig.

There then followed one of the strangest emotional experiences of my life. When Philly opened the door and asked me in, he added, 'I'm so sorry to hear about your mom. Oh, by the way, have you met Elvin?' To my astonishment, Elvin Jones was there.

The next thing I knew I was driving both of them to Chalk Farm, where the connection lived, to score heroin. As usual Philly went in on his own while Elvin and I had to stay in the car for forty-five minutes or more, waiting for him to take care of business. I was in an emotional turmoil. Here I was, sitting in my Dad's old Hillman Minx, waiting for a fix with two of the world's greatest drummers on board, while my mother lay dying in hospital. Elvin, whom I had never met before, was so sweet to me. I poured out my emotions to him and he was very understanding, telling me not to feel bad that I needed something to get through such an awful time. While we chatted, Elvin eulogised about Philly, saying what a good friend he was and how he always helped if he had a problem. It was a brief, very emotional encounter but I was not to meet Elvin again for nearly thirty years.

Eventually Philly appeared. I drove him and Elvin back and, after Philly quietly slipped me a small shot of heroin, I said my goodbyes and made my way home. Dad was surprised and pleased to see me make it back to the hospital before my gig but, as there was no change in Mum's condition, he told me to go to work. If anything changed they would phone. Albert Tolley, the proprietor of the Bull's Head where I had the gig insisted I leave my car at the hospital and he would pick me up and drive me back. I got through the first set and then, in the break, Albert came over and said the hospital had phoned. My mother had died while I was onstage. He offered to drive me to the hospital straightaway, but I thought about it and decided that Mum would have wanted me to finish the show. I played the last set somehow and eventually got home. I didn't see my mother's body. I don't think I could have taken that, by then. Once I got home, all the grief poured out, as I fell into Linda's arms and tried to take in the event and the emotions I had been through. It was a day I will never forget. From the elation of having Philly and Elvin all to myself in the car, to the guilt of going to score while my mother was dying and to the awful truth that I would never see her again.

Once the funeral was over, Dad moved to a new life in the countryside, which he had hoped so much to share with my mum. In fact I don't think she would have adapted to it easily. She valued her few friends in Tolworth and would have found it hard to make new ones. Dad did get to enjoy his new life in Olney where, thanks to his gregarious nature, he made loads of new friends and could be close to my brother. My feelings of guilt about my mother lessened as she had at least seen me begin the road to recovery with the help of Linda, who she thought the world of and, although it would be a while before I was finally free of drugs, I was in much better shape and able to keep the problem just to myself and Linda.

Linda and I were never able to have a child. She was in her mid-forties by the time we considered it and in those days it was thought to be too risky to have a child at that age. We were not too upset as she had her grown-up son and I was not in any hurry to be a father. Anyway, we already had one addition to the family who we both loved to death. When I met Linda she had a small black miniature poodle called Fred. He was part of the package and he was adorable. Highly intelligent, he gained many famous friends all over the world. He was like a child and a pal to both of us. Cecil Payne and Philly Joe fell in love with Fred immediately. One day Philly Joe insisted I come with him to the betting shop to put some money on a horse that had already won twice that week. Philly had backed him and reckoned he won because his name was Fearless Fred. Gambling is the one vice I don't have and, in any case, I figured, if the horse had already won twice he would never win a third time in the same week. Philly knew better and insisted. I was dragged along to place a small wager on the nag. Fearless Fred only damned well won again. Philly said 'I told you he'd win. With a name like that, you should have put a tenner on him at least.' He had so much faith in that horse, and all because of Fred the poodle.

Another time, when Linda was doing film extra work at Shepperton Studios, she and I took Fred for a walk during the lunch break and a gorgeous young chick spotted him and came rushing over. She hugged him, telling us he made her think of her own little dog back in America who she was missing like crazy. It was Goldie Hawn, who was at Shepperton working on a new movie. Then there was the time when in mid-solo at Ronnie Scott's I suddenly felt something pulling at my trousers. It was Fred, who had slipped his lead and to great mirth in the audience, come up onstage. He was a one-off and we were inconsolable when he died at the ripe old doggie age of eighteen years.

Linda got quite a bit of film extra work. Her first job was on *The Magic Christian* and the star, Peter Sellers, actually pulled strings to get her signed up with central casting, so she could do the gig. For the movie they needed extras that looked like some of the 'A' list people of the time. They had John Lennon and Yoko Ono look-alikes and Linda was picked because she bore a passing resemblance to Vanessa Redgrave. Kathy Stobart and Linda often worked together on movies. They did crowd scenes in *Cromwell* and *Scrooge* (both 1970) and Roman Polanski's *Macbeth* (1971) among others.

The film work certainly helped our financial situation, but neither of us could stomach the routine of calling Central Casting at 6 p.m. every damned night, to be told time after time there was no work the next day. Extras are considered the lowest form of life in the film business and in-fighting was the norm with some of the older 'out of work actors' who scratched a living out of the business. Linda watched the antics on set with disgust and some humour, as certain regulars would do anything to catch the director's eye. The reason for this was the day's fee depended on what you actually did. If you were told to blow your nose, put on your hat, scratch your ass, or anything other than just standing in the crowd, you got an extra fee. The fact that she had got into the business through a friend of ours, the assistant director Roger Simon who often came up and chatted, went down like a lead balloon with the more vindictive old hands. After Roger's work dried up, she soon quit the rat race for good.

Eventually Philly Joe Jones moved to France and I didn't hear from him for a while. Then he called from Paris. I had to pay for the call as he was temporarily broke and holed up in an hotel. He wanted me to go over and play a big concert with him the following week. He offered to pay what was a massive sum in those days and told me not to worry about a thing and that he would 'take care of me'. Linda overheard me and got the gist of what was being said. She gave me that 'watch it, be careful' look and something told me it would be wise to stall him for the moment until I could think. Philly knew Linda was there and asked to speak to her, assuring her she needn't worry, but she wasn't convinced. I said I would have to rearrange a couple of gigs and would get back to him. Linda and I talked it over. He was offering me good money and it could be a great chance to raise my profile. Who knows what it might have led to and, anyway, what an opportunity to play with Philly again! On the other hand, he was obviously broke and needed the money from the concert to pay his hotel and probably his drugs bill. I had visions of paying my own fare to Paris, doing the gig and ending up not getting paid and maybe even stranded over there, with a bigger habit and no money to sustain it. I had been trying to get myself straightened out and was making good progress. I knew if I saw Philly I couldn't resist temptation. It was a tough decision and I still don't know if I made the right one, but I called him back and told him I couldn't make the gig. He tried to persuade me but I stuck to my decision, for better or worse. It was nearly twenty years before I ran into him again.

* * *

Life at Beaufort Gardens was becoming a drag. Linda was fed up with having to clean nineteen rooms every day and we needed more space. We lived and slept in just one room, which made it difficult for me to write and use the piano at night. One day I put my foot in it when one of our prostitute friends called me on the intercom. 'Pete, have you got a piece of string?' she asked. Apparently she needed it for a client who'd offered her £50 if she would tie his balls up with it. Amazing what turns some guys on! I couldn't find any, so called up to Linda who was finishing cleaning the last room. Understandably she went mad and yelled down the intercom, 'You called me up to ask me for a piece of string for that! Tell her, for fifty bloody quid, I'll do the job myself . . . All I get is seven pounds ten a week for cleaning nineteen rooms and she can make fifty quid in a few minutes . . . Tell her to find her own bloody string!' Later on, we laughed our socks off at the ways some guys get their kicks.

Things got really scary after that, though. One of the other brasses let us use her room as a bedroom, as she only used it occasionally during the day and was glad to help us out. Being an honest Joe, I asked the landlady if it would be OK. She told us it was alright but we had to put the room rental under one of our own names. I wasn't sure about this but Linda insisted and put it in her name. I had a strange feeling that something was wrong with this arrangement and I soon found out why. I came home from a broadcast one night to find Linda had been arrested. I had to bail her out of the police station. I thought that they must have raided the place and found some pot, but it was worse than that. It was the vice squad. They had been watching the premises for a while and that night they went in for the kill. On discovering Linda was technically paying for the room, which they knew was being used by a prostitute, they arrested her for running a brothel. The landlady had stitched us up good. Knowing the legal angles, she had found a way of covering herself, in case the place got busted.

We had to spill the beans on the landlady. Linda explained the situation to the court and I did my best to back her up when I got a chance, but we were up against a sharp lawyer who tried to tie us up in knots. We didn't want our landlady to get busted after she had given us free board for two years, but it was her or Linda. No contest! In the end there was no real proof against the landlady and her husband so Linda took the rap, getting a small fine and a ticking off for being so naive. Because of her relaxed attitude to the brasses, we always thought the landlady probably had a deal with the vice squad but, if so, it had obviously run out by then. We went back to living in the one room, but only for a short while. The final straw came a few weeks later.

We got friendly with American altoist Lee Konitz, who had just begun a stint at Ronnie's and was fed up with his hotel so we offered him a vacant room at a much lower rate and he took the offer gladly and moved in. We hung out together and talked about Bartók and his book of piano pieces, *Microcosmos*. Lee had recorded some of them and we played a few of the pieces with just two altos for practice. I took him to a specialist music publisher where you could buy a load of French classical saxophone music and he bought a few things including an atonal trumpet study book that he already had a copy of in the States and gave it to me as a present.

Lee made a point of going for a swim in the Serpentine in Hyde Park every morning and very late one night we asked him if he wanted to join us while we took Fred for a walk in the park. To our surprise, he was very nervous about it, saying 'What? At three in the morning? Man, you can't do that. We'll get mugged!' We told him this was Hyde Park in London, not Central Park in New York. I told him, 'Nothing like that ever happens here, Lee. It's quite safe. We do it all the time.' 'OK, if you're sure,' he said and we went off for a nocturnal stroll. Lee really enjoyed being able to do that, without any bad shit happening. But I had been rather premature saying how safe London was and two days later I had to eat my words.

Linda and I arranged to sleep for just one night in one of the newer prostitute's rooms, right above ours. She was going away for the weekend and, as the room wasn't rented in our name, we thought we were safe. The next afternoon, back in our own apartment, we heard movement upstairs. We figured our friend had returned early, to do some business. All of a sudden there was a blood-curdling scream and she was yelling our names and pleading for help. We found her lying on the bed almost naked, covered in blood. She managed to blurt out that a client had just stabbed her in the guts! He had hidden in a toilet but then he escaped through the front door just as I rushed into the hallway to phone for the police and ambulance. Linda stormed out into the street to look for the guy, who had left his shoes behind in his rush to escape. She spotted a man in stocking feet getting into a Mini and, with her usual lack of fear, yelled, 'Hey! Stop, you bastard!' He floored the gas and headed towards her, mounting the pavement and aiming straight at her, but she managed to jump clear and the guy got away.

The girl was still fully conscious as the ambulance rushed her to hospital and later she had an emergency operation. The police tried to calm us down and began taking statements but a plain clothes detective arrived and started giving Linda a real going over. Because of her previous brush with the law, he decided she knew more than she was telling and really started giving her the bad cop routine. I flipped completely and went for him. Restrained by the other cops, I yelled at him to leave my wife alone or I would not be responsible for my actions. I am a pretty timid guy most of the time but seeing the way he was laying into my poor wife, who had been through far too much already, I had an attack of the red haze and went berserk. Amazingly, he backed off, trying to calm me down. The girl got through the operation and soon made a full recovery. We had no more aggro from the police after that but it had been touch and go for her and, if she had died, things could have got pretty ugly again.

In the middle of all this, tenor player Stan Robinson called me about a gig. Linda answered the phone and told him, 'We can't talk now, Stan. Someone just got stabbed!' I think he thought we had all gone mad, but managed to blurt out, 'What! Stabbed? Ehem. OK, I guess I'll call back later then . . . OK?' I felt I also had to tell the news to Lee Konitz. How he resisted saying

'I told you so,' I'll never know. After the pleasant walk in the park, the whole situation was suddenly crazy. Things got scary again a couple of days later when Linda, who was on her own, answered a ring at the main door to the building. A huge, menacing black guy burst in, holding a gun. She was terrified and convinced he had been sent to shut her up about the stabbing. We never found out who he was but, as luck would have it, two croupiers, who had a room at the end of the hall, rushed out sensing Linda was in danger. At the sight of them the intruder turned tail and ran out the door. God knows what would have happened if they hadn't been there.

The police caught the man responsible for the stabbing and we had to go to the trial. But he pleaded guilty, so we weren't required to give evidence. After dealing with the landlady's lawyer, we didn't relish facing another cross-examination in court. He was an officer in a Guards regiment who hadn't wanted to pay the girl for her services. When she protested, he put a knife in her stomach for her insolence, the bastard. After Linda's brush with the law, plus the stabbing, the guy trying to run her down, and maybe another possible attempt on her life by the black guy with the gun, we'd had enough of Knightsbridge. Without telling the landlady, we packed all our belongings and left the flat and the job, in the dead of night with nowhere to live. To our great relief, Stan and Jackie Tracey came to our rescue and offered us sanctuary while we recovered and tried to look for a new home.

8

'Excuse me, can you direct me to Ronnie Scott's, please?'
Red Rodney

Leaving Beaufort Gardens meant we lost not only our free flat, but also the small wage that Linda received for the housekeeping job. Although I was doing odd gigs with Maynard Ferguson and Tubby Hayes, plus a few solo appearances and the occasional studio gig, the thought of paying rent again was a daunting prospect, especially as a lot of my earnings were still being frittered away on drugs of one kind or another. Before we had to make our hurried escape from Knightsbridge, Stan Tracey had asked me to join his new quartet. It was thanks to our friendship with Stan and his wife that we were able to turn to them for help when we had to leave our flat so suddenly. They told us to bring our stuff over to their place in Streatham and move in, while we looked for somewhere more permanent to live. Although we knew Stan and Jackie well already, my working in the quartet and the four of us living together brought us closer and led to a lasting friendship. While we were living with the Traceys, Linda and I would help out sometimes by keeping an eye on their young kids Clark and Sarah. Young Sarah was always easy to look after but Clark, who was only about six or so then, could be a little bugger sometimes. Clark and I often have a good laugh about that now. Over the years, I watched him grow up from a rather sullen six-year-old into a fine drummer, composer and friend, and a bandleader in his own right.

I began playing alto again, partly because both Maynard and Tubby now needed a section leader and partly because I wanted to see if the time I had spent playing tenor would give me a fresh approach on my original horn. For a while I used both instruments but I wanted to concentrate on the smaller horn again.

I have always believed you have to devote all your energy to one instrument to really develop a personal style. Of course, many fine musicians can play more than one horn brilliantly but very few achieve true greatness and individuality on more than one instrument. There are exceptions, such as John Coltrane and Lucky Thompson, who were great individualists on tenor and soprano. But I needed to concentrate on one, for a while at least, and, after all, the alto was my first love. In fact, it's a tough instrument to play well. It doesn't have the tonal weight and masculinity of the tenor and it's hard to get a really good sound, especially in the lower register; there is often the temptation to play too many notes to make up for the lack of tonal weight. Another, more practical, point may have played a small part: there were always good tenor players around but, in those days, not so many good altoists. Now things are different: there has been a proliferation of great young alto players arriving on the scene, especially in the UK, France and Italy. Shit, I guess it had to happen eventually, I'd had it too easy before. But that's fine, a little fresh competition stops you from getting old too quick!

Stan's new quartet comprised myself on alto, Dave Green on bass, Bryan Spring on drums and Stan on piano. With a tough line-up like that, we soon had an album recorded and began working. It was great to do a gig and then come back and relax with Stan, discussing music till the small hours. We listened a lot to his large collection of records, especially to Duke Ellington, and it was interesting to watch him working on new compositions and arrangements. He would occasionally ask my opinion on some musical idea he was having trouble with. He found any kind of writing an agonising ordeal, probably because he was a perfectionist and felt, once the music was committed to paper, it could come back to haunt him. Stan's whole raison d'être is improvisation and he would often turn on a tape recorder and just play for an hour or more. Then he would listen to the result, looking for possible ideas to develop into a new composition or arrangement. This was a revelation to me and made damned good sense. But, much as I would have loved to try the same thing, I couldn't play the piano so it was impossible to go down that route. In fact, the more I tried to write, the more I wished I had stuck to the piano when I was a kid. Although I've written a fair amount of music over the years, it wasn't until I got into computers that my composing developed more fully.

Around the time I was working with Stan the new avant-garde (free) music began to take off. Long before anyone in Britain was aware of Ornette Coleman and the new sounds from the States, Joe Harriott had been experimenting with what he called free form music. Many of us were derisive about what he was doing at the beginning of the sixties, but Joe was an awesome alto player and had a great band which included a fantastic West Indian trumpet player, Shake Keane, and Phil Seamen on drums, so we had to respect what the band were doing, even if we weren't convinced about the direction Joe was taking. It was funny to see Phil's reactions to the music and there were many stories of running battles between him and Joe. Although Phil would mockingly call it 'Fucking Free Form Five Six' music, his contribution to a truly great and original band was immense.

In the years that followed, a new generation of free players, guys like drummer John Stevens and altoist Mike Osborne, carved out their own path. One night, at the 100 Club in London's West End, the Stan Tracey Quartet was booked to play a gig that also featured Mike Osborne's group. Ossie was on before us and tore the place apart with his wild music. The audience reaction was mixed. Some weren't keen on the new sounds but a large contingent of free music fans went wild at Mike's set. I was not looking forward to following him but figured there must be people who wanted to hear us too. When the time came to start there was no sign of Stan. There was only one thing for it: I would have to go on without him, with just bass and drums. I was pretty angry about it. It was tough enough having to face an audience of free jazz fans but, without Stan's strong piano, it would be a hell of a lot tougher still. I couldn't figure out what had got into Stan. I knew he wasn't looking forward to playing, but he was always a real professional and normally would never walk out on a gig like that.

We got through the set and the response was OK but certainly not ecstatic. I couldn't wait to get out of there and back to Stan's place. I wasn't even sure he would be there. Maybe he had really freaked out and was wandering around the streets somewhere. I was pretty mad in the car driving back and as soon as I got in, there was Stan looking sheepish. I asked him what the fuck he was doing, leaving me in the shit to face the gig on my own. It turned out he just couldn't face playing the set and had got the night bus straight home. He apologised for leaving me roasting and I soon forgot my anger as we talked at length about the situation and the ramifications of the new music.

I felt the music world was in a kind of crisis; that everything was rapidly changing around us and not for the better. It was difficult to think that we might end up being seen as musical reactionaries, after priding ourselves on being trailblazers who had rebelled against dixieland and swing. Things were indeed changing as we moved towards the seventies. Free jazz found a small but enthusiastic audience and it wasn't long before jazz rock hit the scene in a big way leaving many fine, hard-core jazz musicians struggling to find work for ten years or more. It's a strange and sad thing that, throughout history, so many once-revolutionary artists end up being the old fuddy duddies to a new generation of trailblazers. The only thing that eases the trauma is the fact that fashions are always changing and the cream of every generation is often rediscovered after a few years to take its rightful place eventually in history. This is why it's so important to plough your own furrow and stick to what you believe in, whilst working hard and being open to any new developments that you can incorporate into your own art. I think it's important to be selective, though, and not just jump onto the latest bandwagon. In the long run there is only good art and bad art and, to survive the test of time, it has to be of the finest quality and originality. All you can do is hang in there and try to believe in yourself.

Everyone has to deal with situations in their own way. I think Stan decided to go along with the new music, for a while at least. To my astonishment, he very soon went fully into free jazz, working and recording with Mike Osborne and others. I was a little pissed off about it at the time and felt rather let down, especially as he had been so completely against the whole idea of what those guys were doing. But now I realise Stan must have done a lot of soul searching before temporarily committing himself to the new music. Osborne was a great innovator and the albums Stan made at that time are seminal works that have, indeed, stood the test of time. He probably did the right thing then, but I had to go through a long period of self-doubt, disillusionment and even despair before I began to grope my way towards a new direction as a musician.

All the time we were living with Stan and Jackie, we hunted for somewhere of our own to set up house. One day my brother-in-law Alan called to say he had a possible place for us to live. When he wasn't on police duty he did a bit of moonlighting with a builder friend. They were renovating a small terraced house which would soon be available at a modest rent. We rushed round to look at the property, which was in a run-down area of Putney, close to Wandsworth, and right next to the railway. In fact. you could wave to the train drivers as they passed by, a few feet from the bathroom window. The house had a tiny garden and needed a lot of decorating but we figured it would do until we could afford somewhere better. We had no idea we would still be renting it almost forty years later! We were very worried because the landlord wanted to increase the rent every year by two and sixpence, to allow for inflation. The area has become prime real estate now and similar tiny terraced houses sell for nearly half a million pounds. Our new landlords, Michael Engering and his wife Margaret, turned out to be the sweetest people. Nearly all their tenants were musicians or actors. I found out several years later that Margaret taught violin, using the Suzuki method. She had actually studied in Japan with Mr Suzuki himself.

Linda was the driving force in getting the home in order. One night she told me, 'Stop the car!' She'd spotted an old armchair left out on the street as rubbish. 'Get it in the boot, quick,' she shouted. We got it home and had somewhere comfortable to sit, while we faced, with great excitement, the only two walls we had been able to afford to paint, and watched television. It's a great way to set up home. You appreciate every new tiny improvement and, with my attempts at 'do it yourself', we felt we achieved something. Linda had a genius for finding high quality secondhand things. When well-off, smartly dressed ladies remarked on her latest dress or earrings or my latest suit, it was a great buzz to see their incredulous look when Linda explained she got these things in the local Oxfam shop for two quid. In those days you could find amazing high quality stuff – for next to nothing and in perfect condition – that some rich idiot got fed up with and chucked out after a few weeks. At last we had a real home of our own, even if we still hoped to move to a bigger and better place. We never did, but that's OK, because today people would kill to get their hands on a little place in Putney like ours.

One day Bill Le Sage called me out of the blue asking if I would form a new band with him. He proposed to call it the Bebop Preservation Society, or BPS, and wanted to play a lot of classic and lesser-known bebop tunes, along with originals in the same style. He felt that now, at the beginning of the 1970s, there was an audience for a bebop revival band, to keep the flag flying and appeal to the diehard fans. To be honest, this was the last thing I wanted to do at this stage of the game. I felt I had to move on somehow, to compete with the changes that were taking place in the jazz world. I told Bill how I felt but he was very persuasive and soon talked me into the idea. There was no imperative to stick to a bebop style once we started improvising and Bill had lined up some great guys: Bryan Spring on drums, my old pal Hank Shaw on trumpet, and Spike Heatley on bass. The result was a group that worked with great success, musically and business-wise through the 1970s and beyond. The Bebop Preservation Society is now a legend and people still come up to me raving about it. It turned out to be a good move. The group had a wonderful social atmosphere, played great and was very popular. Bill also had good connections in the recording scene and we made several successful albums.

After our first one, Tony Williams asked us to record for his new label, Spotlite Records, Later, Tony was the first guy to record me under my own name, for which I am eternally grateful. One of our Spotlite recordings, in 1975, featured ex-Charlie Parker trumpeter Red Rodney. The way this came about is quite a story. Back in the late-forties, Bill Le Sage was working 'on the boats' – playing on the transatlantic liners – with the express purpose of getting a couple of days in New York to hear the new modern jazz. On his very first trip he went straight into town to catch Charlie Parker at Birdland. Not sure how to get to the club, he stopped a young, redheaded guy carrying a trumpet case and asked if he could direct him. The man said he was going to Birdland himself and told Bill to come along. It didn't take long for the conversation to get around to Parker. Imagine Bill's amazement when the young white guy with the red hair said his name was Red Rodney and he was working that very night with Bird himself. Bill spent the first of many amazing nights listening to Bird and other giants of bebop. This is only part of the story though. Over twenty years later, after Bill had started the Bebop Preservation Society, he was walking through Soho one night when a short, portly man came up and said, 'Excuse me. Can you direct me to Ronnie Scott's Club, please?' Bill told him to come with him as he was going there himself. To Bill's amazement it was Red Rodney! Bill reminded him of their first meeting in New York all those years before. They could hardly believe this strange quirk of fate and rapidly became good friends.

Before long a record date was fixed with Red as a guest with the band. Hank Shaw was also on the date and he was professing to be pretty nervy about having to play trumpet with Red Rodney. Although Red had been off the scene for many years, serving a long stretch in the States for drug offences, he still played great. He was amazed at the standard of the group and had to pull out all the stops himself to keep up with Hank. The result was electrifying. You could sense a certain tension between the two trumpet players, but it was one of those friendly, adrenalin-filled situations that made both of them play at their best. It reminded me a bit of when Sonny Stitt and I had jammed together at Ronnie's.

Talking of Sonny reminds me of a neat little trick he taught me that had nothing to do with music. Most of the Americans in those days were real sharp dressers and we tended to follow their example as best we could. Sharp suits and ties were de rigueur. Sonny and I were sitting in the tiny office at the back of the old Ronnie Scott Club one night when he noticed I had dropped some ash from my cigarette and was trying to wipe it off my trousers with my hand. 'Hey, man,' he said, 'Don't do that. You'll get sweat on it and make it worse. I'll show you the right way.' Sonny demonstrated how to take the sleeve of your jacket and use that. The idea is to get another piece of the same material and use it like a clothes brush. A neat little trick, it works like a charm and I still use it.

Drugs played a dubious role in my relationship with Red Rodney. He was out on parole at the time and had been allowed to travel to the UK for a short British tour as part of his rehabilitation. The deal was he had to return to the States after a certain specified time. Of course, while he was in the UK, he had further offers of work in Europe which would have overrun this period. He contacted his parole officer and was granted leave to extend his stay. The problem was that, after a few months, when he finally returned to America, the guy had been replaced by a much less tolerant parole officer. The result was Red was promptly re-arrested for parole violation and had to serve a little more time in prison. But, after his release, he got his own group together, re-established himself as the great artist he was and toured the world with his excellent band, up until he finally died of cancer.

Of course, partly because of drugs, it took no time at all for Red and me to become close. We would get high together and he stayed at our home in Putney a few times. We talked a lot about music and he told me crazy stories about his life and his time with Bird. Everyone knows the story of how Bird tried to avoid racial trouble when they toured the American South by billing Red as 'Albino Red'. Red told me what it was like from his perspective. As they drove into the first town on their Southern States tour, Red noticed a big poster which read, 'Charlie Yardbird Parker Quintet, featuring Albino Red, blues singer'. He was terrified when Charlie explained what was going on but he had no choice but to go along with it. At the first gig he managed to get away with the highly risky ruse. That was frightening enough but the next morning, as he walked down the street, a big 'redneck' Southern cop, with a gun at each hip, who had seen him at the gig, stopped him and asked angrily, 'Hey, is you really a nigger?' He obviously didn't believe Parker's pantomime. Red was scared. All he could think of was to blurt out, in a phoney southern drawl, 'Yassa boss. I's a nigger!' The cop stared at him, scratching his head, and said, 'Well, I guess no God-fearing white boy is gonna walk around these parts pretending to be a nigger, if they ain't. So I guess you must be a goddamned nigger.' To Red's relief, the cop walked away, still bemused.

The BPS did quite a few gigs with Red and in 1977 we also recorded *Namely Me* with trumpeter Jon Eardley. Jon had taken over from Chet Baker in the Gerry Mulligan Quartet but was now living and working in Germany. He also had a 'habit', so of course we got pretty close for a while. As well as the gigs with the BPS, I worked with Red on tours around the UK with local rhythm sections. One night, on one of these trips, I discovered another little-known titbit about Bird. Red suddenly called the tune 'Love Letters'. I only knew it as a rather average pop song that became a big hit for singer Ketty Lester. He could see I was not keen on playing it but told me it was a good tune and that it was one of Charlie Parker's favourites. Although Bird never recorded it, he played it a lot on gigs. I saw the song in a different light after that. In fact, it's a pretty tune with nice harmonies.

Red and I kept in touch through the years and I often went to see his latest quintet when it appeared at Ronnie Scott's Club. I was a bit disappointed not to get an offer to join his band, as he was always singing my praises. But I guess it would have been difficult for him to do this, as a lot of the work was in the US and it wouldn't have been cost-effective to bring an unknown English guy all the way over there. In any case, he always had a great band and a string of young up-and-coming saxophone players, which he always liked my opinion on. I often sat in for a couple of tunes when he was in town, which was nice. Not long after he first formed his quintet he discovered a young, brilliant multi-instrumentalist from Australia, James Morrison, who was then virtually unknown outside his own country. Red told me how it happened but, knowing his sometimes dubious stories, I never quite believed him until James confirmed the story was true when I worked with him years later.

Red was playing in Sydney and having breakfast in his room on the fourteenth floor of a plush hotel when he heard a noise coming from outside the window. Someone was playing a trumpet and sounding just like Dizzy. Suddenly a face appeared, upside down, right outside Red's window, blowing a damned trumpet! Fourteen floors up! It was James Morrison. Already a big star in Australia, he was promoting a new album. He was also a qualified pilot, rally driver, marathon runner and a bit of a wild guy all-round. He had abseiled down from the roof of the hotel, hoping to find Red's room and pull off a publicity stunt for his record company. It sure worked because Red offered him a gig touring the world and the international jazz scene was soon raving about him. Years later, James told me it was a hit and miss adventure because, although they knew Red was staying in the hotel, they had no idea which room he was in, so James had to work his way down from the roof, dangling from his rope and checking each window until he recognised Red sitting in bed quietly enjoying his breakfast. James was a brilliant technician on nearly every instrument you can think of, but Red reckoned – and I agreed – that he played best on the euphonium, of all things. He played saxes too in Red's group but on the brass horn he forgot about sheer technical brilliance and played more creatively.

* * *

Around this time the UK government decided to ban Methedrine completely. There would be no way of getting it, even on the street. Although I didn't find it nearly as addictive as heroin, I looked for a suitable substitute and started buying another amphetamine, known as 'speed'. It meant paying black market prices but it helped a bit. In fact I found withdrawals could be nasty and I was still scoring heroin when I could get it. It was becoming a drag all round and I turned once again to Dr Smith. The only thing he could suggest was methadone, a powerful substitute for heroin. Sometimes, if I couldn't get heroin, I would get hold of a few 5 mg Physeptone tablets to cure the withdrawals. This was just a trade name for methadone and it worked OK, but you didn't get much of a buzz from it. Smith said he would prescribe as much as I needed so after a few weeks I was taking the massive amount of 150 mgs a day; 5 mgs is the normal dose to cure severe pain. If you take enough of the drug you do get an effect very similar to heroin and it lasts you most of the day so, on a regular legal prescription of 150 mgs a day, I was feeling pretty good. The reason this is still the standard drug used to wean addicts off heroin is because it's prescribed in linctus form and so impossible to inject. Also the palliative effect of the drug lasts for more than twelve hours. The idea is you can take it just once or twice a day and then feel well enough to carry on a normal life. What they don't tell you is, because it stays in the blood stream for so long, it's far more invidious than heroin and, when you do get withdrawals, they last much longer. This makes it, from my own bitter experience, a lot harder to kick than heroin.

I settled down to a reasonably stable existence, still working with Maynard Ferguson, Stan Tracey, Bill Le Sage and Tubby Hayes, and doing the usual round of solo spots with good and bad rhythm sections. There were also a few studio dates that came my way. Linda was also working in various boring office jobs when she could get them so we were scraping a living, had a roof over our heads and I could rely on a regular supply of methadone. I even had a little money left to score a bit of cocaine, speed or heroin, but only as occasional recreational drugs, of course.

Our financial situation improved even more in 1970 when Maynard got the band a twenty-six week spot on the new *Simon Dee Show* on television. Simon was a top radio disc jockey who was given a chance to do a chat show. This was regular work, reasonably paid, and we met many celebrities while we were doing the show. Unfortunately, Simon made a bit of a hash of it all and was unceremoniously dumped after just the one series, which was a drag for the band as we had hoped it might last for years like the *Parkinson Show*.

In those days *the* gig to have was with drummer Jack Parnell's band. Jack was deservedly the king of the Elstree television scene and the guys in his band all made big money for years off the back of their work in programmes like the *Muppet Show*. Jack and all those guys were great musicians and deserved every penny they made but when you get a job like Jack's gig, it's easy to lose sight of your passion for playing jazz. When that band finally broke up, most of the musicians carried on doing session work and had financial security until the session scene finally dried up. After that, many of them ended up doing boring pit band gigs, with little chance to play much jazz.

It became more and more apparent that the seventies were fast becoming a nightmare for our kind of jazz. Interest in it had waned dramatically and other things like rhythm and blues and jazz rock were taking off in a big way and leaving people like Stan Tracey, myself, and even Tubby, to pick up the leftovers. This wasn't true only in the UK, it was happening everywhere, even in the USA. The one British band that did manage to keep going throughout this time was the BPS. I guess it kept the bebop flag flying and so always had a small but faithful audience, even though they were getting older and I was beginning to feel jazz was dying fast. In fact, I was getting more and more disillusioned with music and was finding playing hard and unrewarding. I was bored with churning out the same old tunes in the same old way but couldn't find either the energy or the creativity to move in a new direction. I couldn't work up any enthusiasm for jazz rock and the guys going in that direction probably reckoned I was stuck in a rut and they didn't want an old bebopper with a drug problem tagging along with them anyway. What made it worse was some of the guys I knew and had worked with were now starting to do well in the new climate. Ian Carr had a great jazz rock band, Nucleus, and along with Ian, musicians like John Taylor, Kenny Wheeler and John Surman were finding a new audience in Europe and the USA, playing either jazz rock or what was now becoming the new European style of jazz. Even my old friend, Gordon Beck, was soon making an international reputation for himself with Phil Woods and his new European Rhythm Machine. I guess I was too tired and messed up by then to learn new licks, get off my ass and get in on the action. If I ever had a chance to build an international reputation, that was the time to go for it, but it wasn't to be, until I finally tried to get my act together ten years later.

Instead, I struggled on doing routine gigs and grabbing any commercial work I could get. I had been trying for years to get more session work but, although I could play clarinet, I was a lousy flute player. I did my best with the flute, and took any work I could get to survive. I got quite a few sessions with a group that John Cameron had put together, called the CCS Band. It was a good band with a lot of great musicians in it – people like Tony Coe, Les Condon, Derek Watkins, Danny Moss and Ronnie Ross – and we played good rock and blues based music, some of which made it into the pop charts. We recorded a few things with the pop group Hot Chocolate and also the theme tune for *Top of the Pops*, which was used for years after that. John also wrote for films and he booked me on as many sessions as he could.

I started to get other sessions, playing backings and the odd solo on minor pop recordings. These could get frustrating at times, especially when some young would-be pop star or producer would start telling me how to play. Most of these guys had no idea about music, let alone my music, but had heard from somewhere I could play solos. So they would get me to put something down over some horrendously naff backing track and say things like, 'We loved those two notes you played there but could you do the same kind of thing all over the next eight bars? Then could you go up really high and play something really screaming on the *outro*.' Boy, how I hate that word! Why don't they just call it by its proper name, the *coda*? It could go the other way, though. I might lay down a tentative solo and wait for the usual endless postmortem or I'd wait for them to say, 'We've got plenty now. We can cut lots of bits out of it and stick it together the way we want it,' only to have them look totally gob-smacked and say, 'Wow! Fantastic! Cool man! . . . That's it. Thanks. Man, that was brilliant!' But those sessions were OK. Ten minutes in the studio and I got my cheque and ran. The weird thing is you hardly ever knew who the hell you were working for on those gigs. All you had was a pair of headphones, a

With Elvin Jones and Bob Wilber at a festival in the north of England, mid-1990s.

backing track and a few young kids who often treated you like some kind of paid skivvy. For all I knew, the records could have ended up top of the pop charts. I stopped taking any notice of the 'Top Ten' chart after I fell out of love with Elvis' music, so I would never have known what happened after I left the studio.

In this depressing period I had, long before, ceased to do much practice. Most of my spare time was spent studying classical music, including the twelve-tone techniques of Arnold Schoenberg and Alban Berg. I had also obtained a brilliant book on Béla Bartók's six string quartets. Translated from the Hungarian, the book by János Kárpáti was a brilliant study, not only of the string quartets but of Bartók's whole compositional technique. It was a revelation to me and informed my classical studies for years to come, studies that eventually were to reach fruition when I composed *Janus* in the 1990s. As for practising jazz, my playing had become virtually automatic by then and it was hard to figure out what new things to practise anymore. I didn't start again until I began to work during the eighties on a more modal and pentatonic approach under the influence of John Coltrane and McCoy Tyner, who were to become my new inspiration, after years of being dominated by Bird.

Talking of practice reminds me of a story about Elvin Jones.

A few years ago I introduced a great drummer friend of mine, who shall remain nameless, to Elvin and he went to see him some time later. Now this guy was obsessed with practising and he told me he got on fine with Elvin until he mentioned the 'P' word. He told me he felt a complete fool because he couldn't resist asking Elvin what he practised. Now Elvin Jones was the sweetest guy and would never have tried to make a fool out of any genuine fellow-human being but, apparently the question totally threw him. He looked at my friend with a bemused grin, waited a bit, then said, 'Practise? . . . Oh yeah . . . I used to practise . . . Then I found I could *do it*.'

Along with the usual grind of boring gigs, the few connections I had for commercial work led to some interesting jobs in orchestras, backing some big-deal artists. This entailed concerts and tours and a couple stick out in my memory. In 1971 I got a call to work in a backing section of horns, with James Brown, the giant of soul music. That was quite an experience. We attended a rehearsal but James was not present. It was weird, but very gratifying, to be in a section of British white guys playing with one of the leading icons of the Black Power movement. There was no feeling of being out of place and, although we never met James except to see him onstage, it was an uplifting experience all round. I was nervous about possible racial tension because, when Martin Luther King was assassinated, I was asked to play a memorial concert on the steps of St. Paul's Cathedral in London with Philly Joe Jones, Dakota Staton and Jon Hendricks. It was a scary day and there were riots in town and many angry blacks were marching to the Cathedral. I had all this sea of black faces staring at me and then one yelled out at me, 'What the hell are you dong up there, Whitey!' Thank God Philly Joe came to my rescue and yelled back at the guy, saying I had more right to be up there than he did and to, 'Sod off, motherfucker!' Coming from a fellow-black brother, it did the trick and we got through the gig OK. I got out of there pretty quick after that, though.

We did just two London concerts with James Brown, one after the other on the same night. The first was at the Royal Albert Hall. The audience must have been two-thirds black and it was the first time I had ever seen the many balconies of the Albert Hall filled with black people, all dancing their asses off! The concert was electrifying. James was awesome to hear and see. He made his usual entrance, wearing his trademark long dressing gown, which he took off with a huge flourish, to screams of delight from the audience. He generated incredible energy and power and had to do several encores. This caused a bit of a problem as we were supposed to start our second concert at around midnight, in another venue in the East End. We finally arrived and hit to rapturous applause, at about 2.30 a.m, and finished about 5 a.m. I was totally exhausted, but elated with the adrenalin generated by the night's music and spectacle.

On a rather less spectacular note, I also did two or three long tours with singer Sacha Distel. Sacha had originally become known as a jazz guitarist in his native France but one night a young Brigitte Bardot, the French film actress who became the world's hottest sex symbol during the fifties, came into a club where Sacha was working. Bardot was idolised by every hot blooded male who saw her movies. Sacha himself was also an extremely good-looking guy, who spoke English with the kind of French accent that brings out the passionate side of women. Before long the newspapers were filled with the story of Brigitte's relationship with this unknown jazz guitarist. He was the envy of millions of guys worldwide. He had a good voice and was soon in demand himself, but as a singing star. His jazz guitar took a back seat as his fame increased to massive proportions and he hit the top of the charts with a naive little jingle of a tune called, 'Rain Drops are Falling on my Head'. He became the new French heartthrob and women swooned over him throughout Europe and especially in Britain.

On the road, years later when I toured with him, he had a good French MD and rhythm section. They were nice people to work with and Sacha turned out to be a great guy, very down to earth, and had still retained his love of jazz. He was fun to be around, and always being mobbed by beautiful women. The guys in the band enjoyed hanging out with him, partly in the vain hope that some of his charisma would rub off on them. Sacha was quite happy about this because he had long since split up with Bardot and married another beautiful and elegant woman with whom he was very much in love and had a daughter. So we were welcome to anything we could get. Needless to say, it never happened that way – they only wanted Sacha. It was all innocent fun. Sacha was a contented family man, so the adoring female fans were on a hiding to nothing.

He had good guest artists on the shows. We specially enjoyed the company of an Italian comedian who had us in stitches every night with his jokes, delivered in an over-exaggerated Italian accent. He was one of those guys, like Tommy Cooper, with the extraordinary ability to make you laugh without even opening their mouths. Offstage the accent almost disappeared, leaving just his clown-like, dry sense of humour.

In all, we did three British tours and, for the last two, Sacha's old friend violinist Stéphane Grappelli did a short guest spot in the show. Sacha got his guitar out of mothballs and did a passable job accompanying him. They had played together a lot in the old days in Paris and Sacha thought the world of Grappelli, as we all did. The only thing that used to piss us off a bit was Stéphane's insistence on stopping for a full two hour lunch on the road, at specially chosen and expensive restaurants which we couldn't afford. Normally, on coach journeys like this, you would grab a quick bite somewhere and get to the next town as quickly as possible to eat and rest up a bit before the concert. It was all right for Stéphane to luxuriate in cordon bleu food and visit the local antique shops – he was a connoisseur and avid collector – because he never went on before the end of the first half, and then for only about fifteen minutes a night. But the band had to make a sound check and were onstage for the whole show. We would have a go at him about this but, of course, we always forgave him as soon as he started to play every night.

On one of Sacha's tours, a new young girl singer did a spot. She had made a minor hit record and although we had not heard of her, she was absolutely gorgeous-looking and was a very sweet person. Her name was Olivia Newton-John and a year or two later she became a megastar in the movie *Grease* with John Travolta. In fact, although she had a pleasant voice, she was shy for such a beautiful girl and had very little stage presence. Sacha took her under his wing and gently coached her in developing her persona. It must have helped because, by the time she starred in the movie with Travolta, she had her stage presence well-honed. With all the guys pumped up watching Olivia every night and picturing Brigitte Bardot in their minds every time we looked at Sacha, we couldn't resist tackling him about what it had really been like being being with one of the sexiest women on the planet. 'What, guys? You mean what was Brigitte like in bed? Oh, she was all right, but she was a bit too thin for my taste; all skin and bones.' Some people take a lot of pleasing!

9

'... where are you going to find another guy like Bogie?'
Lauren Bacall

So the infamous seventies had arrived and, apart from infrequent gigs with Tubby, Stan, the BPS and the occasional session, all I had as regards jazz playing were a few guest appearances, often with horrendous out-of-town rhythm sections. It wasn't enough to pay the rent so I had to look for other work. With virtually no qualifications outside the music business and being in no fit physical state to do a labouring job, my options were limited. I could drive of course, so maybe a minicab job could have been a way out. After all, many more famous jazz musicians than I have had to resort to driving a cab at certain times in their career. The thought was there but I never got around to following it up and Linda and I just bumbled along, getting deeper in debt, hoping things would improve.

I worked a lot with dance bands, something I had already had plenty of experience doing. In particular, one earlier gig had set me up well for that kind of work. During one of the tougher spells in the late sixties I had been only too glad to take up the offer of a residency with Cyril Stapleton's band, on tenor. There was little or no jazz involved but it was regular work, starting with a season at the Streatham Locarno. Although by then Cyril's band was reduced to working 'holiday relief' spots in various ballrooms on the Mecca circuit, it had been one of the top outfits during the heyday of the big show bands. It's hard to imagine now but, in the forties and fifties, bands like those led by Cyril, Ted Heath, and Jack Parnell, along with the Squadronaires, were regularly in the pop charts and many of the singers who worked with them became huge stars, with thousands of young teenage fans. Denis Lotis, Frankie Vaughan and

Lita Roza pulled in massive crowds and made many hit record-ings. The musicianship was superb too and many great jazz play-ers came out of that early big band scene. So, although these bands were no longer in demand like they used to be, I still felt happy about the chance to work with Cyril. I felt it might add to my musical education, as well as helping to pay the rent.

One very useful result of that gig was the development of my sound on tenor. I had been trying to get a big powerful, cutting tone, using ever more open-layed Berg Larsen mouthpieces similar to those used by Coleman Hawkins and Don Byas. I had visited the Berg Larsen factory to the north of London, where the legendary Mr Larsen would spend hours showing sax players round the factory, letting them try out mouthpieces and even reworking them on the spot. When they were in London, Hawk, Ben Webster, Don Byas and many other jazz stars would hang out and experiment the same way and Larsen told me stories about them and what 'setup' they were using. I had been using a metal Larsen on my alto for quite a while and soon acquired a '150' lay metal tenor mouthpiece. Guys like Hawkins and Webster had incredibly strong chops and played very wide tip openings on their mouthpieces, with very hard reeds. In fact it was rather a macho thing with sax players and a lot of guys felt you had to build your chops up by playing ever-harder reeds and more open mouthpieces, in order to build a big sound. An aver-age tip opening would be about 120 (0.12 inches) so a 150 was pretty open and hard to play. Word got around that some of the black guys in the States were using massive 250 lay Larsens (that's .25 inches at the tip). I actually had a 200 that I would practise on, but it was too hard to use on a gig. My chops would be shot to hell after a couple of tunes. In fact it was all a bit stupid as you can make a huge sound with a much softer set-up. Cannonball Adderley used a pretty close lay and very soft reeds and no one can say he had a small sound. .

Many tenor players started changing to Otto Link mouth-pieces, and the sound they made was acknowledged as warmer and yet just as powerful as from a Larsen, once you got used to them. I had toyed with the idea of using Links but found them rather dull-sounding. Saxophonist friends had told me you had to play them in for a while to get the full benefit. The gig with Stapleton was just playing in the section most of the time so it was the perfect chance to try one out. I didn't solo much and the endless sax section passages enabled me to get used to the new mouthpiece. It worked, just as the guys had told me. At first, because of the cavernous internal shape of the Link it felt like blowing into a big empty hole after the narrower tone chamber of the Larsen, with its raised baffle, which was designed to give edge to the sound. About half way through the second night with Stapleton I found a way of projecting the air through my oral cavities so that the mouthpiece started to resonate. Suddenly my tone projected better and came alive. I had found the sweet spot and from then on I was able to get the same power as from the Larsen but with a richer, more focused tone. After that I used metal Otto Links on tenor, and eventually alto, for many years.

Working in dance band sax sections and in the studio, you have to be able to play quietly and sweetly at times, so you need a mouthpiece that is to some extent a compromise. Using the Link and a medium soft reed gave me this to an extent, but on occasions I still felt I wasn't doing it right. I would sometimes work on sessions with Ronnie Chamberlain, one of the great lead alto players. Ronnie was highly respected in the business and was always friendly and encouraging to me, offering advice if he thought it would help. I'm sure he meant well but he would often suggest I try a mouthpiece like the one he was using, saying it would blend better in the section and I could always blow it harder to get extra edge when I did a jazz gig. I finally followed his advice and changed to an ebonite Meyer on alto for a while, after I had reverted to this horn as my main instrument. Meyers are good mouthpieces and many top jazz artists use them to good effect. I got pretty comfortable with it for a while but, on a gig one day with my old buddy, tenorist Alan Skidmore, I found I couldn't match up to his big fat sound on the horn. It seemed as if all those sessions and dance band gigs had made my tone weak compared to Skid's.

One day I was chatting to Ronnie Ross about this and what Ronnie Chamberlain had told me about mouthpieces. Ross, who was one of the greatest baritone soloists in the world, was shocked. He told me I was crazy to take any notice of anyone who tried to tell me what mouthpiece to use and that I should ignore them and do what I felt was best as a jazz player. He added, 'You don't want to end up sounding just like all those other studio players do you?' I made up my mind then and there: no more compromises. I would pick a mouthpiece that gave me power and a sound of my own and, if I had trouble playing treble pianissimo in some studio gig, what the hell.

Cyril Stapleton had the reputation among musicians of being an old square. He came from the old school and was not a great jazz lover. The guys in the band would rib him and talk in derogative terms about how in the past he used to insist on playing the violin when leading the band. Most bandleaders of the old school were treated with suspicion and derision by their musicians, often with good reason, but I heard only praise for leaders like Jack Parnell, Vic Lewis and Ken Mackintosh. Most big band musicians were jazzers at heart and the idea of standing in front of a band waving a stick about and getting your kicks from seeing your name on the music desks was anathema to most self-respecting jazz guys. There was a great story about one old bandleader who, when some of his musicians tried to follow his attempts at conducting – or rather posing for the punters, yelled at them with a look of horror, 'Don't follow me, guys, for Christ's sake!'

In fact I found Cyril to be a nice man at heart and I respected him. He was very tolerant of me even when I once fell asleep standing up in the section. Junkies have a knack of doing this, closing their eyes and going into a state that looks like sleep, yet still able to remain standing, even if in a rather slumped position. Paul Gonsalves was expert at it and could often be seen fast asleep in the Ellington sax section with his horn still in his mouth and his fingers on the keys.

I got off to a good start with Cyril, maybe because of the way I played corny old waltz tunes. It would have been tempting to take the piss and play with an exaggerated camp vibrato and twenties-style tone. Instead I played dead straight, but with a nice warm sound, a subtle vibrato and a few tasteful but minimal embellishments. He liked that and I felt it was a challenge to play the straight melody with some genuine feeling. He was also quite generous. I had my week's wages stolen from the band room once while we were resident at Hammersmith Palais and Cyril gave me an extra half week's money to get me through until the next pay day. There was no reason for him to do that. It was purely his humanity showing through.

While I was working with the band, Gordon Beck called me about a broadcast he had managed to arrange for us. Jeff Clyne, a fabulous bass player, was with us but I forget who was on drums. The idea was to write some original tunes for the quartet and a small string ensemble. It was a great opportunity but my knowledge of string writing was limited and I wanted to use double stops (stopping and playing on two strings at a time) to beef up the sound. Knowing Cyril was a violinist I asked him for advice on how to write for bowing and multi stops. He was cagey at first, as he probably knew only too well the mirth his violin playing had caused in the past. However, when he realised I was serious and wanted his professional advice, I think he was touched. He told me morosely he wasn't much of a violinist, although he had always loved the instrument, and that maybe the best way he could help was for me to write some music first. Then he would have a look and see if the multi stops were playable on the instrument. For the next week or so that's what we did and he taught me quite a lot as he checked the parts. I began to feel quite warm towards him as he was obviously delighted to be asked for advice. The broadcast went well and the parts worked fine with no protests from the strings, who seemed to enjoy the whole thing.

Just before I joined the band, Phil Seamen had worked with Cyril at Streatham Locarno. He was his usual chaotic self and there were many tales of his antics during his time. Much of the music had to be played in strict tempo for the elderly dancers who frequented the place, especially during the afternoon tea dances. Quicksteps, foxtrots and waltzes had to be at the 'correct' tempo, or the old dears would come up and complain. Well, Cyril had a habit of checking the tempi on a wind-up stop watch and this used to drive Phil mad. One day he yelled at Cyril in his deep-throated roar, 'What the fuck d'ya think this is, Cyril? Brands Hatch?' The whole band cracked up, but poor Cyril didn't get the joke. He put up with Phil's antics pretty well, but one night he couldn't take it any more. Apparently Phil arrived back late from a break and clambered onto the bandstand just in time to take a short drum break. Instead of playing the four or eight bars that were written, he went into a long drum solo. As if this wasn't enough, a load of young couples gathered round the stage to listen, giving him a rapturous round of applause at the end. That was the last straw for Cyril and he fired Phil as soon as the set finished.

Another insight into Cyril's nature was a story he told me when I asked him about Phil's stint with the band. I expected Cyril to bad-mouth him, but instead his expression warmed. Phil had caused problems, but he admired his talent and told me this revealing tale. One afternoon when the band was playing a tea dance an old couple requested a tango. After the number had finished they came up to Cyril, thanked him profusely and said it was the best tango they had ever danced to. Cyril told me the reason it sounded so good was because of Phil's beat: he wasn't only a great jazz drummer but an expert on the various types of tango rhythm. Phil had chosen just the right tempo and feel for that particular tune and the couple had instinctively picked up on it, not realising it was all down to Phil's knowledge of the dance form.

I had a narrow escape myself one night. Mecca ballrooms had revolving bandstands. As the relief band played its final tune, the stage would slowly turn through 180 degrees and we had to be seated before the 'revolve' so that we would appear in our full glory when we faced the audience. We even had to play the same tune, so the change over was seamless and the music never stopped. That night, I arrived through the main door just as the stand was about to start its gyration. I ran through to the back stage area as fast as I could and had to take a desperate flying leap, jumping over two or three other sax players, to gain my moving seat. It could have ended in disaster with the whole sax section in a heap on the floor. But I made it and, as the band slowly arrived facing the audience, there I was sitting in my place and playing as if nothing had happened. I found out from the other guys that the ballroom manager and his cohorts were watching me with glee as I rushed through the hall. They were convinced they had me and couldn't wait to get me fired. Their faces dropped like lead balloons when I appeared, sitting in my rightful place. The guys were knocked out that I had robbed the 'Mecca Gestapo' of their moment of glory.

I was with Stapleton for quite a while. After the residency in Streatham, there were several short stints at other Mecca venues around London, like the Hammersmith Palais, the Orchid in Purley and the Lyceum, where Don Honeywell had been working with Oscar Rabin's Band when I had lessons from him in the late fifties. Luckily, bands like Stapleton's still did regular BBC broadcasts, so it was worth making the best of a sad musical situation. We had to play the latest Top Ten hits when they came out every week. This meant someone had to arrange them, so I earned extra money churning out big band charts at a rate of about two a week, so that the singers in the band could cover the latest pop records as soon as they hit the charts. It was soul-destroying work, but I could scribble the arrangements out fast and they helped pay the rent and get us out of debt. I was beginning to think commercial work would be my life from now on. Dave James' words back in Guildford all those years before, about having to play New Year's Eve gigs for the rest of my life, rang in my ears again and started to haunt me every day.

After a while the Mecca residencies dried up and we had to play one-nighters out of London, with all the endless coach journeys. Over the next few years I worked with several once top-line dance bands which, like Stapleton's, were losing out to the *Top of the Pops* generation, but most gigs were out of town as Mecca were cutting down on musicians in the London dance halls and turning to small guitar-based bands. Now you could hire a few kids, plug them into the wall and they made more noise than a big band, as I believe Humphrey Lyttleton once succinctly put it. Eventually even these guys lost their jobs when the Mecca chain got pretty much out of the music business altogether and turned their premises into bingo halls. There's progress for you.

Working with dance bands kept me going through the seventies and, although the music was often depressing, I made the most of it and there were some good memories. If nothing else I kept chops in shape playing all those waltzes and there were still a few jazz gigs. I did stints with Harry Bence who had a good band, was a good lead alto player and did quite a few broadcasts. I also got a call from Bill Eyden who told me he was working with Ray Ellington's band and Ray needed a sax player. Bill was a good friend and a fabulous jazz drummer. He was a driving force behind several of Tubby's groups and a lot of other top guys. He accompanied many of the Americans when they came over. For me he was right up there with Phil Seamen. He had that great relaxed feel, and inspired you with his driving swing and hip accents. I loved playing with him and jumped at the chance to hang out with him again.

Ray was a great guy, too. Probably best known for his featured spots on *Goon Show* radio broadcasts, he had an excellent big band and was a good man to work for. He was great-looking too and proud of his fabulous physique; he worked out regularly in the gym. And he had a fair voice. His signature tune was 'For All We Know', a song I had fallen in love with after hearing Billie Holiday's heart-rending ballad on *Lady in Satin*. Every time I think of Billie's version, shivers run down my spine at the way she sang the words 'Tomorrow may never come, for all we know'. You couldn't escape the feeling that she knew she would soon die in circumstances that will always be a blight on the conscience of any American with an ounce of human decency. Unfortunately, Ray's version, through no fault of his, brought me down with a bump. He just sang the song at a medium swing tempo, without any real feeling, and I had to face the fact that it was after all just another tune. Billie could take any mundane song and convince you it was a work of poetic genius.

Some of my fondest memories during these times were of sessions I did with Ken Mackintosh's band. Ken was highly respected both as a bandleader and as an alto saxophonist. He was a 'hands on' front man who often led the sax section himself. He had a beautiful powerful saxophone sound and a great technique and it was a privilege to play second alto to his lead. He was the only man I knew who still insisted on the saxes using a matched vibrato. It had become a lost art even then and was hard to pull off. All the saxes had to match the speed of their vibrato to the lead alto, so the whole section sounded as one. When done properly the sound is vibrant but I found it difficult to do and actually prefer the Ellington approach where the overall sound is made up of different and very personal styles. The trouble is that you need to have guys of the calibre of Johnny Hodges, Paul Gonsalves and Harry Carney to really make that work. It's a matter of taste and I respect guys who could make the matched vibrato style sound good. Ken Mackintosh's musical talent lives on in his son, Andy, who not only looks like his dad, but has inherited Ken's tremendous sound and musicianship. Andy is also a first class jazz player and very highly respected and loved by all who know him.

I did the odd date with Annie Ross and began to get work backing some other well known artists. I got a call in mid-December 1971 to do a record session with Eartha Kitt, who was then living in England. Eartha had an international reputation and her quirky singing voice and tongue-in-cheek, sexually-charged personality, were much in demand. She seemed to enjoy working in the huge new nightclubs around the North of England, places like Batley in Yorkshire. It was hard to figure out why such a sophisticated artist would like working in what were really just massive working men's clubs, but I guess they paid good money and the audiences loved her. I expected her to be difficult in the studio as I had the impression she was a bit of a firebrand. But she was fine, very relaxed and a lot of fun. At the end of the session a strange scuffling sound turned out to be her many miniscule chihuahua dogs. It was well known she adored these creatures but to see them suddenly appear like a load of mice all round the studio was quite a shock. They were cute but a little crazy, like their owner. Eartha bundled them in her arms and swept out of the studio, giggling and waving us goodbye.

In 1972, I bumped into Marlene Dietrich again. Not surprisingly she didn't remember me. In fact, I don't think anyone in the band got within a mile of her this time. She did a week in London at the Queen's Theatre on Shaftesbury Avenue and I was in the backing orchestra. It was a weird gig. She kept to herself and no one was allowed near the backstage area from which she made her entrances. It was ostensibly to protect the highly expensive white fur coat she wore in her act but it may also have had something to do with the fact that she was showing the results of too many face lifts. From a distance her face looked, for all the world, as if it was made of plaster of Paris. Nevertheless it was fascinating to watch her work and she had the audience, eighty per cent of which was young homosexual men, enthralled every night. She was a huge gay icon by then and had an incredible aura; her unique place in films and cabaret, and her sheer historical significance, commanded respect. She was loved by millions of Germans and by the Allies during the War, a truly unique achievement.

Another legendary artist I worked with was Liberace. Again, I never met him, because he was not at the orchestral rehearsal and was surrounded by fans when we left the theatre. He didn't need to rehearse, as he was a true professional who knew his act inside out. He was known for his outrageously camp stage manner and flamboyant stage outfits, each of which cost thousands of dollars, but he also had a prodigious piano technique in many different styles, from classical to boogie-woogie. He must have been a courageous man because when he first appeared in the fifties his homosexuality was pretty obvious and homosexual conduct was illegal in most countries. He tried to pretend he was straight for years and that his camp manner was just part of his act, but when the attitude to homosexuality softened he became an iconic figure in the gay community. In 1987, he died tragically of AIDS. At the time I worked with him, Liberace joked onstage about how he had always thought of himself as completely outrageous, but now had a job trying to keep up with the new glam rock stars and felt quite an old square beside them. In fact, considering the viciously anti-homosexual climate in which he rose to fame, he was a far more rebellious iconoclast than any of the young latter day rock stars and, unlike most of them, he was adored not only by the young, but by their moms and dads as well.

* * *

In the early 1970s, my relationship with Dr Smith deteriorated. Registered addicts are at the mercy of their doctors' whims. After insisting I should decide how much medication I should get, he changed his approach completely and for no apparent reason. I was coping fine on my self-prescribed 150 mgs a day, but he suddenly decided to put me in hospital to cut down the medication. I went through hell for about ten days and came out struggling to survive on only about 60 mgs. Tough as this was, it was not the reason our relationship eventually broke down. After all, I figured he was only trying to wean me off for my own good. But my respect for him took a dive one night when I had a television gig accompanying a guest artist on some chat show. I invited him along to see it and he brought his father, who turned out to be a wonderfully lively, distinguished-looking old gentleman. After the show everyone was invited to the hospitality room for drinks, so Linda and I invited Smith and his father to accompany us. Linda had got on great with his dad and he was really up for hanging out after the show. Smith, however, put a damper on the whole thing and whisked his father off, making the excuse that his dad was tired and that he himself had to get up early for work in the morning. It was only about 10 p.m. and Linda was furious with him, as his dad was clearly looking forward to it. Dr Smith seemed almost ashamed of his father's enthusiasm.

An addict's relationship to his doctor can be difficult at the best of times, as one wrong word and the addict can have his supply cut off. It's usually a battle of wits because the addict is always assumed to be an inveterate liar, even if he isn't. It's a vicious circle as the doctor is always trying to give the patient less medication while the addict's tolerance to the drug tends to increase all the time. I've always tried to be truthful with doctors but, when they don't trust you, you are sometimes forced to be 'economical with the truth' to get what you need. At the television show I discovered that my psychiatrist, who had such power over my own life, seemed unable to treat even his father with understanding or compassion.

My opinion of Dr Smith had become specially negative when I had to deal with him over the death of a friend of mine. One day in March 1969 I was at his clinic when, to my astonishment, a friend I shall call Billy Trente walked in. I hadn't seen him since I was with Cyril Stapleton. Billy had been a minor pop star at the beginning of the 1960s but had fallen on hard times and,

unknown to me, had been a patient at Smith's clinic. It was good
to see him again and I took him to our place to hang out for an
hour or two. He told me he had been on heroin but Smith
wouldn't give him any more. He was sick and wondered if I
could give him a little methadone. He said he could get heroin
later and would turn me on as repayment. I was reluctant to give
him any but I knew how he felt, so gave him just a little and he
went off into the night. I was looking forward to getting a taste
of 'horse' later if he scored, but he never returned, that night or
any night. A couple of days later the police came round to question me about our meeting. His mother had found him dead in
bed and suicide was suspected.

I was horrified. He must have told his mum he had been at
my place before he went to bed and that's why the police
came round. I told them the whole story as far as I could. I was
pretty sure the amount of methadone I gave him couldn't have
killed him, but I was wracked with guilt, fear, and sorrow at
losing a good friend. I arranged to meet Smith to discuss things,
as there was going to be an inquest. His attitude shocked me. He
seemed unconcerned about Billy's death and when I told him
how guilty I felt at having given him methadone, he just said,
'Oh? Why do you feel guilty?' The inquest was a nightmare. I
was questioned about Billy's visit. The local press were there and
my own addiction was now in the public domain. Legally the
whole thing was a mess too. The doctor who signed Billy's death
certificate and his psychiatrist, Dr Smith, were in deep discussion. A small quantity of methadone had been found in his body
but no heroin, so he obviously never scored any after he left me.
The doctors agreed the real cause of death was barbiturate poisoning. He had taken a lethal dose of sleeping pills.

To both doctors' dismay the coroner brought in a verdict of
death by drug addiction, a totally bogus terminology, as there
was no such legal cause of death. The coroner clearly wanted to
make a point about drugs with this verdict, which was very hurt-
ful to Billy's memory and especially to his mother. I decided to

face her and offer my sympathy. But she was in shock at her son's death and hardly took in what I was saying. I felt terrible but when I tried to talk to Smith, he was still in deep discussion with the other doctor about the verdict. They seemed more concerned about the coroner overriding their professional judgment than about Billy's death. I left in disgust to try to cope with my own troubled conscience.

The final straw in my relationship with Dr S. came when I asked him to help me get off drugs by trying an apomorphine cure. A friend of mine, an eminent bass player who had been a heroin addict, told me he managed to kick drugs with the new treatment. Author William Burroughs was also a staunch advocate of the experimental apomorphine cure and wrote about it in one of his books. Apomorphine was used mostly as an aversion therapy for alcoholics. One normal shot makes you violently sick but, if used in tiny amounts, vomiting is avoided and it apparently acts on the metabolism that opposes the effects of opiates. But a private cure was too expensive. I told Smith about the treatment, hoping he could arrange for me to try it. He was very unimpressed, but I finally persuaded him and he arranged for me to go into hospital.

As is the norm with the treatment, I had to stop opiates completely while undergoing the cure. A large and intimidating male orderly came round to give me my first shot of apomorphine, but to my horror it was the standard aversion dose. The result was that after a few seconds I threw up violently. I protested, saying the whole idea was to use minimal doses to avoid vomiting but Dr S. refused to change the sadistic regime. The result was ten days of absolute hell with four-hourly injections. Wracked with withdrawals, I had to spend hours vomiting into a bucket. Sleep was impossible and I couldn't eat, so I lost about a stone and a half in weight. Linda was furious and we agreed Smith was trying to teach me some kind of lesson. How dare I question his advice not to try the apomorphine cure? I signed myself out and after ten days without methadone, it was a relief to go home, still with mild withdrawals but no more vomiting. Gradually I put on weight, started to feel better and was off all opiates, but it would have been easier to have just gone cold turkey at home. Linda wrote a furious letter, telling Dr Smith what she thought of his treatment. After that there was no way I could return to his clinic, even if I had wanted to.

I couldn't throw off the long-term effects of withdrawal and looked for a legal alternative. This turned out to be a family remedy that contained a tiny amount of some form of opium. The product was known as Dr Collis Brown's Chlorodyne. When I was a child, my parents would give me a few drops in a glass of water if I suffered a stomach upset. Now I found that drinking half a bottle or more helped a bit. But it's such an evil-tasting, stomach-burning liquid that I had to take it in a large glass of water with a couple of tablespoonfuls of demerera sugar. To this day, I hate brown sugar in my coffee. Eventually the friend who had recommended the apomorphine cure managed to get me an appointment with the nursing sister who had treated him. She was horrified at what had happened to me and showed me how you are supposed to do it. She gave me about a quarter of a tablet to put under my tongue and I had no nausea at all. However, just one day is not enough to have any effect so I still continued forcing down two whole bottles of Chlorodyne a day along with the odd shot of heroin if I could get it.

Around this time I got an unexpected call to go to Majorca with a band put together by pianist Harry South which included Ronnie Scott, trumpeter Les Condon and bassist Phil Bates. The gig was a six-week residency at a big theatre in Palma, accompanying star acts like singer Matt Monro. It was well paid and we started rehearsals. But unfortunately a dispute arose between the Spanish and British musicians' unions which turned into a minor diplomatic incident involving the respective governments. At this time Spain was still a dictatorship under Franco. The problem started with the British union. A Spanish flamenco act had come to the UK for some concerts and naturally brought their own guitarists with them. The Musicians Union stupidly put the blocks on this and understandably the Spanish union in retaliation refused to allow a British band to accompany the star acts in Majorca, insisting that inexperienced musicians from the Spanish mainland were used instead. We continued to rehearse and played the first night, hoping that sanity would prevail and the problem would be sorted out. Instead, things went from bad to worse with neither side willing to compromise. The British and Spanish ambassadors got involved, it became a major diplomatic problem, and the gig was off after just one night.

I had left my horn in the venue but on the second night was told I was not even allowed to enter the theatre, which was heavily guarded by police and strange men in dark suits, who were obviously badly disguised Spanish secret service agents. After a lot of high level negotiations I got permission to pick up my horn, but had to be accompanied by an armed guard. It was bizarre in the extreme. We were going to get paid in full, but would not be able to stay in the free hotel accommodation. However, because of the nature of the contract, some of us who had arranged to rent flats for the six weeks would be allowed to remain for the duration, rent free. This was a great bonus: six weeks wages with a holiday in the sun. Linda and I, Ronnie Scott and the others who stayed on had a ball and I got a much needed rest and a chance to clean up and recuperate. I swam a lot, got a good tan and discovered through some friends who lived in Majorca that you could buy dexadrine tablets legally, over the counter. I was having trouble sleeping and was advised to try another freely obtainable drug, Mogadon. This worked great and was then considered totally harmless. However the drug was to prove a big problem for me a few years later.

Ron Rubin, his lovely wife Marie and their children were living on the island and Ron was playing solo piano in a bar where we often hung out till the early hours. I would play sometimes to keep my chops in and Ron introduced us to the American pianist Art Simmons who was living on the island at the time. Art would often play a set to give Ron a break. He was quite a legend and one of the first American modern jazz musicians to move to Paris in the fifties, along with Kenny Clarke and Bud Powell. He had also been Billie Holiday's accompanist. One night Art and I persuaded Linda to sing a few tunes. She had hardly sung a note since we first met so it was wonderful to see her doing her stuff again. Linda was pretty nervous so we didn't tell her Art had worked with Billie. One tune led to another and Art wouldn't let her offstage; he loved her singing so much. When she finally came off, we told her about Art and Billie and she nearly fainted. Linda had insisted she was through with singing when I met her. She disliked girl singers who married musicians to further their own careers and felt that too many fine players had ended up as just an adjunct to their wife's acts. She wanted none of it. So it was wonderful to see her so happy that night. Also, singing with Art and getting a warm reception from the few late-night punters at the club restored a little of the confidence she had lost since giving up the profession. I hoped she might consider working again when we got back to England, but things never worked out and her wonderful talent remained a secret.

Back in London, I was offered a regular gig in a new production of the show *Applause*, which was about to start rehearsals at Her Majesty's Theatre in the Strand. It would be regular money for the run of the show and a chance to escape from the constant hand-to-mouth existence, waiting for the phone to ring. The show entailed playing a lot of flute which worried me, but the MD was a nice old stick and the flute parts were not too hard, so I could bluff my way through, and I figured my flute playing had to improve after a few months in the pit. The story was about an aging Broadway star whose career was on the wane. It was a great part but needed a strong personality, with plenty of vindictiveness to carry it off. The part was to be played by the legendary Lauren Bacall, so we knew it was going to be special.

Bacall had always been respected as a fine actor so I expected her to be brilliant in the lead role, which seemed perfect for the charismatic, still very attractive lady. I did wonder if she might be hard to work with. In fact nothing could be further from the truth. She certainly gave the part all the neurotic maliciousness it demanded, but did it with great humour too. Offstage she was a really charming person. She knew what she wanted, and how to get it, but always worked as a team player. During the 'first night party' Lauren was getting an ear-bashing from some hangers-on when she spotted me looking for an opportunity to introduce my wife. She interrupted her conversation, gave us a welcoming smile and offered her outstretched hand to Linda when I introduced her. I left them chatting away like old mates and Linda told me later, to my horror, that she asked Bacall whether she planned to marry again one day, now Humphrey Bogart had died. Their marriage was reputed to have been one of the happiest in Hollywood, despite their legendary, spectacular fights. Lauren was not fazed at all by Linda's question and just replied quietly, 'No. I mean, where are you going to find another guy like Bogie?' I believe she did eventually re-marry so her new husband must have been pretty special.

Unlike me, Linda would go up to anyone and start a conversation. She was in Ronnie's one night when Rudolf Nureyev came in with a team of minders. Since she always adored ballet, she waited her chance and then went right up and introduced herself. The minders stood up menacingly but Nureyev was so taken aback by her directness that he invited her to join him. He loved it when she told him her mother had once worked as a cleaner at the Birmingham Royal Ballet and used to steal discarded ballet shoes from the dustbin and bring them home for her to wear. He knew about poverty. Linda asked him about a prominent scar he had on his lip and why he had never had it removed. He told her he got it when he was a small boy in

Russia. Everyone was starving so, when the news came that there was meat in another village, his father made him walk miles in the snow on his own to try and buy some. While he was bringing it back, he saw a starving dog and bent down to give it a piece. But the dog was so hungry that it attacked him and stole all the meat, biting a chunk out of his lip in the process. When he got home minus the meat, his father beat the hell out of him. He told Linda that he never had that scar removed because he never wanted to forget how poor he had been as a child.

One enjoyable thing about the year I spent in the show was making friends with the guys in the string section. It was a great chance to talk about classical music and I started working hard at the clarinet again so I could play a few straight pieces with the pianist and the strings between shows. One of the players brought a relative in to deputise for one of the violinists. His name was Christopher Warren-Green and he was a brilliant young musician who went on to become a fine soloist and orchestral leader. I was renewing my interest in the violin and how to write properly for it, so Chris gave me a lot of advice and encouragement and even lent me a violin for a while. I hadn't touched the instrument since I was at school and soon realised why I'd given it up but it was very useful to get a feel of the violin again. It would be valuable in years to come.

Although I now had regular work, I was still using Chlorodyne from the pharmacist. The guys in the orchestra thought I was 'clean' but, while in *Applause*, I became friendly with a Canadian musician who was a registered addict and, once a week, he would give me a shot of heroin. He was also registered on methadone linctus. My stomach got so bad from forcing down too much Chlorodyne that I had to find a better solution, so he suggested I try to get fixed up at the clinic he went to. It wasn't easy but, after some emotional telephone calls from my wife, I got an appointment. They put me on 60 mgs of methadone a day and told me I could remain on it for life if necessary. It was a huge relief, even though I realised there would be some problems working outside the UK. I could relax more and, as far as everyone else knew, I was free of drugs. I lived a secret life of evasions and half-truths that took a huge toll on my self-esteem. It gave me no satisfaction when people congratulated me on how I had kicked drugs and survived. Only my wife and the clinic knew the truth and Linda had to endure years of subterfuge and anguish, which she stoically kept to herself. I know of no other woman who would have tolerated the immense secret burden she carried for those years.

Gradually the clinic rules tightened up a lot and they began insisting everyone pick up their script every day from their local pharmacy. Previously, I used to get a week or two at a time and could easily make it last. In fact, without telling the clinic I actually reduced my dose and managed to save enough to give me a spare supply. The new regime meant I had to take my secret spare supply with me, when I went to France for instance, leaving my poor wife to go every single day to collect my official script. This had to be done without telling the clinic or they would have taken away my spare supply. It was huge burden on Linda that went on until the European Union brought in new regulations that allowed registered addicts to carry methadone into any EU country. I had to have a letter from the clinic each time I travelled in Europe but was soon trusted enough to take up to two weeks supply with me.

When *Applause* eventually came to an end, I was out of regular work again and went back to waiting for the phone to ring. One way and another I managed to pay the rent and there were good gigs from time to time. I now had some contacts in the pit orchestra scene and the pianist from *Applause* got me a Christmas gig, a pantomime at Richmond Theatre. It wasn't the West End, but it was a new experience and had its good side. The six-week stint led to three consecutive years of work over the often barren Christmas period. They always had old-style traditional pantomime at Richmond and, although it was hard work with matinees every day, it was great to see old music hall pros like Arthur Askey strutting their stuff day after day to an audience of unruly kids. But Dave James' words rang in my ears again. As if Christmas party gigs were not bad enough, I was now reduced to playing in pantomime and even enjoying it. My connections in the pit soon led to another West End job, a short stint in Michel Legrand's *The Umbrellas of Cherbourg*.

I did have a few memorable jazz gigs during the seventies, especially with American guest artists who toured with British rhythm sections. Alongside work with Red Rodney and Jon Eardley, there were dates with Slide Hampton, trumpeter Nat Adderley and ex-Monk tenor man, Charlie Rouse. What sticks in my mind about Slide was not only his brilliant trombone playing and his quiet, kindly demeanour, but his obsession with his horn. He would spend hours every day practising in the hotel and again just before we went onstage. We got on well, except for one thing. He was anti-cigarettes and would shame me into not lighting up in the car. This was before the days when all smokers were made to feel like the lowest form of life and it was tough for me to sit for hours on the road without a fag, even if Slide was such good company. But it was a great tour and Slide played beautifully, due no doubt in part to his endless practising.

I first met Nat Adderley when he came to this country not long after his illustrious brother Cannonball had passed away. Nat, who had done very well out of his composing royalties with tunes like 'Work Song', told me he had not wanted to play with another alto player since his brother's death. He described how he had struggled night after night to keep up with Cannonball's awesome talent and felt that any other alto man was a big anticlimax after that. So he paid me a big compliment when he told me I was the first alto player he enjoyed working with since his brother died.

Charlie Rouse was quiet, self-effacing and a pleasant man to work with. I got the impression he had struggled to get recognition outside of his famous work with the Thelonious Monk Quartet. It seemed a shame that he had few British dates. I did just one or two concerts and a BBC broadcast with Charlie, accompanied by the Stan Tracey Trio. Stan's knowledge of Monk's music helped put Charlie at ease and the gigs were very enjoyable.

Another trumpet player I worked with was Howard McGhee. I was interested to meet him as he had played trumpet on Bird's ill-fated 'Lover Man' session in Hollywood in 1946. Although I rather regret it now, I was never one for collecting autographs or photos. I did have a lovely signed photo of Ben Webster which I lost somewhere but, apart from a snapshot taken with Elvin Jones, I have very little memorabilia. However I came across an old promotional shot of Howard in my belongings, which has the rather quaint inscription: 'Howard McGhee, internationally famous trumpeter'. It's signed and dedicated, 'To Pete'.

Howard McGhee

The only other memento I have is from when my quintet played opposite Billy Eckstine, at Ronnie Scott's in the eighties. I had been listening a lot to Coltrane's amazing solo cadenza on his recording of 'I Want to Talk About You'. My pianist, John Horler, asked if I knew Eckstine had composed the tune. I didn't so I asked Billy if he had an old song copy of it I could study. He hadn't, but said he would get back to me. The next night he gave me a piece of manuscript on which he had written the whole tune, with all the lyrics and chords, signed with a lovely dedication. I mentioned to Billy how much I loved Coltrane's version and he told me 'Trane had sent him a copy of his album but he couldn't figure what the hell he was doing in the cadenza. 'Trane must have hoped for his approval but, although Billy admired him, I think that long cadenza was a bit too far out for the composer!

A new source of work appeared when organist Mike Carr asked me to join his new trio. He had worked in Ronnie Scott's trio, but Ronnie had disbanded it and Mike felt it was worth carrying on with the trio format as they had established a lot of useful connections in Europe. There was no bass player because Mike is one of the few organists fully capable of sustaining the bass line on the foot pedals. He is very underrated and I consider him to be one of the best there is. A young South African, Bobby Gien, was with us on drums. We toured extensively in England, Germany, Belgium, Switzerland, Denmark and Sweden, playing at some of the best European clubs and concert venues. Bobby couldn't always make the gigs due to his other work, as a dentist, so we had other drummers along the way including, for one tour, ex-Basie man Sonny Payne.

That tour was a lot of fun until Sonny and Mike had a big falling-out over – wait for it – tennis! Yes, tennis! They were both enthusiastic players and fixed up to play a game one day. Afterwards, Sonny came to my hotel room and told me Mike had gone crazy, cussing him out so bad that they stopped the game and drove back, arguing the whole way. Then Mike got me on my own and raved about Sonny not giving him a serious game. Sonny expected just to have some fun and knock a ball about for exercise, but Mike took the whole thing as seriously as if he was John McEnroe at Wimbledon. Poor Sonny was upset at the whole thing and for the rest of the tour Mike never forgave him, which put a damper on things. But we all enjoyed playing together in spite of this and, at one party gig, Sonny showed some of his vaudeville skills, bouncing his sticks off the wall behind him with great aplomb during a drum solo.

I had first played with Sonny at a jam session several years before, when he was still with the Basie band, before he left to make more money with Frank Sinatra. At the jam session the legendary tap dancer 'Baby' Laurence Jackson, 'sat in', with Frank Foster and a few more of the Basie guys. Sonny was good friends with all the famous black tap dancers, many of whom had worked at the same venues as Basie. Back then drummers had great respect for good dancers and often shared new rhythmic ideas with them. Phil Seamen, who was also hip to the relationship between dancing and drumming, had been married at one time to a beautiful 'hoofer'. Anyway, in the middle of one tune Sonny yelled out with a glint in his eye, 'Eights, with me and Babe.' There followed an incredible show of skill, as Sonny and Babe traded eight-bar breaks, Babe tapping out the most amazing rhythms, while performing all kinds of spectacular gymnastic feats, including full somersaults. It was a revelation. Phil had taught me the importance of dancing in jazz, but this was the first time I had seen anything like this. Babe Laurence was reputed to be the greatest tap dancer of all time. He made stars like Fred Astaire look pedestrian by comparison, but black dancers were not allowed into the white world of film stardom and their talents never received the international acclaim they deserved.

I worked with Mike Carr's trio right into the eighties. It was not my ideal choice musically and it really needed the weight of a tenor sax to complement the power of the Hammond organ. But we had some great times, including a week's stint at a Scottish festival playing opposite my old friend Yusef Lateef and his group, and a spell at Ronnie's supporting Dizzy Gillespie's quintet. This was the only time I came close to being friendly with Dizzy. We used to play 'Dizzy Atmosphere' a lot, which I assumed was one of his tunes. I transcribed it for the band and I wasn't sure of a couple of the notes so I asked him one night if he could check them out for us. He had a look, took his trumpet and slowly fumbled his way through the difficult up-tempo tune as if he had never seen it before. Finally, he said, with a slightly bemused look, that he couldn't remember what the notes should be but that what we were playing sounded fine to him. Dizzy would say hello to me every night, but then, when I ran into him later, he ignored me again, as I said earlier.

Before the 1970s drew to a close I had an interesting recording session with Californian pianist Hampton Hawes. I was playing opposite him at Ronnie Scott's and so we would hang out a little between sets. He had a great trio and I was impressed with the way the group worked together as a unit. Hampton always led, but there was a lot of freedom in the music. One night, Johnny Hawksworth, who was Ted Heath's bass player but also ran his own publishing business, asked if I would do a session on the Sunday. He had written some tunes and was to record them for De Wolfe, a music company which then specialised in stock recordings for films and television. He wanted me and Hank Shaw to do the session with the Hampton Hawes Trio. Hampton must have been short of cash because to my surprise he accepted the poorly paid gig but Hank could not make the session, so it was just a quartet. The result was released under the unwieldy name of *Johnny Hawksworth Presents Anglo American Jazz Phase 1.*

For one track Johnny wanted a free piece so he asked us to make something up ourselves. This caused a bit of consternation but then, suddenly, Hampton picked up an empty beer bottle and started walking around the room tapping out rhythms with it, on the wall, a radiator and on anything else that looked interesting. The rest of us gradually joined in and it turned out to be one of the most interesting tracks on the album. The musicians composed the piece all by themselves but Hawksworth, sharp business man that he was, claimed all the damned royalties. I was used to shit like this but surprised that Hampton didn't kick up a stink about it. I guess he felt the same as me: do the gig, grab what money you can and get out. I was beginning to wish I had stuck to aerodynamics. But, luckily, things were about to improve, once we saw the back of the infamous seventies.

10

'Are you straight?'
Philly Joe Jones

I had not been involved in the new 'free' jazz but one day I got a call from drummer John Stevens who wanted me to make a record with a band he was to call 'Free Bop'. I had played many times with John and apart from an odd reluctance to count the bars during sixteen or eight bar breaks, he had a great feel on drums and a massive drive and swing, reminiscent of Elvin Jones, whom he greatly admired. John had been heavily involved in the new free music and wanted to record an album using both free and more bop-based musicians. The idea was to play bebop inspired melodies but, while keeping the improvised passages mainly in tempo, to do away with any harmonic structure, leaving the musicians to play whatever came into their heads. John's talents must have been gaining more recognition because the album was to be recorded on the famous Affinity label. Along with myself, he had hired Gordon Beck on piano, with Paul Rutherford, known for his avant-garde trombone playing, and some other excellent free musicians. Gordon and I thought it would be an interesting project and we were both looking forward to a chance to do something different. It turned out to be quite an experience and the resulting album called *Freebop* received wide acclaim, even getting a good review in *Down Beat*. This, while welcome, galled me a bit as, good though the record was, I didn't think it should have had more attention than many other excellent British albums that never got reviewed at all in the magazine. I had a lot to learn about how the business works and what constitutes a good album. Looking back on it, it was a challenging and stimulating experience.

Although I enjoyed the recording session it was not without a few tense moments. Gordon and I soon got into playing free, especially when we were given our heads and let loose on a piano and alto duet with no tempo. However, some of the melody lines John had written for the horns sounded to me a little naive and lacking in real substance. A lot of friendly banter went on between Gordon, John and me about this. In fact the reason I gave John a hard time was more to do with what I considered to be his lack of harmonic knowledge, rather than his melodic writing. Of course there were no chord sequences behind the tunes and that was fine, but John insisted on harmonising some lines by simply having us play exactly the same parts, doubled up in parallel thirds. Loving harmony as I do, this seemed pointless to me. I offered to construct some kind of functional harmony, at least behind the tunes but, rather than that, I felt the lines would sound better and have more freedom if they were all in unison.

Eventually, I got so pissed off, I snapped, 'For fuck sake, let me re-harmonise the damned tune, properly!' John always kept a sense of humour and he completely disarmed me by saying, 'Hey Pete! You're getting angry with me, aren't you?' 'Well, yes,' I said, 'I guess I am.' To which he replied, 'Great! That's what I want! I want you to get angry. I like that tension when we play. It makes the music better and gives it a kind of edge. Know what I mean?' I broke out laughing. What else could I do after that curve ball? He knew exactly what he was doing and I think he was winding me up with those damned parallel thirds on purpose, just to get my adrenalin up. It put me in mind of when Miles once picked a fight with his producer, Teo Macero, during one of his record dates, just to psych himself up, to make something different happen with the music. John gave me one of his big bearhugs and I got into the music again with a more upbeat attitude.

I loved his adventurous spirit, even though he could drive me mad at times. He could be outrageous too. One day he came up to me in a crowded club, grabbed my face in his hands and kissed

me, full on the lips! I loved the shocked looks from some of the
bemused punters. John had a heart as big as a mountain and did
wonderful work with his Spontaneous Music Ensemble. His
rather off the wall teaching skills helped to develop the talents
of many young up and coming musicians, including saxophonist
Courtney Pine. I was terribly shocked when he died suddenly,
long before his time, in 1994. It was a great loss and I wish I had
spent more time in his sometimes abrasive but always stimulating company. He was a one-off; a genuinely free spirit.

In the mid-1970s Linda and I had difficulties in our marriage
for various reasons. Although I was now relatively stable on
methadone, I still messed around with speed and cocaine and
had difficulty taking care of business. After Linda's mother died
things got considerably worse. In a very short space of time we
lost Linda's father, her mother and then my father, who died of
lung cancer in 1977. Her dad passed away suddenly but peacefully at a ripe old age, but her mother's death was a prolonged
and agonising ordeal. Linda felt the loss very deeply and began
losing control of her own life. Gladys was not only her mom but
her number one fan and best friend and Linda never fully recovered from her passing. She started going out on her own a lot to
parties, began drinking too much and became accident prone,
breaking both wrists during her period of worst anguish. Both of
us were spinning out of control and all these problems finally led
to me being fired for the first time in my life.

I had been working with a new octet that Stan Tracey put
together in 1976. It was a great band and we made an album or
two and did quite a few gigs. Unfortunately, because of my rather
chaotic state, I sometimes had difficulty getting to gigs on time.
On 21st December 1976 I was supposed to be at a broadcast with
the octet but, after a row with Linda, I arrived very late. As it
happened the BBC had some technical problems and recording
had not yet started, but Stan had already hired another guy to
take my place. They were also filming the band for a documentary during the broadcast. I apologised profusely to everyone

and, although there were a few sad and knowing looks at my late arrival, I had the feeling not too much harm had been done. I knew I had let the side down but I was not prepared for what happened ten days later as Stan hadn't seemed unduly put out. I was shocked when I opened the post on New Year's Day to find a cold and uncharacteristically officious letter from Stan, saying my services with the octet were no longer required. I was desolate. Linda felt, wrongly, that she was as much to blame as me and was furious about the dismissal letter. I resigned myself to the news, figuring I had gotten away with it all for too long and was finally getting my just deserts. I later discovered that Stan had felt bad about firing me but thought he had little alternative. One thing was certain, it was a serious wake-up call and I resolved not be late for a gig again if I could possibly help it.

The start of 1977 was tough but things soon changed for the better. In September I got a call to start rehearsals for a new West End show, *Bubbling Brown Sugar*. It was a fine project and kept me in regular work for the next two years. We had a great band, which included Les Condon and Duncan Campbell on trumpets, Stan Robinson on tenor, and my dear friend trombonist Keith Christie. Tragedy struck, though, when our excellent young drummer died very suddenly of cancer; the only positive thing was that Bill Eyden took over the drum chair. The big 'C' hit us again when Richard Leonard, the musical director and pianist, also died suddenly of the same disease. He was a great guy, a brilliant classically trained musician who had worked closely with Leonard Bernstein. He had me do one of the band arrangements for the show and always encouraged me in orchestral writing, even asking me to write an arrangement for full symphony orchestra to be used on a big concert at the Royal Albert Hall. That was his last performance as he was desperately ill by then and died shortly after. His place as MD and pianist was taken by Colin Purbrook, also a fine, classically trained musician, better known as a talented jazz pianist. He already knew the show, having done a lot of the rehearsals and conducted the band occasionally when Richard had a break.

The show was full of good jazz and the cast was made up almost entirely of top class African-American dancers and singers. Two of its brightest stars were Helen Gelzer, a stunning-looking black girl who was over six feet tall, and the legendary Billy Daniels, famous for his original hit recording of 'That Old Black Magic', which he also sang in the show. Gelzer charmed and amazed us all. She was pure dynamite, with a powerful, show-stopping, singing voice. She had beautiful legs, so long that she could cover the whole stage in about four steps. We told Helen her talents would surely rocket her to stardom, but she just smiled and said she knew two dozen other girls in New York as tall as her, better looking and better dancers and singers, and all unemployed. She must have been right because, despite rave reviews about her stunning performance, we never saw or heard of her again. I hope she continued her career after the show ended.

The male dancers included Charles Augins, the archetypal tall, bald, mean-looking black dude. He stayed in the UK after the show. Another of the dancers, a beautiful Adonis of a guy, with a great physique, made a big show of warming up onstage before the curtain went up, wearing just a skimpy G-string. At first we all figured he was gay, but he turned out to be straight and had a beautiful girlfriend. The real truth came out one night when we musicians were having dinner with some of the cast between shows and the male dancers were looking at gay porno magazines. The penny dropped: they were gay, but the guy in the G-string was not. I figured Mr G-string was just winding the other guys up with his nightly demonstration of his Harry Belafonte looks.

One night Bud Freeman, the legendary tenor player from the old Eddie Condon Chicago jazz scene, dropped by. We got him an extra chair and he sat right in the band with us, for the whole night. His enthusiasm and vitality were amazing, especially considering he had been playing from way back in the early days of jazz in the twenties. We had a ball in his company and he was our honoured, if very self-effacing, guest for the night. Bud was a hell of a player. Although not a great technician, he swung like mad. He was a seminal figure on tenor and had been a big influence on the young Lester Young.

Although the show was fabulous, something was happening to me that led to a mini crisis at the end of the run. I was getting too used to regular work and all I wanted to do after the show was go home and watch television or listen to classical music. I found myself preferring to stay in my comfort zone with the show and becoming more and more reluctant to take other work, unless it paid much better money. I was regularly turning down offers of jazz gigs, with one notable exception. One afternoon I got a call from Pete King, business partner of Ronnie Scott. Stan Getz was refusing to appear for a Saturday night gig at their club. Pete asked me to deputise and, of course, I jumped at the gig thinking that if Pete considered I was the best guy to take on that prestigious challenge, it should be worth decent money for once. I did the gig. Ronnie Scott's was packed and not many walked out when Getz didn't show. At the end of the night Pete thanked me and put some money in my hand. When I checked it later it was a measly £30, the same money I would have got for working with the relief band. I knew Getz was charging a fortune to work at the club so, to put it mildly, I was not amused. I was too scared to argue with Pete though, so I skulked off home, more than a little disgusted.

In those days I didn't fully understand the economic realities of trying to keep Ronnie Scott's Club afloat. Later, when I played there for minimum union rates, I knew that was really all Pete and Ronnie could pay and I would never quibble about fees. Once I realised the struggle they were having keeping the place open, and knowing they always put taking care of musicians at the top of their list of priorities, I happily worked there for the honour and prestige of playing at one of the finest jazz clubs in the world. In view of the acclaim Scott's has had from so many high powered politicians, I reckon it should be subsidised by the nation as a national treasure. In most European countries, an institution like Ronnie's would be considered vital to the artistic and commercial well-being of the capital and given huge government funding. Britain, under Thatcher and right up to the present day, puts me in mind of Hermann Göring's cynical and oft quoted remark, 'When I hear the word culture, I reach for my revolver.'

All good things come to an end and finally *Bubbling Brown Sugar* was due to come off. We musicians had plenty of warning about it but I was dreading being out of regular work again and the last few weeks became a bit of a nightmare due to a sudden deterioration in my mental condition. For many years, my GP had been prescribing Mogadon, a mild and supposedly harmless sedative. It helped me sleep and like its close relative, Valium, helped to keep my nerves under control. Then, out of the blue, he quit his practice and I could not get any more. The worry of being out of work again began to get to me and I started to feel more and more nervous, so Linda insisted we go to Greece for a holiday before the show finished. Although we both needed a break in the sun I didn't look forward to it. I was worried about spending money, with the show due to come off. Also, the journey to Paros, an island in the Cyclades, involved a seven-hour sea crossing. By the time we came back, I had lost weight and had been drinking Ouzo and Greek brandy for my nerves. Although I had a good tan, I felt weak, my nervousness had worsened and I was showing signs of mild paranoia.

The remaining few weeks in the show were horrible. I began imagining the guys in the band were talking about me behind my back. I had lost all my confidence and even worried about making mistakes, playing music I knew backwards by then. Of course the guys hadn't even noticed. It was just my paranoia. I struggled through to the end of the run and went home to lick my wounds, but I was so depressed by then I couldn't even face the few gigs I had in the book and pleaded with Linda to cancel them for me, scared of even speaking on the phone to people. I became suicidal and drove around looking for high buildings I could possibly jump from. Things got so bad I began having problems with my digestion. Any food I managed to force down passed right through me. I had continual diarrhoea, lost weight fast and couldn't sleep. I was worried enough to call a doctor, imagining all kinds of terrible illnesses I might be suffering from. A very pleasant GP came to see me, listened to all my woes and told me I was just suffering from nervous dyspepsia. Seeing my obvious distress at this innocuous diagnosis, he assured me that this mild-sounding condition could be very debilitating. He prescribed a mild stomach medicine and gave me a few Mogadon tablets for my insomnia. I took one and immediately felt a hundred times better. The penny dropped: a lot of my suffering over the last few months was because I had become addicted to Mogadon without realising it.

I signed on with the new GP and he continued prescribing a low regulated dose, under close supervision. By this time the addictive properties of drugs like Valium and Mogadon were recognised and many people began suing the pharmaceutical companies for foisting large quantities of what were thought to be harmless drugs on unsuspecting patients, who later found they had become helpless addicts. I considered doing the same but figured, I wouldn't have a leg to stand on.

I had been experiencing classic symptoms of tranquiliser with-drawals: inability to sleep, depression, nervousness, feelings of inadequacy and paranoia. The amazing thing is that the suffer-ing was not even alleviated by my regular daily intake of methadone. But now that I realised what was happening, and could obtain a small but regular script, I was able to put this painful interlude behind me and face the future once more.

Eventually the clinic decided they were going to get me off methadone for good and began reducing my dosage as part of a very slow process to get me off the drug, once and for all. It was such a gradual regime that I hardly noticed it until I had reduced from 60 milligrams to less than ten a day. I started to panic as those last few milligrams were reduced to less than five, but the doctor said ten milligrams was not even an addictive dose and I should be feeling no withdrawal symptoms. But the mind can play tricks on you, as I mentioned before, and I was fighting with imaginary symptoms for quite a while after. But I had no choice. The doctors were adamant and I wanted to be free of all that shit, so after a gradual six to twelve month reduction plan the day eventually came when I was signed off the programme.

After a lifetime of addiction, the thought of using nothing is terrifying. It's like losing a close relative. It leaves a massive hole in your life and a feeling close to bereavement. I had to get used to the idea that all the nasty symptoms I was still getting were no more than bad nerves. In fact, when I felt rough, just sitting down with a cup of tea and a sandwich could often make me feel better again. I began to realise I had often suffered from the same feelings of discomfort before I ever started using opiates; it's just that heroin or methadone bring such complete relief from them. I still have to cope with these bad feelings occasionally, but I know now they were not withdrawal symptoms at all. It had been a long hard battle that I believed I could never win but, when I finally made it, miraculously my health was still intact. I was free at last! Free of living a double life and being unable to talk to anyone about it. And best of all, Linda was finally free of carrying her terrible secret burden. The day came when I could travel freely and concentrate on music, and I was determined to make the most of the rest of my life.

* * *

Meanwhile, other circumstances changed, and I had to take some long overdue professional decisions. After some twenty years in the business I had established myself as a decent jazz saxophonist having worked with many top-line musicians, British and American. But I began to realise that this was not enough in the eyes of promoters and recording companies. It's all very well being known for your work as a sideman in other people's bands and on other artist's records but you need your own name on the posters and on the album covers to make real progress. A few people had pointed this out to me over the years and I realised it was time to go against my nature and think of starting my own group.

Several years earlier, pianist Pat Smythe, who I first met when he worked with Joe Harriott, had been very helpful in this respect. Pat was a fascinating man, who had been a fighter pilot in the war. I had heard a bit about this from others, but was told he would never talk about it. In fact he was a very quiet guy and the word on the street was that his nervous disposition was caused by trauma suffered as a fighter pilot. One day I brought up the subject and my interest in everything to do with aeroplanes. To my surprise he was quite relaxed about it and told me some wonderful stories.

Pat was an excellent pilot, qualified to fly more than twenty different types of plane, including Spitfires, Hurricanes, Mosquitoes and Beaufighters. He told me about the incidents that eventually led to his loss of nerve. Both occurred during night fighter training on Beaufighters and Mosquitoes. The first incident was due to a mistake by one of the ground crew. Pat crashed at the end of the runway, writing off the plane, but both he and his radar operator escaped more or less unhurt. He told me the golden rule in flying was always trust your instruments over your instinct. He was accelerating down the runway, watching his air speed indicator and by the time he realised he was travelling at full take-off speed, instead of the 40 mph the airspeed indicator was telling him, it was too late. The plane ploughed right off the end of the runway at some 100 mph. He shrugged that incident off, saying it was just one of those things. Aircrew worked under enormous pressure and the crewman had not removed the canvas cover from the air speed indicator tube properly. That was what caused the faulty air speed reading. Pat said he felt sorry for the poor guy, who got demoted because of it.

The incident that finally freaked him out happened when he was posted to a base near Newcastle for more training. He arrived after dark and had to fly his first practice mission that night, having never seen the aerodrome in daylight. He took off, with his radar operator, in total darkness and suddenly noticed his altimeter was reading below zero. Unable to see anything, he frantically pulled back on the stick and applied full throttle, until the altimeter started to show a positive reading. He managed to land the plane, but the experience broke his nerve and he was taken off flying duties. What happened was this: unbeknown to Pat, there was a deep valley just beyond the end of the runway and the plane had dropped slightly, into the abyss. The altimeter was set as usual to read zero at the height of the airfield, so when he flew into the valley it gave him the terrifying negative reading. It was the last straw after too many stressful hours in combat.

Pat told me some funny stories as well, like the time he had to fly a five star general somewhere in a Lysander, a very slow, short-take-off-and-landing, high-winged army co-operation aircraft. He had never flown one before and, when he pulled back on the stick to climb, the damned thing did a complete loop, a manoeuvre considered impossible in that aircraft. Pat was not at all phased by the antics of the plane but was terrified that the military big shot would get him court-martialled. The general, however, thoroughly enjoyed the whole experience, blissfully thinking it was all quite normal.

Pat Smythe was a sweet man and a great musician and he helped me a lot. He was even shyer than me, but he encouraged me to work with my own band. He arranged several BBC *Jazz Club* broadcasts with himself on piano, and me as the nominal leader. He convinced me that being the bandleader occasionally was not so scary. Of course, I had had a regular quartet of sorts in the early days at Ronnie's, but the personnel was always

The Peter King Quintet, early 1980s: Spike Wells, Henry Lowther. PK, John Horler, Dave Green

changing and we only ever played standards. It really was about time I got down to writing original tunes and putting together a group with a creative voice of its own, with my own name on the album covers and the billboards. Being in demand as a sideman was very gratifying and helped to pay the rent, but it was getting me nowhere in developing my own musical style. I needed to surround myself with musicians who wanted to help build a group with its own identity. There was only one problem. No one had shown the remotest interest in recording me as a leader. But, in 1982, thanks to Tony Williams and Spotlite Records, that changed.

Tony suggested I make an album of my own. I felt I was beginning a new life as a jazz musician so we came up with the title for the album: *New Beginnings*. Next, I had to select some guys to help me build the nucleus of a new group, both for the album and for any gigs that might come as a spin-off from the recording. I wanted guys who were both good players and people I felt comfortable with socially. For the piano chair I turned to John Horler, with whom I had become good friends. He is a fabulous pianist and composer and shares my interest in classical music, having had a 'legitimate' training. Heavily influenced by Bill Evans, John is also an excellent sight-reader and much in demand for session work. I chose Spike Wells to play drums. Spike had made a big impact when he joined Tubby Hayes' quartet. He was an amazing guy: one of those rare people who, although in great demand as a jazz musician, always remained a semi-professional. He had studied philosophy and law at Oxford University and had a lucrative day job as a legal expert in a bank. Fortunately, because of his position, he was usually able to get time off to play and even go out on the road. I loved his relaxed feel on drums, his exciting rhythmic ideas, and his intellect. A totally natural jazz drummer generating tremendous swing and drive, he has an offstage personality that exudes the rarefied air of the university professor.

Apart from his love of jazz, Spike has also indulged in other strange passions over the years. While he was with my band his obsession was collecting rare books. Later he became a connoisseur of bullfighting, regularly flying out to Spain to attend fights and study the world of the matador. As if this were not enough, a few years later I received an invitation to his ordination as a priest. He had given up his job at the bank and was about to have his own parish. In spite of all this, he still plays the shit out of the drums. Spike is a law unto himself.

For bass I turned to my old friend Dave Green, simply one of the finest in the world. Dave worked with the house band at Ronnie's and backed countless American stars, from Ben Webster to George Coleman and everyone else in-between. He once had a similar experience to the one I had when Philly Joe and Elvin were in the back of my dad's old Hillman Minx. In Dave's case Ben Webster and Coleman Hawkins were in the back of his old Ford Anglia.

All I needed now was a good trumpet player and I got Dick Pearce, undoubtedly one of the most underrated musicians ever and one of the most natural jazz trumpet players I know. It was great to have him in the group. In fact, although he played on *New Beginnings*, he was not available to work with the band later, so we booked Henry Lowther to take his place. Henry is also a great player, but with a very different style from Dick. He is a fine composer too and also much in demand as a classical musician as well. As it turned out, Henry became my regular trumpet player after that. It was unfortunate for Dick and I still feel uneasy about him missing out on the venture, but Henry's contribution both as a player and as a composer helped to define the sound of what became my regular quintet.

New Beginnings turned out to be a reasonably good album, but it was in some ways a tentative start. It took a while to develop a distinctive style for the band but the many new compositions in the book, by Henry Lowther, John Horler and myself, helped a great deal to develop our sound. Fortunately that first album got us work and some good tours over the next few years and Tony Williams followed it up with more albums, including a live recording of a gig in the wood-panelled hall of Spike's old college in Oxford. I like to think that album, now long deleted, managed to capture the quintet when it had settled into a well-integrated unit.

Stan Tracey must have had second thoughts about firing me and, although neither of us remembers the exact chain of events, I was soon back playing with his octet and his big band. I have continued to work with him, on and off, right up till the present day. The trio with organist Mike Carr and drummer Bobby Gein was also still working and we did a few dates in Bobby's home country, South Africa. This was quite an experience as apartheid was at its height and the British Musicians Union had put a ban on working there. I decided to go only because several black American musicians, like saxophonist James Moody and singer Dakota Staton, had played there. The pianist Chick Corea had also done some concerts. I figured it would be morally OK if they had been out there and I also hoped I might get a chance to say what I thought if I ran into any racism along the way.

I was just kidding myself really but, amazingly enough, on the very first gig I found myself facing shit I didn't like and to my astonishment I tried to do something about it in a very small way.

Our first concert was in Bloemfontein, a stronghold of apartheid. It was a big modern theatre and the organisers were very nice people but, when I was told that a black gentleman had been refused admittance after driving fifty miles to hear the music, I refused point blank to go on, and proposed that I would play two concerts, one for 'Whitey' and one just for him. The show was held up for a while as everyone tried to persuade me to relent. I did in the end after it was explained to me that, although the local race laws did not allow blacks to enter the concert hall, everyone in the small audience was just as upset about the guy as I was, he had already long gone and there was no way we could get him back or alter the sad situation. I would be letting down the rest of the audience, so I started the gig, but a little late. At least I tried to make a point and apparently gained the respect of the audience and promoters, who were mostly very anti-apartheid anyway.

We stayed in Bobby's lovely house outside Johannesburg and commuted to the few gigs we had. We did get to meet several local black musicians who wanted us to go and jam with them in Soweto. They were allowed to come to the Jo'berg Jazz Club to see us and I would have loved to have gone to see them in their own environment, but the whites kept trying to put us off, saying it would be too dangerous, they would have to give us an escort and no one was prepared to take the risk. It wasn't long before I found myself getting mad again at some more bullshit. We did a television show and Mike Carr told me he was trying to manhandle his Hammond into the studio when some racist bastard from the television station said, 'Hey Mike, don't do that. We have blacks here to do shit like that!' Luckily I was not there or I would have had to say something to that asshole. It was a shame because we met some really wonderful people, but you had that racial stuff at the back of your mind all the time. I found out, years later, that the Musicians Union knew all about my trip but decided not to blackball me. I also found out, and this was far more upsetting, that when those US musicians got back to the States things got ugly for some of them. I heard that Dakota had some hardline African Americans picketing her house and she even had to move out till it blew over.

Although I didn't realise it at first, the summer of 1981 was an important turning point for me. In July, I was offered a three-month stint at the Chichester Theatre playing in the pit for a show called *The Mitford Girls*. Linda and I had a nice flat as part of the deal in a lovely old manor house, with a big twenties-style swimming pool in the extensive gardens. Les Condon and Bill Eyden were in the band, along with a real nice bunch of musicians, dancers and actors and we all had some great times socially. Bill, his wife Maureen and their cute Norfolk terrier, Rags, would often come over and share the garden and pool. Linda's young grandsons also spent some time with us, which was wonderful and it was good to see Linda so happy again.

I wasn't going to let myself get into the same downward spiral as when *Bubbling Brown Sugar* came to an end, so I took every jazz gig I could, as long as I could get a dep for the show. In fact I had very few jazz gigs so the theatre job, which ended in September but went into the West End for a few weeks in the autumn, was very handy. However, one day in August, right out of the blue, I got a call from a guy in France. Gilles Eckenschwiller, a teacher of English in a French school in Rennes, who wanted me to fly out and play some gigs in Brittany. Bobby Wellins and the brilliant pianist Peter Jacobson had been over there and recommended me. To be honest I was nervous of going to France, my old phobias rearing their ugly heads, I guess, but I felt it could be an important step for me. The guys in the band egged me on to go for it so I arranged a dep and took the gig. It was the best thing I had done in years and opened up a whole new phase of my life.

Gilles and his wife Françoise became great friends and through him I met a whole chain of useful contacts in France. I got a wonderful reception, made a load of new friends and was soon flying over to France nearly every other month. I seemed to have become just part of the scenery in the UK by now, and the chance to build a new following in a foreign country was not only good for work abroad but in time started to increase my credibility back in Britain. It's amazing how it works: I often had to tell people, calling me for gigs in England, that I was sorry but I had a tour in France. Could they offer me a different date? At first they just sounded put out, but then the attitude changed as it sunk in that I was beginning to build a more international reputation. Maybe, they thought, if I was in so much demand abroad I could pull in more punters at home. Unfortunately it doesn't always work like that.

The most important effect of that first trip across the Channel was on my confidence and above all my playing. I had become so tired and jaded, playing the same few old gigs in the UK, that I was just going through the motions, except for the odd date with my quintet. When I found myself playing with some great musicians to a growing and appreciative French audience, I came alive and really enjoying playing again. It had been a long time and *Bubbling Brown Sugar* had left me exhausted and drained of any inspiration.

It wasn't long before Gilles introduced me to Philippe Briand, another English teacher, living in Quimper and an excellent drummer. Philippe arranged for me to play with him in Paris, at a club called Le Petit Opportun. It was the first time I'd been back there since the sixties, when I sat in with Bud Powell. Playing in the French capital was an important breakthrough. Le Petit Opportun was on the Right Bank in the rue des Lavendières-Ste-Opportune, in Châtelet, across the river from Notre Dame. That amazing street name is French for 'Street of the Washerwomen of Saint Opportune'. The Petit Op, as we called it, was a tiny cellar with a bar above and a wonderful atmosphere. All the best French and American musicians hung out there till four or five in the morning, six nights a week. The owner, Bernard Rabaud, a gentle giant of a man, would sometimes come down to the basement and play really good stride piano after the gig was over. The place was a mini *Who's Who* of the jazz world and the bar was covered in hundreds of little brass plates inscribed with the names of the famous musicians who had played there. Bernard was friends with them all and you never knew who would drop by after hours. After a while he paid me the honour of adding my name to the illustrious list. I met many old friends from the States and new ones too, as well as fine French musicians. Sometimes I would bump into Lee Konitz, when he was working in town. He seemed a bit concerned that he rarely worked at the Petit Op and would say ruefully that they seemed to like my playing more than his. I told him I found that hard to believe, but I think Bernard was not keen on Lee's esoteric style. I also got friendly with Steve Lacy who worked a lot in Europe. Steve was a great soprano saxophone player with a style all his own and was very popular on the Continent. Paris had been through a lean period, like everywhere else during the seventies, but now it was buzzing again and the Petit Op was at the hub of the action.

I'll never forget what Bernard did for me. Once he heard me play, he was a fan for life and he soon called personally to invite me back again, this time to play with some of the best Parisian musicians. For my first gig at the club Philippe Briand managed to get me 400 francs a night (about £40), which was not bad considering they had never heard of me in Paris. On my first return gig, Bernard booked me for a whole week, paid my air fare and put me up in a decent hotel. Before I went on for my first set, he came up and gave me 1,000 francs in cash. It threw me at first and I asked him rather worriedly, 'Is that for the whole week, Bernard?' 'Peter, of course not,' he said, rather taken aback, 'That's just for tonight: I always pay each night, before the first set.' He's the only club owner I ever met who voluntarily gave me on a return gig more than twice what he paid before and it was the first time I had ever been paid £100 for a night, let alone for six nights in a row!

The rhythm section was led by pianist Georges Arvanitas whose trio was highly respected and loved in France. He became a good friend and helped me get a load more work, including broadcasts on Radio France. A strange thing happened after one of those broadcasts. It was a live show that went out about 6 p.m. and after it had finished André Francis, the famous jazz connoisseur and radio producer, told me a lady wanted to speak to me on the phone. I couldn't think who it could be and and was worried in case Linda had some trouble at home. I picked up the phone and a voice said 'Peter, it's Chan Parker here. I was just listening to your broadcast and wanted to call to say how great you sounded.' I was pleasantly taken aback. I had never met Chan, Charlie Parker's widow, but thought she might just know about me through Gordon Beck. He had been playing with her second husband, altoist Phil Woods, and his European Rhythm Machine. We had a long chat and Chan wanted me to say hello to her daughter, Kim Parker, a good singer doing a lot of work, who seemed to want me to do some gigs with her. Chan invited me to her place but, as it was in a tiny village about a seventy kilometre train ride from Paris, I said I would call her

Chan Parker

back later in the week. In fact, it would be several years before I finally got to Champmotteux to see her

I met more and more French musicians as the word spread and I started getting work all over France. At first much of it was centred around Brittany where I started, but then I started getting offers from all over the country. The local musicians gained too, because often someone could put together a good rhythm section to do a few dates, but needed a horn player with a higher profile to sell a package to the promoters. And I guess I was getting a bit of a name because it seemed to work well. The Petit Op and other places like the Hot Brass in Aix-en-Provence – where I now often worked on tours in Southern France – regularly featured guys like Johnny Griffin, George Coleman, Chet Baker, Hank Jones and Horace Parlan. I found myself in direct competition, as a featured soloist, with some of the best guys in the world and this made me work on my playing again. I think it made me a better artist and gave me more confidence.

When you follow someone like Johnny Griffin into a club, you need to have a certain aura if you are going to be taken seriously so I tried to learn more about projecting myself and my music to an audience. This also meant structuring the sets well and having control over what your rhythm section was doing. It's second nature to guys like Griffin. Call it showmanship if you like, but most good artists have a certain presence onstage. For a rather retiring person like me that can be tough, but you don't have to tell a load of jokes or strut around the stage like Mick Jagger to make an impact. Just a few words to the audience, including them in what's going on, can make a big difference. There are tricks of the trade that you pick up, like not speaking over the applause, talking a little more slowly with a slightly lower voice, and getting a good visual rapport with your musicians. People feel better when they see a band enjoying each other's contribution to the music. Then all you have to do is let the music do the talking. I have always tried to communicate my emotions through music, and I believe you can do this without making compromises if you get the audience on your side. Unlike my multilingual brother, I am useless at languages, but I did remember a little French from school. People really appreciate it when you try to say at least a few words in their own language, and I'm sure that helped in building my small but faithful following in France.

It's one thing to get gigs as a soloist with local French musicians, but I still didn't have enough of an international reputation to tour abroad with my own band. However, my regular British quintet did get a one-off booking at the Paris Jazz Festival. That was really nice and it was good to play our own quintet programme outside England for once. But apart from that, most of the French guys I worked with were excellent and I began to feel more at home in France than in the UK..

One particularly memorable gig, in March 1984, was in Lorient on the west coast of France. Philippe Briand arranged a concert in a beautiful concert hall, and the performance was also broadcast on a radio station, part of the media group Ouest-France. Along with Philippe on drums and Peter Jacobson on piano we had Italian bassist Riccardo del Fra so it was a truly international band. Riccardo was Chet Baker's regular bassist and we worked a lot together, becoming quite close and sharing an interest in classical music. He was a fine musician and went on to write a lot of symphonic music. We rehearsed in the hall the evening before the concert and, at the same time, set up the sound for the broadcast. That meant that by the time we played the concert we had the music well-rehearsed, the radio had a great sound balance and we felt really at home onstage. The concert was relaxed and wonderful and I managed to set up a deal later, between Spotlite Records and Ouest-France to release the concert on a record in the UK. The album, *Hi Fly*, came out on vinyl but was later re-released on CD.

I spent so much time in France in the eighties that Linda and I seriously thought of getting a second house there if things continued to improve financially. We had many good friends who wanted us to come over, but we never managed to afford it. I loved France and it was almost like a second home by then. Whilst I was working there I was also able to pursue my interest in aviation and meet others with a similar enthusiasm. In Avignon the director of the local airport had a small collection of historic aircraft and one day he took me up in a Tiger Moth, the ubiquitous old biplane that every World War Two RAF pilot had made their first solo flight in. It was 'real' flying: sitting in an open cockpit complete with helmet and goggles, I experienced what it was like to have the wind in my face and hear it whistle through the ancient bracing wires on the wings. Real Biggles stuff.

I was also interested in the great painters who had worked in France, especially Cézanne and Van Gogh, who did some of his greatest work in and around Arles. The first time I worked in Aix-en-Provence, I couldn't wait to make a pilgrimage to Cézanne's studio and to see his beloved Mont Sainte-Victoire. What amazed me about the mountain and the Midi countryside in general was the famous light and the colours. Mont Sainte-Victoire really did look the way Cézanne painted it and the olive trees looked like writhing flames in a fire, just the way Van Gogh had seen them. Cézanne's studio had been kept exactly as it was when he died and I was the only visitor that day. It was as if he was still there. The objects that appeared over and over again in his still lifes were all there on the shelves. His cape and umbrella, his easel, were just as he left them and I found it all profoundly moving.

Cézanne's friendship and tragic falling out with author Emile Zola is part of art history and I was amazed when the old lady in charge of the studio showed me, in an old glass-topped chest of drawers, a visiting card she thought I would be interested in. Roughly translated it said 'Dear Paul, arriving Tuesday, 20th October. Meet me at the railway station at 11.30 [Signed] Emile

Zola'. It meant more to me than playing Bird's saxophones a few years later!

One Monday afternoon I was rehearsing for a week at the Petit Op when who should walk into the club but Chan Parker. She popped in to say hello on her way to the New Morning club, where Philly Joe was playing that night with his own band. I told her I hadn't seen him for years and asked if she could try and drag him down to the Petit Op after his gig as my last set wasn't until 2 a.m. Chan said she would, but I didn't really expect they would show up. That night, however, I had just finished my first number of the last set when I saw Chan and Philly Joe, sitting in the front row, less than five feet from the bandstand. At the end of the set I went straight over to them and, after the usual pleasantries, Philly, who looked in good shape, gave me one of his evil grins and whispered in my ear, 'Hey, Pete, are you straight?' After all, as far as everyone else knew, I had been straight for a long time. 'Yeah Philly, I've been straight a while now. How about you?' Philly looked at me knowingly and said, 'Oh yeah, sure, I'm straight too.' It was funny. He obviously didn't believe a word I told him and figured I didn't believe him either, but he must have thought: OK, let's both pretend we're clean if it makes us feel better. We chatted, then said our farewells and off they went off into the night. I never saw Philly again. Not that long afterwards he was dead. I felt a part of my life had died with him.

* * *

During the eighties American pianist Al Haig came to Europe to do some gigs. He had been off the scene for many years but was playing again. When he came to England I got a call to work with him. I think it was in Manchester. Our first meeting got off to a shaky start. I had been travelling around the country and he had just travelled up from London. We were both tired and had to figure out what we were going to play. My heart wasn't in it and the novelty of playing with Americans had lost its edge a bit by then. I couldn't think of anything so suggested the first thing that came into my head, 'Perdido'. I was thinking of the way

Bird played it on the Massey Hall concert. Al, who didn't know me from Adam, snapped back, 'No, not "Perdido". Bird was the only guy how could play that damned tune right.' 'OK, so fuck you,' I thought and said, 'Well, you pick something then.' Things lightened up a bit once we figured out a set. I think Al must have had a shock when he heard me, because he was as friendly as hell after that and asked if I'd play on his other gigs in the UK.

I became good friends with him and his wife right up to when he died. Spotlite recorded a nice concert we did at the University College School in Hampstead, with me and Art Themen on saxes. The record was re-issued on CD, followed by a second volume from the same gig. It seemed I was collecting piano players who worked with Bird. To date the list includes Bud Powell, Al Haig, Duke Jordan and Bird's old bandleader Jay McShann. In addition to Red Rodney, I'm lucky to have also hung out and even played with many Bird alumni such as Kenny Clarke, Max Roach, Roy Haynes, Lucky Thompson, Dizzy Gillespie and Howard McGhee. I wish I could have added Miles Davis to that list but it wasn't to be. Charlie Parker died before I started playing so I never met him or heard him play live but, knowing all those guys along with two of Bird's partners Chan and Doris Parker, I now feel as if I knew him pretty well and Chan once told me Bird would have really dug me and my play- ing. If someone had told me in 1959 all this was going to happen, I would have laughed at them.

Al Haig may have appeared abrupt at first, but he was a nice guy when you got to know him. Stan Getz, on the other hand, had a reputation for being a total asshole. I never got to know him well but, except for one occasion, I didn't have a problem with him. On our first meeting I drove him back to his apart- ment. He was friendly enough and invited me in but I politely refused as I had to go somewhere else. The next time, I was playing at Ronnie Scott's and Stan seemed to be yelling some kind of abuse at me while I was on the bandstand. I never did find out what he was on about. The funniest meeting came later.

I was playing at Ronnie's one night and, when I finished the set, I noticed Getz had dropped by and was standing at the bar talking to Linda, who he hadn't met before. He had a terrible reputation for pulling guys' wives, so I went over to see what was going on. I knew he would get nowhere, but figured I ought to 'rescue' her. When she saw me coming she told him she was my wife. Stan turned to face me, smiled and said warmly, 'Hi Pete, how are you? I was just talking to your lovely wife.' A couple of times in the past he had completely blanked me, but now suddenly we were on first name terms. Linda told me afterwards he was trying to chat her up with the corniest line of bullshit she'd ever heard. She took the wind right out of his sails and must have put at least a little dent in his massive ego. He was lucky I came over, or Linda would have probably told him to 'go stick it in the ground and run round it,' her usual line for guys who tried taking liberties.

The last words I heard from Getz were, believe it or not, complimentary. I had done a broadcast in Hilversum, Holland, as featured soloist with a Dutch radio orchestra. Pat Smythe did some lovely ballad arrangements for me and Rob Pronk, a fine trumpet player who had worked with Duke Ellington's band, was conducting. Pat had a copy of the broadcast on tape and one day he called me to tell me Getz, who was a close friend of his, had been to his house and heard the tape. He wanted to tell me Stan had really liked it and was very complimentary about my playing, particularly remarking on my 'good intonation'. Getz hated anyone who played the slightest bit out of tune and considered that very few alto players met that requirement.

Apart from bringing new hope for my career, the eighties brought the so-called jazz revival. I hoped that, with my slightly higher profile, the renewed interest in jazz might lead to me finally getting a recording contract, one with decent international promotion. After twenty years and more I had had enough of trying to live on the kind of money a plumber would scoff at. Unfortunately, it never turned out that way. The whole thing was a case of short-term media hype. At the centre of it was saxophonist Courtney Pine, with a few other, exclusively young, musicians following behind. Andy Sheppard, Steve Williamson, Philip Bent, Julian Joseph, Jason Rebello and a host of other talented musicians were suddenly propelled to stardom, with massive promotion and big-deal recording contracts. Although Courtney and others have stayed the course and matured into great artists, once the big record companies realised they weren't going to sell a million CDs each year, many of them lost their contracts and had to aim a bit lower.

Some of the new wave of players were black and I was very happy to see their interest in jazz, but it seems there was some racial animosity around at the time. Probably under the dubious influence of the Marsalis family, there was a feeling that these young guys had had a tough time breaking into the jazz scene. I could never understand why that should be as, when I was growing up in the business, black players like Joe Harriott, Shake Keane, Bogey Gaynair, Dizzy Reece and Harold McNair were all highly respected and loved. I was rather out of touch with the jazz scene at that time and I find it very sad to think there might have been any racial antagonism. The whole idea is so alien to me. In fact I found it very stimulating to have guys like Courtney and pianist Julian Joseph around, playing fresh sounding music, even though I can't personally identify with the introduction of reggae and rap into some of their music. That's just my own musical taste; you can't dig everything. In fact, there was quite a bit of bad feeling from my generation of players about the way these young guys were making names for themselves, while we appeared to be getting sidelined, but I always kept an open mind and figured it was better to check out what these guys were doing musically. I soon realised they were a pretty talented bunch and made it my business to get to know them as much as I could. It wasn't their fault they got instant recognition, while we were still struggling. That was just the way things were then.

I first met Courtney when I joined the new big band put together by the Rolling Stones drummer Charlie Watts. In fact, when I was asked to join, I didn't even know who Charlie was and was distinctly underwhelmed when they told me he played with the Stones. I didn't know then what a loveable guy and huge jazz lover he was. The band he put together was truly enormous, with three drummers, two bass players, two vibraphonists and God knows how many saxes and brass. The number of saxes seemed to change from one gig to the next, but was never less than about ten! Charlie wanted all his favourite British players in the band and kept adding new ones, regardless of whether or not he already had too many drummers or bass players. At the first rehearsal I found myself sitting next to a young, tall, intense-looking black kid playing tenor. It was Courtney. I had been hearing derogatory comments about how he was riding on a massive wave of media promotion and that he couldn't even play his horn. In fact he sounded damned good to me and I told him so. He had a big strong sound and had obviously put a lot of time in on the instrument. But I didn't see him much after that first rehearsal as he quit Charlie's band a few days later. I think his management had figured he wouldn't sell enough records, buried in an over-large big band, even one run by the drummer with the Rolling Stones.

Some of the tension between the 'new young Turks', as they became known, and us old-guard beboppers became obvious at a gig I did in the early eighties at the Edinburgh Jazz Festival with Red Rodney. Red and I were booked together with a variety of different and often incompatible rhythm sections, doing up to three gigs a day. On one of these we went on at a large, jam-packed venue just before Courtney Pine's set. We seemed to go down pretty well. At least there was a lot of reaction from the audience. But, when Courtney went on, there were huge screams of excitement from the large young contingent in the crowd. It dawned on me that we had walked into a kind of battleground and our two bands seemed to be the focus of the war. Courtney obviously had a big following but a lot of the audience was on our side too. It was a bit scary and it made me realise these new young Turks were here to stay, plus Courtney's whole band sounded really good. I realised the rest of us had better get used to it and up our game, or we were going to end up as just another page in British jazz history. At least, that's how I saw it and it made me think hard about what the future had in store.

The Edinburgh Jazz Festival programming policy in those days was a joke. They had a load of American solo stars and the 'usual British suspects', thrown together in all kinds of stupid combinations. The biggest joke of all was a gig Red and I did with Art Hodes on piano. Art was renowned for his piano playing in Eddie Condon's Chicago-based dixieland jazz scene. Red went ballistic when he saw the line-up. How were we going to find any common ground? When we met Art, he felt the same way of course, so democracy ruled and Red and I suggested we should just stick to twelve bar blues and 'I Got Rhythm' changes all night. Art agreed but then asked us, 'Hey guys, do you know "Aunt Hagar's Blues"?' Red and I looked at each other in desperation. 'Aunt Hagar's Blues' is an ancient blues that came out of New Orleans, probably in the twenties. We had figured we could at least play 'Now's the Time' and stuff like that. With goodwill and professionalism on all sides, we managed to get through the gig.

11

'Watch out for that Pete King, he'll cut yo' ass!'
Sonny Stitt

Tommy Watt, a well-known bandleader who did a lot of BBC broadcasts and liked to use top jazz players as much as he could, would sometimes bring his young son, Ben, to hear me play at the Bull's Head in west London. Some years later, in the 1980s, Ben asked if I would play a couple of solos on a recording he was doing. He had landed a contract to make an album with his pop group. I only agreed as I needed the work but, when I got into the studio, I discovered he had quite a talent. He played guitar well and had written some nice tunes. The pop band had a sophisticated approach and I remember thinking the recording was too good to sell to a pop audience. The group was called Everything But The Girl; it made quite a name for itself and Ben asked me to overdub solos to each new album they put out. I wasn't on their touring payroll, but did one short British tour with them, mainly in universities, where they had a big following.

Once Ben was established, he persuaded Blanco y Nero, a subsidiary of Warner Brothers, to let him produce a Peter King album. Everyone hoped it would get me recognised by a wider audience. It was to be a crossover record, with tunes specially chosen by Ben. The songs he picked were mostly from the pop repertoire but included some jazz themes like 'Blue Monk'. I did the arrangements in consultation with him and also wrote a couple of originals with a jazz rock feel. After struggling to make the tunes work, we ended up with the album *Crusade*, recorded in 1989. The musicians were from the pop world but were talented and professional. Blanco y Nero liked the result and as I was free to play plenty of jazz solos over the backing tracks, I felt the final mix was pretty good. For a few months things looked exciting, with photo shoots, interviews in the press and some promotion outside the UK. The problem was, although everyone loved it, they handled the project all wrong. Instead of aiming at a young non-jazz audience, they pushed it as a jazz album, which it was not. Pop fans weren't interested and jazz fans probably thought I'd sold out.

It soon became clear it wasn't selling, on top of which some changes in the company management messed everything up and *Crusade* got left on the shelf. They never even released it on CD. It was a shame because, with the right promotion, it might have had a chance. In fact, while we were on holiday in Greece, Linda got a friend who ran the local taverna to play it on their sound system. To our amazement, many of the younger holiday makers started dancing excitedly to the music, right there on the beach. Everyone was asking about the record and they thought it was fantastic. These were not jazz fans, so I know it had a wider appeal. I guess the record company thought it would sell on the back of the so-called jazz revival, but it should have been aimed at the pop market, with a good video and a single. Funnily enough, I discovered years later that Ben's group was a huge hit in Spain, and when I started playing out there I had quite a fan base because of those old Everything But The Girl albums.

I had to sign a complicated contract with Blanco y Nero. There were pages of it, with many sub-clauses, but it didn't require me to sign exclusively to the company – something I would have been very wary of after years in the business. While negotiations were on-going I was approached by a typical young eighties-style would-be entrepreneur, with all kinds of big ideas. He must have spent a small fortune wining and dining all kinds of people, generally hustling on my behalf and employing expensive lawyers to deal with my contract. I told him straight I had no money to spend on lawyers, but he insisted on picking up the bill himself and was adamant we would both make a load of money from the album and its spin-offs. He almost convinced me but, of course, it came to nothing. He probably ended up bankrupt.

I soon realised the so-called jazz revival was going to ignore my existence totally and, in my next brush with a major label, one reason became painfully clear. This time, Alan Omakoji, a young black whiz kid, who had landed a job with a British or European branch of Blue Note, contacted me with a view to signing me up. Scottish saxophonist Tommy Smith and others had contracts with the label, were making records, doing big concerts and getting massive publicity. I had several meetings with Alan but they never seemed to lead to anything but more meetings. He finally told me he was having a lot of trouble convincing his bosses about me. In the end he looked at me, with more than a hint of exasperation, and explained. If only I was younger and good looking they could sell me but as it was, in spite of being a 'great artist', they couldn't figure out a way of promoting me. That was that, the end of any hope of getting on a major record label. These days, if you are not signed to a big label, it's impossible to get on any big international festivals. Even Red Rodney tried to spread the word about me a bit with record industry friends in the States, but ran into the same bull-shit. The major companies were only interested in signing new young artists. If you were over thirty they didn't want to know, unless you already had an established international following; a real catch-22 situation.

Things could have been worse. Many musicians of my genera-tion were now considered old hat and past it by the younger jazz generation, but I gained some good friends among the up-and-coming players, who seemed to respect me not only for what I had done in the past, but for the way I was still trying to move forward. I started to book younger guys, like drummer Winston Clifford and pianist Jason Rebello, on my gigs and was glad they seemed to enjoy them. I was anxious to learn from them and I guess they picked up a few things from me too. If I was to be ignored by the record and festival moguls, I could at least try to up my game and reach a younger audience.

I appreciated the fans of my own age and older, but I was getting a bit tired of them still wanting the same old music I played twenty years before. I began to feel, rightly or wrongly, that I was just a poor imitation of Bird to a lot of them. I enjoyed working with the Bebop Preservation Society, but I was trying to move on and found it harder and harder to play the same old stuff with conviction. On gigs where I had to work with local rhythm sections, just playing the old standards, I felt I was playing worse than I had been twenty years earlier. I had played all those things to death, but not many punters seemed interested in anything different. I had to get to new listeners somehow, even if it meant losing a few diehard fans.

I have to thank pianist Julian Joseph for helping me gain acceptance with a new audience. I first met him at a party at John Dankworth's place. Julian had worked with Courtney Pine and studied at the Berklee School of Music in Massachusetts. He knew many of the young Americans, having worked with saxophonist Branford Marsalis for a while before settling back in London, and he was now signed to a major label. I became good friends with him and his family and it turned out he had been a fan of mine since he first started playing. A neighbour of mine, a teacher at a local primary school, used to tell me about a young black kid in her class who was learning piano, loved jazz and was thrilled to bits to discover that his favourite teacher knew me. That young kid had been Julian. Years later, I had been particularly impressed with Courtney's pianist on the gig I did with Red Rodney in Scotland, but hadn't realised it was Julian. I went over to his house, very near mine, in Wandsworth, and he gave me his latest record. I liked his compositions, transcribed some of them from the album and wanted to try them out with him. I hadn't transcribed anything since I studied some of Chick Corea's fascinating tunes. I particularly liked Julian's free approach to harmony, which opened up new possibilities for my own composition. It was a very productive setup. His music was challenging to play. I learned from him and I think he did from me too. I remember that when he first accompanied Johnny Griffin at Ronnie's he called me up to check the chords of a standard Johnny wanted to play and generally asked my advice about accompanying him.

Rehearsing with him was interesting. He didn't have any alto parts so I transposed some of his tunes I particularly liked, comparing them with my own transcriptions. He got me to learn everything by ear, as he played things through, bar by bar. It was a tough process but I knew from experience that this was the best way to learn any tune. It was exactly how I learned Jon Hendricks' music all those years before and it was a stimulating exercise getting those tunes under my fingers. I put aside any negative thoughts about having to learn something this way, from a kid who was half my age, because I recognised how much talent he had. Anyway it was good to see him working that way. Most young players tended to bury their heads in the 'Real Books' and learn by reading the notes and chords instead of using their ears. He told me he had a lot of respect for the way I still tried to develop my playing, while many guys from my generation were content to play the way they always had and keep their regular audience happy. Certainly he had a high regard for them, and rightly so, but he thought I was a little special, I guess, because I remained open to new ideas. I'd have to add that this was so only if I felt they had some real musical interest for me.

I booked Julian on some of my quartet gigs and he reciprocated by asking me to take Jean Toussaint's place in his group when the former Art Blakey tenor player left to concentrate on his own band. I had first met Jean when he sat in with me at the Petit Op in Paris and we had often played together in Britain and in France. I did several quite high profile dates with Julian's quartet and big band, including a concert at the famous Concertgebouw in Amsterdam, culminating with the big band's appearance at the BBC Proms at the Royal Albert Hall in London. The Proms date was televised and I was interviewed on the programme, which was valuable publicity. It was a prestigious concert for Julian too, only the second time jazz had appeared on the Proms, and it gave me some access to a new, younger audience. It's nice to have young kids come up and say they became fans after hearing me at that concert. Now perhaps I could afford to lose one or two of my older followers who felt wrongly I had forgotten my roots in bebop. I tried gradually to move on from that music, but its influence is still there, burned deeply into my psyche.

Julian and others spread the word about me among their American contacts too and, although I was still passed over by major record companies and booking agents, I seemed to be getting a bit of a reputation among some of the younger American musicians. One incident that sticks in my mind was being introduced to the American saxophonist Joshua Redman. He shook my hand and said politely that it was an honour to meet me. Christ! I thought he was he was taking the piss at first, but it seems he did indeed know about me. That was nice, as I particularly admired his playing.

Speaking of reputations, a funny thing happened one night at the Bull's Head. Tenorist Red Holloway, a close friend of Sonny Stitt, came from the US to do some gigs in England and I was booked to play with him. I was getting my horn out when Red, whom I had never met before, walked into the club. He made a beeline for me saying, 'Hey, are you Pete King?' As soon as we had introduced ourselves he said, with a big grin and a look of mock anxiety, 'Oh man, Sonny Stitt warned me about you. He told me when you get to England watch out for that Pete King, he'll cut yo' ass!' I guess those jam sessions at Ronnie's all those years ago had left their mark on Sonny after all.

* * *

Around 1984 I suddenly renewed my interest in aeromodelling. Strange as it seems for a jazz musician to be interested in what

we used to self-mockingly call 'toy' aeroplanes, I was not the
only one. I soon discovered a few British musicians had an interest and that US ex-pat tap dancer Will Gaines and pianist Kenny
Drew were both avid radio-controlled model flyers. To my great
surprise, altoist Phil Woods recently told me he had taken up
the hobby again in a small way. When he first started playing, he,
along with guitarists Jimmy Rainey and Tal Farlow and some
other musicians, would spend all night listening to Symphony
Sid Torin's and Bob Garrity's New York jazz radio stations, while
they built model planes. Then, when it got light, they would go
and fly them in Central Park. I also discovered that several
American aeromodellers were also very keen on jazz. One guy in
particular, Hardy Brodersen, had been friends with tenorist
Lucky Thompson and vibraphonist Milt Jackson. Lucky and
Hardy both went to Cass Technical High School in Detroit,
where jam sessions took place during the lunch period, in a
sixth floor music classroom with a piano. Milt Jackson would
come over from Central High School and jam. Hardly surprising
that Hardy's model planes had names like Salt Peanuts and
Loverman. Later, when doing his army training in Maryland, he
would travel to New York in the hopes of hearing jazz at the
Three Deuces or other 52nd Street clubs. He first saw Bird in
Chicago, at the Bee Hive on 55th Street. I also discovered that,
as well as musicians, several famous Hollywood movie stars were
into model planes too, including James Stewart and Clark Gable.
You have to appreciate that back in the forties and fifties most
kids had a go at building and flying model aeroplanes. In those
days young boys were as excited about aviation as they are about
computer games today.

What I find so satisfying about aeromodelling is the fact
that you get a definite result in a competition. If you win it's
because you had a good model and flew it better than the rest on
that day. There is something clear cut and satisfying about that.
You don't get this playing jazz. You just do your best and hope
people like it and that you get booked again, and the two things

don't necessarily go together. But now, if I have a bad gig, instead of brooding over it for days I just put the horn in the car and think about how to improve the design of my next model. It's an extraordinary feeling, and needs a tremendous amount of skill and perseverance, to design, build and trim your own model, launch it into a perfect climb pattern, then see it centre into a thermal that your experience and sixth sense alone told you were there.

The other great thing for me is the fresh air and exercise you get. Because I compete in free flight (not radio-controlled), the models just continue gliding in wide circles, drifting with the prevailing wind and can end up landing a mile or more away if the wind is strong. I really struggled at first as my physical shape was abysmal but, when you see your model, which may have taken a hundred hours to build, disappearing into the distance, you somehow find the strength to trudge off downwind across ploughed fields to bring it back and then do it all over again for the next round. I would be completely wrecked after a big event at first, but the physical demands soon began to pay dividends and my strength began to come back, and this helped my playing too.

The free flight class I fly is F1B and the models are powered by twisted strands of rubber. The Wakefield Cup, originally donated by Lord Wakefield in the twenties for all types of model, is now specifically awarded to the World Champion in F1B and is still the most coveted trophy in the sport. Although usually referred to as a hobby, free flight aeromodelling is now officially classified as a sport and because of the considerable physical effort and skills required in flying and retrieving, it has, believe it or not, finally been recognised as such by the International Olympic Committee.

In the 1980s, new Russian designs revolutionised F1B aeromodelling. The most brilliant of the Russian F1B flyers, Alex Andriukov, was a young engineer from the Antonov aircraft works in Kiev. Alex, whose father had been a Russian general

PK launching the F1B (PK10) during the 2007 British Team Trials at Sculthorpe. Photo Martin Dilly.

involved in the USSR's ballistic missile programme, decided the best way for him to fulfil his ambition to travel freely, both in the restricted USSR and abroad, was to become a regular member of the Russian team. To do this he worked long and hard at developing the ultimate F1B. This led to him representing the USSR at nearly every world and European championships since 1980 and he became World Champion, European Champion and World Cup holder on more occasions than any other flyer.

I was one of the first British modellers to incorporate some of his techniques and in 1989 they helped me beat the opposition to become the British F1B Champion. I finally met Alex when he came to fly in the UK, staying as a guest in our home. We met up again in 1991 at a big French international meeting, where I had the dubious honour of being beaten into second place by the great man.

It wasn't long before I renewed my interest in the theoretical side of the hobby and studied everything I could find on aerodynamics. I soon found myself contributing occasional technical papers for modelling forums and magazines. Fellow-aeromodeller Ian Kaynes, a top boffin at Farnborough, taught me a lot and showed me how to use an optimum climb simulation he had originally programmed on a large mainframe computer. I went on to devise my own modest additions to the package and between us we developed quite a complex analysis tool, capable of predicting the relative performance of various model designs. After I bought a computer – firstly for writing music with – I became pretty adept at working with spreadsheets and am now regularly asked to contribute to several publications, including the US-based *National Free Flight Society Annual Symposium*. The *Symposium* honoured me with a Model of the Year award for one of my models which won the Aeromodeller Trophy in 1997, and also for my writings on model aerodynamics.

I am only an amateur aerodynamicist so it's pretty intimidating to contribute papers alongside professionals. Many of the US contributors have retired from top jobs with NASA, or other prestigious organisations like Boeing and McDonnell Douglas. In fact there is so little research on aerodynamics, at the very low speed that our models fly, that some useful work can be done by relatively untrained people like myself, and when it comes to flying model aeroplanes barriers between professionals and amateurs soon break down if you have something interesting to say. I have met some amazing people, especially since using email. I was talking to one modeller who, having worked at NASA, suddenly let drop he was one of the guys who calculated the first lunar landing orbit for the US space programme. Then there is Bill Bogart, without whose pioneering work on flutter analysis the space shuttle would never have left the ground.

Another man, Masaru Koike from Japan, who contacted me about a paper I had written, turned out to be head of aerodynamics at Mitsubishi Cars and a lifelong John Coltrane fan. We eventually met in Tokyo when I was on tour with Charlie

Watts. He introduced me, via email, to Dr Werner Würz who was in charge of the ultra-low-speed wind tunnel in the highly prestigious aerodynamics department of the University of Stuttgart. Masaru had persuaded Dr Würz to revisit earlier tests on model wings they had done in the eighties and Masaru and I were able to suggest new tests that would make best use of the severely limited wind tunnel time available. Dr Würz was very grateful and only too happy to follow our advice. This was a real thrill for me and I felt very honoured to have contributed, if only in a very small way, to furthering aerodynamic knowledge. The results of the tests were published in a paper by Masaru Koike and Werner Würz. Before publication I received all the test data from Werner in person, and he kept me 'in the loop' in case I could offer any more advice on progress. It's all a far cry from playing jazz but, for a guy who as a kid longed to be an aerodynamicist, this was pretty heady stuff and a fulfilment of a childhood dream.

* * *

In 1985 I went to the US with Charlie Watts' new big band. Working with Charlie was great fun but totally mad and the tour was fabulous. We played New York, Chicago and other major cities. I had to fly back early from Philadelphia with Dave Green and Evan Parker because we all had gigs in the UK and Europe. In Philly, we discovered saxophonist Michael Brecker's mother and father were living in a suite at the top of the hotel where we were staying, so after the concert we spent time with them, before taking a train to Grand Central Station in New York. We finally caught the 'red-eye' flight to London where I got straight on a plane to France. The total journey was about twenty-four hours. I was exhausted but very happy to have finally gotten to the States.

One day I got a call from pianist Mike Pyne. He had made a recording with a band called Straight Eight for the new Miles Music label which was dedicated to promoting British jazz talent. They were doing a promotional gig for the album and

Tommy Whittle, the saxophonist who had been on the recording, was unavailable. Mike asked me if I would stand in for him and knowing my old interest in racing cars, told me the company was run by John Miles. John, the son of Sir Bernard Miles the actor and founder of the Mermaid Theatre, had driven for Colin Chapman's legendary Lotus Formula One team. He went on to work at Lotus Engineering where he soon established himself as one of the world's most brilliant chassis engineers and test drivers. Meeting John revived my interest in motor racing and I became close friends with him and his partner, co-producer and sound engineer Peter Watts. These friendships developed into a long and productive partnership in which I have produced what I consider my most creative recorded work to date.

John was with the Lotus F1 team during 1969–70, in the days when you risked death at every race or test session. He himself lost four of his best friends that year. He had been Jochen Rindt's teammate when Rindt was killed qualifying at Monza in 1970, becoming that year the only man in history to win the World Championship posthumously. John wasn't interested much in talking about his racing career and he would say, 'Peter, it's like me asking you if you remember a gig you did at some pub twenty years ago.' I understood that completely, but still wanted to learn about his days as a Formula One driver. I had always been fascinated by the psychology of bravery, especially how sometimes the most sensitive and modest people can cope with fear and mortal danger better than more typical 'gung-ho hero' types.

John eventually opened up and told me about that tragic day at Monza. The story goes that Rindt was killed when something failed on his car under breaking. John had experienced a brake shaft failure in Austria two weeks before, but survived without injury. After Monza, Miles was replaced in the F1 Team after a row with Colin Chapman about Colin ordering John to remove the wings to make the Lotus 72 go faster down Monza's straights. John still remembered every word of his row with

Chapman. John's reluctance to drive the already dangerous car without testing it with no wings led to him leaving Team Lotus.

For me the all time greatest drivers, like Tazio Nuvolari, Juan Fangio and Ayrton Senna, are true artists, with talent verging on genius. They move and inspire me almost as much as Bird, Coltrane, Beethoven or Bartók do. Just as there are seminal moments in music, like Louis Armstrong's solo on 'West End Blues' or Bird's on 'Embraceable You', there are in Formula One too. For example, Senna's legendary and mesmerising first lap in the rain, during the 1993 European Grand Prix at Donnington. For me, that lap was on a par with Coltrane's 'Giant Steps' solo.

One of the biggest thrills of my life was at Silverstone where, at a big test session, I was allowed to spend a day in the pits watching Alain Prost, Nigel Mansell, the young Michael Shumacher, and above all Ayrton Senna, working at close hand. I stood on the pit wall and watched them drive past a few feet away at over 190 miles per hour. The deafening sound of the engines and the mind-numbing speed so close by were beyond anything you can experience watching on television. The sensations I felt will stay with me for ever and served as inspiration for my album *Tamburello*.

I often think playing jazz, especially really fast bebop, is a little like driving a racing car. Of course, in the old days there was one very big difference: you were not likely to end up dead if you played a wrong note on 'Cherokee'! F1 today is far less dangerous, with crash-proof structures and safer circuits, but both activities involve taking risks. Improvising is often a process of taking a chance in the search for fresh ideas. In a sense, that is what racing is all about and years ago some drivers used to go to jazz clubs to unwind after a big race. I think they felt an affinity with what we did up there on the bandstand. The great world champions are the ones who can also plan a race strategy. It's not enough just to be blindingly quick. All the drivers are super-fast. The trick is making split-second decisions whether to take that big risk or wait another lap to make your move. Nowadays, if you make the wrong choice you'll probably just end up in the gravel trap but, in the old days, you could very likely end up dead.

Ayrton Senna developed a reputation for total ruthlessness on the track, mentally dominating all the other drivers to such an extent that they would often just move out of his way rather than have an inevitable collision with him. He was one of the first to realise cars had become safe enough to withstand the most horrendous crashes and he used this knowledge to his advantage. However, as he explained in an interview, throughout a race he would continually make decisions regarding risk. Only in situations where his championship chances depended on it would he take the 'big' risk and go for a do-or-die overtaking move. If he decided on taking the big chance, he embraced his naked fear of death. At Imola in 1994, during the San Marino Grand Prix, he was fighting to stay in the lead ahead of Michael Shumacher, risking everything. He finally stepped over the precipice, lost control, crashed into a wall at 180 mph and was killed when, by a tragic quirk of fate in what should have been a survivable crash, a piece of debris pierced his visor leading to catastrophic brain damage. It had been twelve years since the last F1 race fatality, but that terrible weekend brought home again how dangerous F1 can be.

Ayrton was arguably not only the greatest driver ever; he was revered almost like a god, especially in his beloved Brazil, where he was a national hero of mega proportions. He had done so much to promote his country, to improve its image in the eyes of the world and to help its poor and starving children to have some hope for the future. His funeral was extraordinary. Over a million people lined the route and the cortège was grander than for any former Brazilian head of State.

* * *

In 1988 John Miles asked me if I wanted to go in the studio and record under my own name. I jumped at the chance and we began discussing tunes and a line up. I had the idea of writing something in honour of my good friend Bernard Rabaud, the proprietor of the Petit Opportun in Paris. We agreed to call the album *Brother Bernard* as a tribute to the man who helped bring me to the attention of French audiences.

I used the nucleus of my regular quartet, with Alan Skidmore (tenor) and Guy Barker (trumpet) added on some tracks. One original of mine, 'Dalin' was dedicated to my wife, Linda. The title is an anagram of her name and also sounds like a colloquial pronunciation of 'darling'. By the time the vinyl album was reissued on CD in 1992, John's father had died and at John's suggestion I wrote and included on the CD an additional Coltrane-inspired tune called 'One for Sir Bernard' as a tribute.

John can be demanding as a producer but he has a very good sense of atmosphere and which tracks should go where. He also has a good 'non-musician's' feel for what turns on the average listener. Just as when he was racing or when he is tuning a car chassis, he is a perfectionist and very creative, often suggesting quite outlandish but stimulating ideas for tunes or for the over-all theme of an album. Peter Watts is also a joy to work with. His knowledge of recording techniques, and his willingness to spend hours mixing and editing, enabled me to take far more control over the production. Instead of just picking a few tunes, record-ing them and leaving the rest for the recording company to sort out, I now became far more involved in everything, from getting the sound I wanted, right through to the cover design.

When John was ready to make a follow-up CD, I wanted to widen my musical horizons. I had long been interested in classi-cal music and my playing was becoming influenced more and more by John Coltrane. Many of Coltrane's harmonic ideas were obviously influenced by Béla Bartók, whose music I loved. McCoy Tyner and Trane were heavily into pentatonic and modal harmony and, on 'A Love Supreme', Trane used a typical Bartókian technique of building the whole work on one simple pentatonic motif, clearly stated in the first few bars. I had been working on pentatonic scales but found, with my regular quartet, that it was difficult to integrate these in the heat of playing. I wasn't able to develop this technique until I later found a pianist who had a more modal-based approach. John Horler had an important role in my quartet but he was not so happy about playing more modal music.

John Miles invited me to a session for an album *Tribute to 'Trane* by Alan Skidmore which featured a lot of Coltrane's music. While I was there I met drummer Stephen Keogh who played on the record. Alan's group really captured the feel of Coltrane's classic quartet. Around the same time, I happened to play with Steve Melling, a pianist who I had heard many times with Clark Tracey's group. I hadn't realised before that Steve, as well as being an excellent musician, was also a great modal player in the McCoy Tyner mould. I wanted to work with him more and had to make a difficult decision about my quartet. I poured out my soul to John Horler about the way I wanted to change direction and, to his great credit, he had already realised what was happening and felt I should move on. I tried to get him to come along with me but he felt it best that I should be free to work with someone else. I felt bad about it but John was very supportive and had plenty of work outside the group, so we parted musical company, remaining good friends and retaining our admiration for each other's ability. Gradually I built a new group with Steve Melling and Steve Keogh as the nucleus. This was the band, with Alec Dankworth on bass, that went into the studio to record my next album *Tamburello* in October 1994. Apart from an occasional change of bass player, it became my regular quartet until today.

With Steve on piano I could develop my modal playing. He laid down powerful McCoy-like accompaniment, and so I began to hear differently and I slowly brought more modal and pentatonic elements into my solos. I liked the freedom that that music can give: so different from constantly running through tightly-defined chord sequences. Before, I had found stretching out on one chord hard but, with the right backing, you are free to explore many harmonic possibilities over the basic tonality. I hoped that, if I stuck to alto, any Coltrane influence would simply colour my style and give me an original voice of my own.

The Yanagisawa company had kindly given me a soprano saxophone and my interest in Coltrane made me want to try the smaller horn. Although my soprano playing is heavily influenced by Trane, I tried to develop my own thing as well. I began to hear a sound that was a cross between a kind of wild Arabic chant and a trumpet; rather like Sidney Bechet in fact, but without the vibrato. I didn't want the usual light sweet sound many guys go for. I wanted more of a wild oriental wail.

We started work on the new album and John Miles suggested I try to do something with, of all things, Henry Purcell's aria 'Dido's Lament'. At first I was not keen but when I really listened to the piece it struck me as very soulful. I started to use synthesizers for the first time and had Steve play the theme on one, with a straight classical feel. Then, after a slow vamp, we improvised on the chords at a slow-medium tempo with a modal feel. It became the first track on the CD. John came up with some odd ideas but they stimulated me into trying new approaches.

Halfway through planning the album I witnessed, along with millions of others, Ayrton Senna's tragic death, live on television. Ayrton loved to fly model aeroplanes and I had hoped that, if I ever got the chance to meet him, he might be interested in talking to a fellow-aeromodeller. Now I would never know. Witnessing his death like that, I just knew I had to compose a tribute to him on the new album. At first John was not too keen but he came around and I started work on a mini-suite.

Another crazy idea I had was to record the exquisitely poignant melody from the slow movement of Bartók's *Violin Concerto*. That melody had haunted me for years and as we had already used a classical piece on the CD, it seemed a good time to have a go at it. Once again I talked John into the idea but first I contacted Bartók's publishers Boosey and Hawkes, to see what the situation was regarding publishing rights. It turned out we had to get permission from Bartók's son Peter, who was in charge of his father's estate. I wrote to him, explaining what we wanted to do and waited for a reply. It took forever but finally Boosey and Hawkes received a letter, which they read to me over the phone. I couldn't believe my luck; here I was dealing with the son of the great man himself. Bartók wrote his famous piano studies *Microcosmos* for his son, when Peter was a young boy learning the piano. The letter gave me permission to use the piece and, as Peter pointed out, his father regularly used other people's tunes anyway. (A reference to the many folk songs he used in his compositions.)

In the event, I decided to have the synthesizer just play the original Bartók orchestration. However, the tune with its exquisitely sad harmonies made a perfect introduction to the Ayrton Senna suite, so I followed it directly with the same chords, sustained on the synth, while the bass and then the soprano improvised over the atmospheric background. We did one take which worked fine but, for atmosphere, I got John to turn all the studio lights down very low and we recorded an even better and quite different version. In another piece I wanted to capture the thrill of driving an F1 car at speed and also hint at Ayrton's love of his native Brazil. I wrote a fast tune, 'Ayrton', where the first four bars were repeated backwards and then the whole first section was repeated in retrograde inversion (upside down and backwards). It was a technique I learned partly from Bartók and partly from twelve-tone music and it gave the tune a fast twisting and turning feel like a car going round a race track. In the middle of the piece we suddenly burst into a wild Brazilian section, complete with Steve Keogh's over-dubbed whistle and a huge Brazilian drum he had borrowed for the session, before returning to the main theme.

Once the tracks were all in the can, Peter Watts and I began a long process of post-production. I had never done it to this degree before and found it fascinating. We hired James

Hallawell to programme the electronic sounds and spent days mixing, remixing and editing the album. When we came to the 'Ayrton Senna Suite' the two versions of the slow music seemed equally good, but different. I remembered how Stan Getz had used two takes of the same piece on his album *Focus* and I persuaded Peter and John to let me do the same. We started with the Bartók piece as an intro, followed by one take of the slow music. Then, after a short interlude, came the fast tune and then, after another more poignant interlude, the other take of the slow music.

The intro I had written for the fast piece was a musical imitation of the blipping sound of F1 engines being revved up. This gave me a mad idea. Why not use the sound of real cars on the record. By a strange coincidence, Peter had made a private recording of the cars and general atmosphere at the Monaco Grand Prix the year before, just for fun. I mentioned the idea to John but he said, 'Are you crazy? No way!' Eventually, he agreed we could try it, but that if he didn't like the result he wouldn't use it. Peter and I spent hours selecting and editing short sections of the Monaco tape and blending them with the music. I think we came up with a good result and John had to admit it worked. The most successful point is at the end where the music fades and you just hear the noise of one solitary car racing off into the distance. After the sound fades away, there is a shocking cry of anguish from the band, signifying Ayrton's fatal crash, followed by descending harmonies into the last slow section which portrays the sadness of the tragic aftermath.

John and I worked a bit on the CD cover and after Nick Warren had produced the final design the album was complete. We named it *Tamburello*, after the high speed corner where Ayrton was killed. We all felt the album was something special and showed new aspects of my music. As it turned out it was well received when it came out in 1995 and won the British Jazz Award for best CD of the year. I was particularly pleased for John, as he had worked so hard building up the label for very little profit. He even got us a review in *Autocar* magazine, as a result of which a few Ayrton Senna fans bought the album. Then one day, I got a phone call from the London correspondent of *TV Globo* in Brazil; he had bought the album and wanted to interview me for the Brazilian six o'clock television news. They had a dubbed Portuguese translation and used footage of Ayrton as the CD played. The effect was stunning and I felt we had really produced a fitting tribute to the great man. To see it covered on the evening news in his beloved Brazil was quite something.

I also sent a copy of the CD to Hermeto Pascoal, the Brazilian musical genius with whose band I had worked on a UK tour. Hermeto, a Senna fan like all Brazilians, liked it. He even liked my tentative attempt at Brazilian colour on the album, inspired as I was by the experience of working in his amazing band. Hermeto is a legendary figure in Brazil and when he worked awhile with Miles Davis, Miles and Gil Evans called him 'the greatest musician [they] had ever heard'.

After the critical success of *Tamburello*, it was difficult to do a follow-up but, by using the same wide range of musical material, *Lush Life*, released in 1999, turned out quite well too. I played the title track completely solo and the great Billy Strayhorn tune has become a regular feature on my live gigs. On the classical side I did an arrangement, with me on soprano, of Wagner's beautiful 'Prelude' to *Tristan and Isolde*, which was, again, something I had wanted to do for years.

Although I was delighted to continue recording for Miles Music, John had not tied me to an exclusive contract, and I was free to make other recordings if the opportunity arose. So, when I played Ronnie Scott's Club in September 1994 with my band, augmented to a quintet with Gerard Presencer on trumpet, we recorded *Speed Trap* for Ronnie's own house label. Gerard was already a phenomenal jazz trumpet player. He just got better and better too, and he is always my first choice when I get the chance to work with a quintet. I first met him when we worked together in Spain with the great Catalan pianist Tete Montoliu. Tete was known worldwide and adored in his own country, having recorded with a string of American stars. He was a musical phenomenon, especially considering he was not only totally blind but almost totally deaf. I would have to shout into one of his ears to converse with him and yet, when I tapped my foot and counted a tune in, he was right on it. He picked up on the vibrations somehow and could play anything all night, without dropping a beat. The Spanish date was recorded and later released as a double album, *New Year's Morning '89* by Fresh Sound, a Spanish label.

I got an unexpected call one day from Charlie Watts, after not seeing him for several years. A small publishing company had asked him to reprint a little book he had written years before about Charlie Parker. It was like a kids' picture book, with cute little illustrations by Charlie himself. He refused to do it unless they recorded an album to go with it. They agreed so he wanted me to write some original tunes, with titles picked from his text. I was to write new themes, but in the style of Bird. It was an interesting project in which I used every bebop lick I could think of in the compositions. The whole package was a success and it was an interesting challenge to find myself playing the role of Charlie Watts' musical director, instead of just being a sideman in his big band. To promote the package, *From One Charlie*, we did some concerts in Britain, America and Japan. The line-up was Gerard Presencer on trumpet, Brian Lemon on piano, Charlie Watts on drums and Dave Green – who had worked in my original quintet and had known Charlie since they were kids – on bass. It became Charlie's regular quintet and led to other projects over the next few years.

One spin-off was an appearance by the quintet in the film *Blue Ice*, starring Michael Caine. While we were shooting our scenes for the movie, I was approached by the man who negotiated the fees for music used in the film. Some of my compositions were used and he said he would make me a special deal. His idea of a deal turned out to be £300 for all three titles. I was told this was an especially good offer, as often composers would donate tunes for free publicity. Oh yeah, I thought: hang on a minute, that sounds a bit dodgy. So I said I would get back to him. I got straight on to Sherry, Charlie's secretary, and she fell about laughing at the offer. 'Leave it with me,' she said, 'and we'll work something out.' Presumably Charlie's lawyers negotiated a deal and towards the end of the next day's shooting I was called off the set to take an urgent call. Sherry had fought all day with the guy and had negotiated another offer. 'Peter, does £7,500 sound a bit better?' she said, and that's what I finally got!

I had to face the guy again, to sign the contract. I looked at him slightly embarrassed and said, 'Is that OK with you, then?' 'Yeah,' he said. Then, looking at Sherry with a sheepish grin, he added, 'She's a hard cow, isn't she?' For once in my life I had some real financial muscle behind me! When I originally worked out my writing deal for the album, the young publisher and I had some problems with Charlie's lawyers over the rights to my own tunes. The small company had offered me an excellent royalty deal, but Charlie's legal team intervened and insisted he should own the rights to all the compositions. Thank God, Charlie had already warned me that, if there were any problems, I should let him know. He was as good as his word. One call to him and everything was mysteriously sorted out in my favour, within the hour.

After the Rolling Stones got ripped off in the early days, they hired a team of the cleverest, toughest lawyers and accountants in the world. I've seen how they work and wouldn't want to get on the wrong side of that team. I sure wish I could afford to have them working for me. Charlie himself wields enormous personal power, of course, but in a very quiet way. Once, in New York, we were booked to appear on TV on the highly prestigious *David Letterman Show*. At the rehearsal, Charlie didn't like something the producer was trying to pull, so he just walked right out the door, there and then, taking us all with him. It caused quite a stir and the story was in all the papers next day. I think Letterman saw the funny side of it, because he kept looking off-stage during the show that night saying things like 'Hey, where's Charlie?' Or, 'Has that rock and roll drummer arrived yet?' Word got around fast and the audience cheered us when we arrived at the Blue Note club that night. No one had ever dared to walk out of a Letterman show. Charlie got more publicity out of doing that than if he had done the show.

I thought Letterman would sue him and I figured we'd never get the chance to do that show again. How wrong can you be? A couple of years later we were invited back again. Letterman was great to us all and when we asked about the producer who Charlie had the dispute with, we were told he got fired soon after it happened. What had caused all the trouble? Well, the guy had thought he could make Charlie appear with the regular house band. I had been warned about this, as it had been a long-running dispute. In the end I had to get involved myself. They wouldn't pay for the string section we wanted to use so I made an amicable arrangement with the leader of the house band. He would play our string arrangements on synthesizer from a part I had written specially for him, and we would play the regular quintet parts. Charlie flipped at the rehearsal when he noticed a bass guitar part for our tune on one of the music stands. The big deal producer was trying to go back on his word after we had already agreed on the musical line-up. Charlie was justifiably furious and let him know who was boss.

My closer relationship with Charlie saved my life many times after that as, every time I was getting near to bankruptcy due to lack of work, he would come off one of his stints of two to three years with the Stones and start a new project with the quintet. This usually entailed a good fee for new writing, on top of well-paid work on the road. We had used a small string section on the first tour and, pleased with the result, Charlie decided on a new project, a Bird with strings tribute. I transcribed several of the original strings arrangements from the Charlie Parker recordings and added a few of my own settings of Parker tunes. We went on the road again, playing *From One Charlie* on the first set and *Bird with Strings* on the second. Our first gig was the opening week at the new Ronnie Scott Club in Birmingham. Bernard Fowler, a backing singer with the Stones who had a great voice and looks to kill, narrated Charlie's short book and was also featured singing 'Lover Man' on the *Bird with Strings* set. He was a wow with the ladies and Charlie's next two projects featured Bernard singing ballads with a full string section.

The new albums and the accompanying promotional tours to Brazil and the USA were beautiful. Charlie picked some wonderful standards, all great ballads, and Brian Lemon and I wrote all the string arrangements. I was a bit nervous, as I had to conduct the strings and rehearse a different orchestra in every city. But it all worked out fine as the orchestras were excellent, easy to work with and enjoyed the music. I'll never make a great conductor but writing for full strings and then directing them, plus playing solos, was invaluable experience. We appeared on the east and the west coasts of America and also crossed into Canada where we played the Montreal Jazz Festival and then appeared at the famous Massey Hall in Toronto, where Bird recorded the historic *Quintet of the Year* album.

During the long gaps between these enjoyable, lucrative and even luxurious stints with Charlie Watts (we always flew business class and stayed in the best hotels), life would return to the usual fight to make a living from ever fewer gigs. I scraped together as much work as I could for my quartet. The group remains an inspiration to me. It's still the best rhythm section I have ever worked with bar none, including the best Americans. At last I had that beautiful relaxed rhythmic feel behind me I always wanted. Steve Keogh's drums, Alec Dankworth's and later Jeremy Brown's bass playing were pure perfection, and Steve Melling is not only a great accompanist but a fine soloist. His deep knowledge of modal harmony, especially, helped me to develop that side of my playing. We have several of Steve's fine compositions in our library too. He also has his own trio which is gradually gaining some of the recognition it so richly deserves. With this group I felt I was finally maturing as a player, discovering a more powerful and individual voice of my own. If I have, my fabulous rhythm section has played a major part in the process.

A few other interesting gigs came in now and again. I had to fly out to Norway and Finland, at a moment's notice, to substitute for American saxophonist Steve Grossman, when he was taken sick. That's how I got to play the Pori (Finland) and Molde (Norway) festivals with Steve's rhythm section, and what a section it was, with John Hicks on piano and Idris Muhummad on drums! Later I met Grossman in London and jammed with him. We became friends and worked together in the 1990s at the Italian Communist Party Festival, a massive affair held every year for a whole week in a huge park in Bologna. The Communist Party is still a powerful political force in Italy, often supporting jazz.

During this period I also played the Berlin Festival several times, with Tete Montoliu's trio, with Gerard Presencer and, another year, with Phil Woods and Jackie McLean. That was a great concert, except Bird's ex-pianist Duke Jordan caused problems. He got drunk between the rehearsal and the concert and disappeared. George Gruntz, the festival's artistic director, finally played piano with us on the gig. The theme that year was 'Kansas City Jazz' so we played a Bird tribute and were also asked to join the Basie band, now under the direction of tenorist Frank Foster, for their last number. We even played 'Scrapple from the Apple' with the legendary Jay McShann. Charlie Parker made his first recording while in McShann's Kansas City-based band. Well into his eighties, Jay still played fine piano, with great enthusiasm and panache.

Jackie McLean was supposed to join us with the Basie Band but decided not to for some reason. Jackie was a sweet and sensitive guy and he reminded me we had first met way back in the sixties, when he came over to London to play and act in *The*

Connection, a play about junkie jazz musicians! After years off the scene, Jackie made a comeback and did some wonderful work, setting up and running a jazz course in Hartford, Connecticut, where he lived. He had to fight a lot of opposition from the ultra-conservative faculty when he started, but he persevered and produced one of the finest jazz education faculties in the States. In Hartford he started a great new band, in which he employed several of his brilliant young students, many of whom went on to become stars in their own right. Surrounded by all this young talent, Jackie played better than ever and made great new recordings.

Just before Hong Kong was handed back to the Chinese in 1997 I went to China on a British Council tour with Stan Tracey's octet. We played in Beijing, Guangzhou, and finally for Governor Chris Patten at the Governor's residence in Hong Kong. Beijing was fascinating; it was shortly after the dress code had been relaxed and instead of the old standardised dull uniforms, everyone was dressed in colourful Western garb. Beijing is very flat and the bicycle was the standard mode of transport at that time. I've never seen so many bicycles in my life. They were stacked ten deep along every street and it was funny to see young Chinese office girls cycling home from work, chatting on mobile phones. My fondest memories of China, though, were of Don Weller who was also a member of Stan's band. A great tenor player, Don is a very dear friend and a really funny guy. Large in build but with a quiet nature, he is not the kind of guy to take much interest in the usual tourist attractions. We were invited on a special trip one day. The transport was about to pick us up but there was no sign of Don, so we called his room and asked him if he was coming with us to see the Great Wall of China. Don's reply was a dour, 'No thanks. I've got a wall in my garden.' The whole band fell about laughing and I told Don he ought to charge people to come and visit his wall. I give him a lift home sometimes and, as he gets out of the car, he often whispers with a twinkle in his eye, 'Hey Pete, d'ya wanna come and see the wall?'

12

'Hey, did you dig "The Nail"?'
Chan Parker

Chan Parker decided, after a lot of soul searching, to auction Bird's plastic Grafton saxophone, the one he played on the Massey Hall concert. She later told me she would often 'talk' to Bird. Not that she was into spiritualism or anything; she just used to imagine he was there and ask his advice on occasions. In a bit of a fix financially, she asked again and he told her to go ahead and sell the plastic horn. After all, she still had the valuable King Super 20, his regular instrument. She slept with it by her bed, wrapped in plastic. I was approached by Christie's, the London auction house, to act as an advisor for the sale. I hadn't spoken to Chan for several years, but apparently she had specifically asked for me to take on the job. I called her at her home in France to discuss it and to see how she was. From then on until her death, we became good friends, calling each other regularly and meeting when we could; sometimes seeing Kim too, when she was over from the States.

On the day of the auction in September 1994 I had to play the horn at Christie's and field questions from the press. The instrument was leaking badly when I first tried it out but I got it fixed well enough to play, at Christie's expense. Had this all happened thirty years before I would have been trembling with awe at the thought of playing Charlie Parker's horn, but by now it was just another saxophone. There was a moment, though, while I was playing at the auction, when I got an eerie feeling as if Bird was there listening, a strangely emotional experience. I found it interesting when I had to examine some of his musical manuscripts, also for Christie's. I got used to spotting pages written in Bird's hand because these were mostly just trumpet parts.

With Chan Parker and Bird's King Super 20 alto which Chan kept safely next to her bed.

The tunes I inspected were all based on standards or the blues, so I figured he needed no rhythm section parts. Bird obviously played his parts from memory and just wrote the line for the trumpet. Tunes that had alto parts were mostly in a different hand, so it was debatable whether they were in fact his compositions, or whether someone else wrote those particular tunes or just noted them down for Bird. Some tunes recorded just after his Scandinavian tour, like 'Swedish Schnapps', may in fact not have been Bird's. I still possess photocopies of the written material, each sheet of which has a large cross penned through it, so it can't be passed off as the original article.

The horn was eventually bought by the mayor of Kansas City who paid around £95,000. I was soon to see it again in the new jazz museum in K.C., also meeting Mayor Cleaver in person when I was invited to play over there. He had bid for the horn himself over the telephone and heard me playing in the background. In fact, Chan ended up getting very little of the £95,000. Apart from having to pay tax and Christie's commission fee, she had got into a legal dispute with Francis Paudras over some photos she lent him. He allegedly used them without her permission in his book *To Bird With Love*. Chan was so angry that she called Paudras a liar on a live television programme in France; so, later, Francis decided to sue her for a large sum of money. Chan was advised it would be a long and messy case to win so she decided not to put up a fight and settled out of court for a much smaller sum. In the end she was able to pay some debts and fix up her house a bit, but I don't think there was much left after that. She wasn't worried though. As long as she could live quietly with her pets, her music, her memories and a supply of good wine, she was perfectly happy.

Chan lived in Champmotteux, a tiny village about an hour and a half's drive south west of Paris. The mayor and the villagers were proud to have such a famous resident and thought the world of her.

In the next village lived one of her closest friends, a lovely Turkish lady called Füsun, who I had met several times at gigs in France. She ran a jazz club in Turkey and invited me to play there and also arranged for me and Kim to play a jazz festival in Antalya, inviting Linda to come too. Chan was to be an honoured guest. We stayed in a beautiful hotel and, driving back to our rooms one night, Linda spotted a cement lorry on the road. She called out in delight, 'Cement mixer' to which Chan and Linda both added, laughing their heads off, 'putty, putty'. These were the lines of an old bebop hit from the forties and when Chan realised Linda was hip to the old tune, they became real close.

Linda often talked to Chan about music, Bird and the problems of living with a 'junkie' musician. She asked whether Bird nodded off in bed smoking a cigarette like I used to: I would often burn holes in the damned sheets like that. 'Oh yeah,' Chan said, 'and when I would try to wake him he'd look up and say, "I'm just resting my eyes, Pudding."' He always called her 'Pudding', probably his nickname for her when she was pregnant. She also told us the story about the time he arrived at her flat in 52nd Street to take her for dinner, riding a white horse! He had some terrible musicians with him playing a corny tune to serenade her outside her window. A great story, but Chan was not impressed and asked him what he proposed to do with the horse while they were in the restaurant. In the end he tied it up in the nearest car park and then rode it all the way back to the stables in the pouring rain, after they had eaten. Bird was always playing the fool like that.

Despite all the really terrible times they went through, he and Chan were deeply in love. She first met him when some musicians brought him to her flat during their intermission and she Jwas up a ladder, painting the ceiling! She loved his playing but was not interested in him romantically at first. But, she told us, 'He was so damned persistent. I couldn't help myself and gradually fell in love with him.' There were good reasons for her to be reticent, not least the problem of racial prejudice. It wasn't easy for a white woman to be with a black guy in those days. When she went on the road with Bird in the American South, she would sometimes hide on the floor of the car, so no one would see them together. In those days they could both have been lynched. I never pestered Chan with questions about Bird, but heard a lot of stories during the course of general conversation. She told Linda many more things in private, only some of which Linda passed on to me. I guess a lot of it was just women's talk.

Chan and I did discuss Bird's interest in modern classical music. He wanted very much to study composition and almost did, first with Nadia Boulanger in Paris and later with Edgar Varèse in New York. But he could never get it together, with his many problems and failing health. When Chan asked him when he was going call on Varèse, Bird would just look sad and make excuses like, 'Oh you can't just drop in, you have to take a bottle of wine and some flowers for his wife. Maybe next week.' He knew it had all become wishful thinking and yet he would have loved to have studied more. Towards the end he was still trying to take his playing in a new direction too. Chan reckoned he would have sounded a bit like Eric Dolphy if he had been able to carry on, but who knows. She did confirm to me that, just as I had thought when I first heard his music, he was a very intelligent and sensitive man. After some of the stories about him I had begun to doubt it, but Chan told me I was right and that he would have really liked me, both as a player and on a personal level. We'll never know, but it's a nice thought.

Bird also shared my interest in painting and took lessons with a New York artist, leaving most of his paintings at the studio, rather than bringing them home. Unfortunately there was a fire in the place and most of his canvases, along with his tutor's, were destroyed. One or two of Charlie's paintings still exist, but Chan thought his best work, which included landscapes done in Central Park, was all lost in the fire. On a wall of Chan's house in France hung a haunting picture of their baby daughter Pree. It was painted by Bird after Pree died tragically in childhood, probably of cystic fibrosis. In that painting, which I saw often, he portrayed her not as a child but as a young woman with a striking resemblance to Chan. Very much in the style of Modigliani, whom he particularly admired, the picture seems to capture all Bird's despair at the loss of their daughter. It is naive in its execution but profoundly disturbing, especially if you know the story behind it. Chan told me Pree's death was the beginning of the end for Charlie. His worsening health, coupled with his grief and feelings of guilt over the loss, took a terrible toll on him and he died only about a year later.

Chan gave us a copy of her autobiography, *My Life in E-Flat*, with a lovely dedication to us both, but it was all in French. My limited knowledge of the language was not good enough to read a whole book, so later she gave us a copy of the original manuscript. Although she spoke fluent French she wrote the book in English, but the only published edition at that time was the French translation.

Chan loved reading but I discovered she also wrote lyrics and played some piano. I persuaded her to write words for 'Please Don't Ever Leave Me', an original ballad I had recorded. I sent her the piano part and she set words to the tune around my original title. As I explained to her, it was supposed to be about a musician who loves his woman and needs her to be there at home waiting, but is always on the road and worried she might leave him. I knew Chan would understand what I meant. She was an extraordinarily hip lady and great fun to be around.

Despite being hounded sometimes by people wanting to talk about Bird, she was usually very polite to anyone not put off by her rather intimidating aura. She summed up beautifully one particularly persistent 'anorak'. When she finally dragged herself away from him, she came over to Linda and me and, aware we had been watching, said 'Hey, did you dig "The Nail"?' We howled with laughter at the thought of this guy, 'nailing' her to the wall, so she couldn't escape while he bent her ear!

As our friendship with Chan was well-known, people began seeking my help as a go-between. The BBC asked me to persuade her to let me interview her for a radio programme. I was able to get her to do it and to advise the Beeb what kind of questions she would or would not answer. We got a good interview and had fun doing it. Not long after that, the Glasgow Jazz Festival asked me to do a Bird tribute with a quintet, plus Phil Woods, and they wanted me to get Chan to come as the guest of honour. I was a little concerned about Chan and Phil because they had been through a rather acrimonious divorce a few years before. Chan was not at all worried about it but, to my surprise, Phil, who had re-married and had not been informed about Chan's presence, was rather angry and nervous when he discovered she would be there. In the end everything turned out fine. After a brief but amicable meeting they kept out of each other's way and the concert went well, with the first set dedicated to Bird. At my insistence, the second set was chosen from my regular quintet repertoire, with Phil joining us on alto. Gerard Presencer was on trumpet. The concert was broadcast by the BBC. I still get asked to appear in Bird tributes, which is OK, but I would prefer to play my band's own music and usually try to insist on that for at least part of the programme. Chan felt the same about it. When she heard about the Glasgow concert she said, 'Oh no, Peter, not another Bird Tribute!' Charlie Parker, of all people, would have preferred jazz to keep moving forward. Let's face it, his music was all about innovation.

After the Glasgow gig, things seemed to open up a bit and some interesting offers came in. My drummer, Steve Keogh, also a fine classical percussionist who worked a lot with the Ireland National Symphony Orchestra, used his Irish connections to set up a major concert for us at the Cork Festival. I was commissioned to write music for my quintet, strings and an American guest artist. I booked Gerard again on trumpet and persuaded the festival to hire tenor saxophonist Johnny Griffin as the guest. I had known Johnny for years but we had never actually played together before. The concert went well and Johnny enjoyed it too. We didn't have enough rehearsal time for the strings though, and there were some minor musical hiccups which we covered up OK. The audience seemed to like the music but one damned Irish critic had a problem with the idea of using strings at all and thought it added nothing to the music. So far I had been pretty lucky with critics but I soon found out that good reviews don't lead to more gigs or record sales. Often the most successful guys with the best promotion and the highest record sales get lousy reviews, sometimes justifiably, so I rationalised the whole thing by thinking, Great, a bad review, maybe now I'll sell fifty thousand CDs!

Another nice gig was at Ronnie Scott's Club, where I was booked to play with another American saxophonist, George Coleman. Julian Joseph was on piano and Mark Taylor on drums. Mark and I had played together a lot and, when he came over to France one time to sit in and hang out, I introduced him to the Paris scene a little. He eventually settled in New York where he has done really well, working regularly with Coleman and then Lew Tabackin. Pete King booked George and me at the club a couple of times and the last gig was recorded for Ronnie's house label, under the name of the George Coleman Quintet.

I had a lot of admiration for George's playing. He was a bit of a 'tough guy', liked to work out in the gym and had a reputation for playing very fast tempos. As I mentioned earlier, he was also renowned for being able to play in any key. I looked forward to the challenge of working with him. We first met when we played opposite each other in London at a gig at the 100 Club. Later he invited me to sit in with him at Ronnie's. I was expecting a Sonny Stitt-type competitive roast-up, but he just asked politely what I wanted to play. I said, 'You choose something and as long as I know it we can play that.' Then my competitive streak reared its stupid head and I quickly added, to wind him up a bit, 'at least as long as it's in a reasonable key.' I figured he would rise to the bait and try to cut me and I hadn't really been in this situation since playing with Stitt. In fact, George picked comfortable tunes in their normal keys until the last number. Then, suddenly, he just started playing on his own, real fast. He played a couple of improvised choruses without telling me what the tune was. I soon realised it was 'Cherokee' but thought, hang on, what key is he in? The bastard was playing it in D-flat! I had practised tunes in every key all my early musical life so figured the adrenaline would get me through. It did, but on the last theme statement he suddenly left me to play the melody during the bridge. This should have been easy, but I hit the wrong first note and had to find my way back to the tune fast! It was funny: I figured, Ha! He finally got me, the oldest trick in the book and I fell for it. You can get away with a lot when you are improvising but, when you have to play the melody, it's got to be right. I wasn't worried, but pride made me quickly run down the melody of the bridge at home the next morning, in all twelve keys. That's the way to learn jazz fast! On the gig each night we just enjoyed playing. I told him I had learnt by playing things in every key after I read that Bird did that a lot. George claimed that when he started playing you had to be able to play in any key or you got kicked off the stand.

The week we recorded, in January 1995, turned out after many years of regular annual gigs to be the last time George ever worked at Ronnie's. When he wasn't soloing he would sometimes wander off to the bar and one night Pete King found him reading a newspaper in the lobby while the band was all playing and recording. I heard Pete read him the Riot Act, right there in the lobby. He was getting paid a lot more than we were so Pete saw red and told him to get back on the bandstand *tout de suite*, or else! Poor Mark Taylor, taking a drum solo, had to keep playing chorus after chorus, while we waited for George to come back and take the tune out. In the end I started playing the head myself and George quickly got his ass back onstage and joined me. At the end of the week, he asked me to oversee the mixing of the album and the choice of takes, as he would be back in the States. I picked what I thought were the best tracks from the various nights and we mixed and edited the CD. I called him in New York when it was finished and he seemed reasonably happy with the result, but Pete King never booked him for Ronnie's again.

In the mid-nineties I met up with Lalo Schifrin again. We became friends and now he books me occasionally in Europe, as a featured soloist for his *Jazz Meets the Symphony* concerts. It all started when I got a call from Pete King. Lalo was in London recording a new work called *Firebird*, an amazing piece for symphony orchestra that cleverly combines Stravinsky's *Firebird Suite* with several Charlie Parker tunes. The soloists were to be Jon Faddis on trumpet and Phil Woods on alto. However, Phil couldn't get a work permit in time, so Pete suggested I could do it and that I should give Lalo a call. When I bucked up the courage to telephone, Lalo told me the record company had insisted on using an established star from America (the old pro-American prejudice once again), and they had managed to get Paquito D'Rivera to fly over at a moment's notice, just in time

In Paris, in rehearsal for Lalo Schifrin's *Jazz Meets the Symphony* concert 2008.
Right: PK with Schifrin (piano). Photo George Korval.

to make the sessions. That wasn't the end of it though. Lalo wanted to hear how I sounded so he invited me to the mixing of the album and asked me to bring some of my CDs. I met him at the studio and we spent a few hours chatting as he worked on mixing the album. He made a point of asking for news about Stan Tracey, whom he greatly admired. Lalo, like Sonny Rollins, considers Stan a genius and a true jazz original. A month or so later I received a surprise letter from Beverly Hills. It was from Lalo, saying he liked my CDs and hoped to use me on future projects if he could.

He was as good as his word and a few months later his management contacted me about appearing as a soloist in one of his concerts. I played Paquito's parts on *Firebird* and other things Lalo had written for full symphony orchestra. James Morrison

Left: As above, with Schifrin's *Jazz Meets the Symphony* concert. PK with Jon Faddis (trumpet). Photo George Korval.

was on both trumpet and trombone and the rhythm section was Lalo on piano, Grady Tate on drums and Ray Brown on bass. I must have done a reasonable job because other concerts came in over the next few years: in Switzerland, Germany, and two in Israel where Lalo conducted the brilliant Israeli Philharmonic. Its regular conductor was Zubin Mehta. Ha! Now I could joke with my friends and say, 'Yeah, guys, I remember when I was with Zubin Mehta's band.' On these concerts Lalo used Christian McBride, one of the most talented of all the younger generation of American bass players, and it was exciting to meet and to play with him,

Lalo and I occasionally discussed my aspirations to write more classical music. We keep in touch by email and I often seek his advice about classical projects I'm considering tackling. He is an amazing musician, classically trained, and one of very few Argentineans to win a scholarship to the Paris Conservatoire, where he completed his studies before emigrating to the States and joining Dizzy Gillespie, for whom he wrote several classic Latin American suites. I got an idea of just how brilliant he was in his hotel room one day, whilst showing him a movement of a string quartet I was writing for fun. He studied the five or six pages of score carefully and complimented me on my knowledge of string writing. Because the piece was harmonically complex and very much influenced by Bartók's more atonal music, I asked him if he would like to hear it on a tape I had recorded from my computer. He looked a bit taken aback and said, 'Oh no, there's no need for that. I just heard it.' I was stunned. Lalo is one of those rare musicians who can read the most complex of modern scores like a book and hear it all in his head. He told me he liked what he heard, which was wonderful for my confidence. I was a beginner in classical writing so his encouragement was very welcome.

In 1996 I was talking to Neil Ferber, who ran the Appleby Jazz Festival in the wilds of Westmorland. It was a great annual event for eighteen years, held in idyllic surroundings and featuring the best in British jazz. Neil had obtained a commission for Don Weller to write a suite for his new big band, to be premiered that year, so I approached him about the possibility of getting a similar deal myself. He asked what kind of thing I wanted to do. I had not had time to think about it so, casting around for ideas, I said rather rashly, 'What about something with a string quartet?' Neil seemed to like the idea and said he would see what he could do. A while later he called to say he would try for two separate commissions, one from the BBC and another, for a smaller scale work, from Northern Arts. Now I had to be more specific about the music, so he could make proposals to the relevant organizations. This was getting serious and, not long after, Neil called me to say we had the go-ahead to fulfil both commissions. Things were deadly serious! I would have to write two whole works for jazz quartet and string quartet. Although I had written music for a string quartet when Gordon Beck and I did a broadcast years before, this would be my biggest musical challenge so far.

I began to get cold feet but couldn't let the opportunity go. Northern Arts only needed about twenty minutes of music, so I proposed a three part work with the overall title of *The Passions*, along the lines of Stan Getz' *Focus* album, using the string quartet to back the jazz solos. For the larger work, the BBC required up to an hour of music. I wanted to make use of what I had learned, studying all those Bartók string quartets. It seemed a good idea but when I actually had to write the damned thing, it hit home what a huge challenge I had taken on. Neil got the Lyric String Quartet, a fine, established group, interested in playing the suite. I was pretty nervous about discussing the music with them when we met up at Ronnie Scott's Club one night but I felt more comfortable once I realised they were really up for doing it. The only worry they had was that I might want them to improvise. They said, rather apologetically, that they couldn't extemporise and were very pleased to hear that I wanted to write purely straight music for them, with a strong

Bartók influence. I was thrilled to discover they had played the formidable first and sixth quartets and they invited me to come to their recording for a broadcast of the first movement of the Bartók *Number 1*.

I really enjoyed the experience and was fascinated to talk to musicians who had actually played this music. I knew the quartets were extremely demanding and they told me they performed only the somewhat easier first and sixth. Playing the whole cycle is limited to a small number of groups who specialise in that music. They also confirmed what I suspected: that the most difficult is the fifth quartet, with its use of very fast Bulgarian rhythms in compound time, such as 3+2+2+3 over 8.

With everything in place, I needed to get down to work. I had begun to use an Atari computer whilst writing string arrangements for Charlie Watts, so I could hear the music I was writing. My inability to play the piano well had made writing an ordeal before but now, with computers, a whole new world opened up. It was especially helpful when writing contrapuntal passages and there would be plenty of these in the new commission, which I decided would be in five movements. After it was completed I called it *Janus*, after the Roman god with two faces. I figured it was an appropriate name as I was looking in two directions, one towards the classical world and the other towards jazz.

After years of searching for a way to integrate some of Bartók's techniques into jazz, I now had to solve the problems and damned quick. I wanted to avoid making compromises, so that the string quartet could do their own thing and my quartet could play jazz the way it always does. Using a classical quartet in this way was challenging, especially because I particularly wanted to avoid any hint of pretentiousness. Fortunately, Bartók's music is full of jazz-like qualities, rich modern harmonies, rhythmic drive, and 'soul'. John Coltrane and McCoy Tyner were obviously influenced by him, particularly by his harmonies, and

I felt I could tap into these elements and make them work in a jazz context.

I treated the two quartets as separate entities for much of the time, hoping this would not only allow each of them to feel comfortable but also create a tense dialogue between them. Throughout most of the work I had the strings develop each new musical motif first; then I would turn that motif into a jazz tune, so my quartet could improvise on it. I tried to bring both quartets together gradually as one unified force during the course of the suite. To pull this off I felt there had to be a tight structural cohesion, so I made use of a typically Bartókian architectural device, the arch form. One of the most rigorous examples of arch form is Bartók's fourth string quartet, from which much of the inspiration for *Janus* was drawn. In this work, movements one, two, four and five are derived from the same thematic material. They are like the outer supporting stones of the arch and the central keystone is the middle, third, movement, which has new material, a harmonic form of the original motif. In fact, the entire Bartók quartet is derived from one six-note chromatic motif, continually transformed and developed. The result is one of the most concentrated, rigorously logical and profound works in the whole of music.

To attempt this degree of architectural rigour in a jazz work would be fruitless, so I just used a basic five-movement form, with a central slow movement forming a kind of calm centre around which the other movements are grouped. The tune in the slow section is similar in general shape to Bartók's slow third movement melody but, unlike Bartók's, my slow movement incorporates a further mini-arch form within itself. For the centre of this arch I wrote a fast strings passage, loosely modeled on the brilliant and virtuosic second movement of the fourth quartet. In *Janus* it becomes a kind of separate storm in the eye of the main storm. Although I spent a lot of time organising the overall musical structure of *Janus*, my main concern was still to let the music flow naturally and, above all, to swing.

The Lyric Quartet worked hard and did a superb job, not only in their featured passages but also in blending with the jazz quartet in the tutti passages. Patricia Calnan played the difficult violin cadenza with great bravura and passion and Dave Daniels brought the solo cello parts to life. Looking back, there are certain string passages I could have improved on but, bearing in mind how little experience I had had in such writing, the Lyric made my music sound better than I could ever have hoped for. At the premier in Appleby and during the subsequent British tour the audiences seemed to like the music and we also performed *Janus* in Spain. One concert, at the Purcell Room in London, was recorded, but it was nearly eight years before the results were released by Miles Music in 2006.

I sent Chan Parker a tape of the BBC recording of Janus and received a beautiful and touching note from her. It was hand written on a sheet of Beverly Wiltshire Hotel note paper. She had some left over from her trip to Hollywood as an advisor to Clint Eastwood about his film about Bird. It is one of my most treasured possessions and this is what she wrote:

Dear Peter
It's beautiful! I think of how Bird would have liked to have the
facility to write for himself like that. I wish I could send it to him.
But maybe he heard it. I do thank you for sharing it with me (us).
You are a grand composer !!

Despite many years trying to find my own voice on the horn, Charlie Parker kept coming back to haunt me. After all, he was my original inspiration on alto and, if people sometimes turn to me for the odd Parker-related project, I guess that is a compliment and every now and again something really interesting turns up. One that stands out was a short tour with the Royal Ballet. I had to play Bird's 'Lover Man' solo – the superior second version recorded by Norman Granz, not the ill-fated first recording on the West Coast when Charlie was sick. The music had been transcribed note by note, even the piano part and Red Rodney's trumpet solo. That was played by Gerard Presencer, whose father-in-law, trombone player and jazz educator Bobby Lamb, was directing the jazz contribution to the Royal Ballet's tour project.

'Lover Man' was just one of several works in the programme and the choreographed steps were performed by a brilliant and beautiful ballerina while the jazz quintet played onstage. I had to stand on my own in the centre of the stage and play the solo while the dancer performed her steps around me. It was quite an experience and I remember being in total awe of all the dancers. People have no idea how much body-breaking work ballet dancers do, let alone the excruciating physical pain they can often suffer. It was a revelation watching them rehearse and perform on tour. They can sustain the most horrendous injuries to muscles and tendons and yet still go onstage, often with the aid of powerful painkilling injections to get them through the performance. The problem is that, although the pain is temporarily relieved, they are in grave danger of doing themselves permanent damage by aggravating the injury. On top of this, they work extremely long hours and, except for the star dancers, earn far less money even than jazz musicians.

It was the Bird connection that hooked me up with a man who became a great friend and benefactor to me in the US. Chan Parker told me about Verne Christensen, from Kansas City, with whom she had been corresponded regularly. Verne and I met via email and this led to a strong friendship with him and his family. He is one of a number of ardent jazz enthusiasts who run a great organisation called the KC Jazz Ambassadors. He had good connections with the mayor's office in Kansas City. Mayor Cleaver, who bought Bird's Grafton sax to install in the new jazz museum there, is now a US Congressman and is much admired for his work in the city. Verne told me that in March 1999 there was to be a special event in honour of Charlie Parker who was, of course, born in KC. There would be a week of events and

concerts and sculptor Robert Graham had been commissioned
to produce a large public statue of Bird. It would be installed
close to the Gem Theater and the jazz museum in the 18th Street
and Vine Street area where all the clubs had been located when
Kansas City jazz was in its heyday.

Of course, very few people had heard of me over there, but
that soon changed when Verne got on the case. He already had
a large collection of my albums but asked for my latest CDs and
some promotional material. He quickly made everyone aware
of my music with the aim of getting me over to play at the Bird
celebrations. Thanks to the sterling efforts of Verne and his
friends, enough money was raised to fly Linda and me to Kansas
City and to pay me for playing at a concert in the Gem Theater,
along with a host of other more famous musicians associated
with Bird. Also present at the festivities were several of Parker's
relatives, including his stepdaughter Kim, and Doris Parker who
was still Bird's legal wife when he died. Chan was invited but
decided against making the long journey from France. I had met
Doris briefly when we played Charlie Watts' *Bird with Strings* gig
at the Blue Note in New York. Just as I was about to go on, I
heard she was in the audience there and the idea of playing *Bird
with Strings* in New York, and with Doris listening, made me
more than a little nervous until I met her afterwards and heard
how much she had enjoyed the show. On that occasion, though,
I think she was more excited about meeting Charlie Watts than

With reedman Bobby
Watson and Verne
Christensen's son, Miles,
Kansas 1999. Photo Verne
Christensen.

chatting to me. Linda and I stayed with Verne and his family in their beautiful house in Olathe, Kansas. He had studied architecture and had designed the place himself. One of his passions is cooking and he made the most amazing food, smoked and then barbequed with a formidable array of BBQ equipment. He would take all day to prepare a meal. The meat had to be smoked for many hours at just the right temperature, before being cooked to perfection for the evening meal. The taste was out of this world. One day we drove for miles just to get some special smoked beans from what he considered the finest source in the world, a dilapidated joint on the edge of town. The old black proprietor opened huge doors to show us inside the massive oven. It was like opening the gates to hell itself. Great carcasses of meat sizzled in the inferno as he reached in for the beans. That evening I realised why Verne had driven all that way. Those beans were unbelievable, like none I had ever tasted before.

Rightly proud of his cooking, Verne invited a host of guests to a special barbeque party the day before the unveiling of Robert Graham's statue. It was a fabulous night and the many guests included Graham and his beautiful wife the actress Anjelica Huston, Kim and Doris Parker, Laurie Spoon from Mayor Cleaver's office, and Tony and Marti Oppenheimer who had donated money from the vast Oppenheimer fortune to commission the statue of Bird. Verne rescinded his no smoking in the house rule for the night, especially so Robert Graham could enjoy his beloved Havana cigars, so it was a lovely relaxed evening at the end of which Linda and I had made many new friends. The only thing I found unnerving was being talked into playing my unaccompanied version of 'Lush Life' for the guests. As a rule I never play at parties, I find it embarrassing, but this was an exception; everyone appreciated it, and anyway how could I let Verne and his lovely wife Stephanie down.

At around midnight, Robert Graham invited us all to drive into town and see the statue, still completely covered in a huge canvas tent. It was stunning: a gigantic bronze about fifteen-foot high, just of Bird's head alone, looking like a Buddha and chemically treated to give it the bright verdigris patina of aged bronze. Robert, renowned for his magnificent and controversial public statues of Duke Ellington in New York and Joe Louis in Pittsburgh, explained that he had started with a small, lifelike, clay model which was then scanned by laser. The co-ordinates from the model were fed into a massive computerised milling machine and the statue was assembled like a jigsaw from hundreds of individually machined pieces of bronze.

One reason Robert had us visit the statue was to place some special items secretly in the base. He unscrewed a small plate and invited Doris and Kim to put some small mementos of Bird, which they had brought specially, in a hidden container within the statue. Linda lit one of the candles we had all been asked to bring and set it by the bronze plate that Robert later screwed back in place, sealing the secret mementos in the statue. The following morning, when we had breakfast at the Jazz Museum, Robert came over and talked excitedly to Linda. Apparently, when her candle burned down it left a small disc of wax on the bronze cover plate. Robert noticed it had taken up a perfect impression of some writing on the plate and, fascinated by this accident, he had added the coin-like piece of candle to the other items before he sealed back the cover. He was eager to tell Linda her little piece of candle was now for all time a secret addition to the statue. We were very touched by his gesture and he gave us an open invitation to visit his studio and new house, which he had built especially for Anjelica, in Venice, a Bohemian area of Los Angeles.

The concert at the Gem Theater was quite something. I met up with two old friends, fellow alto saxophonist Bobby Watson, who I first met whilst jamming with the guys from his 29th Street saxophone quartet in England, and Charles McPherson. I had worked with Charles on a Bird tribute tour in Holland. Bobby was originally from Kansas City and I was delighted to meet his father, a handsome man with great charisma. The artists on the concert included several KC musicians along with Kim Parker, Charles, Bobby, Milt Jackson, Max Roach, Jay McShann and Claude 'Fiddler' Williams.

Fiddler was a revelation. I was totally unaware of him before visiting Kansas but discovered he was a living legend with a US-wide reputation. Well into his nineties, but looking no more than a vigorous sixty, he still played the hell out of the violin. My part in the concert was a couple of tunes with Kim and trombonist Al Grey, and a short set with Charles McPherson and Fiddler Williams, but at the end most of the artists got together for a big jam on one of Bird's blues themes. Milt Jackson and Max Roach, both of whom had played impressive solo features, joined us onstage along with the other artists. I played my solo then looked round to see Max smiling broadly at me from the drum kit. I was hoping to talk to him about working with a string quartet, as I knew he had done the same kind of thing with his daughter, a classical violinist. When we were later introduced, I broached the subject. He seemed interested and we agreed to keep in touch, Max saying he hoped we could work together in the UK some time. We never had the chance but we kept in touch by phone from time to time.

After the concert many of us went to the all-night jam session at the Mutual Musician's Foundation, an amazing place close to the Gem Theater, that used to be the premises of the black musicians' union in Kansas City. It's now a musicians' club where all the local KC guys, young and old, jam together till the small hours. The place was full of history and in one of the rooms upstairs Dizzy and Bird are reputed to have first met and jammed together when Dizzy was passing through on tour with Billy Eckstine's band. Even the beat-up old piano they used was still there. The club also featured in the famous jazz movie *The Last of the Blue Devils*, in which Basie and his band appeared. Verne and Bobby Watson hung out until breakfast time, digging the wonderful atmosphere. Robert Graham and Anjelica

With Anjelica Huston (*left*) and Linda in Kansas City, 1999.

Huston dropped in too. The whole week was fantastic and, although I'm still not really known in the States, I do have a small but enthusiastic audience in KC.

The rest of the week Verne took me on excursions around the area. We visited Bird's grave and the places where he grew up and went to school. He showed me the office building where Bird's mother used to work and we saw the remains of the house where Bird spent his early youth. Before it was demolished, leaving only some foundations, the house stood in what is still a poor, mainly black area on the outskirts of Kansas City. The place that left the most lasting impression on me though was Fort Leavenworth.

The whole town of Leavenworth seems to revolve around its many prisons. Most of its inhabitants are prison guards and their families. There is a women's prison and a young offenders' prison, but we only had time to visit the famous army prison and the infamous Leavenworth Penitentiary. Considered to be the toughest jail in the States, it's where Robert Stroud served thirty years of his life sentence before he was transferred and became the subject of the famous film, *The Birdman of Alcatraz*.

They reckon that many of the inmates, serving time for crimes ranging from fraud to armed robbery, only committed murder after they arrived at the prison. Conditions were so bad and violence from guards and among fellow-prisoners so endemic that many relatively minor criminals ended up killing, just to stay alive, a great example of prison rehabilitation. Even from three hundred yards away, which was as close as we were allowed to park, the place had a menacing aura, with the guards at the gate watching our every move through binoculars. Maybe they figured we were part of some plot to spring one of their inmates. They must have thought we were pretty weird, wanting to include the penitentiary in our tourist schedule. I was quite glad to hit the road back to Olathe and more barbequed ribs!

Actually this wasn't the first time I caused consternation outside a jail. Once, in Berlin, I persuaded a friend who lived in the suburb of Spandau to take me to see the famous Nazi war crimes prison. Rudolf Hess was still incarcerated there, the sole remaining prisoner. The Russians had vetoed all attempts to get him released, not so much for any reasons of justice, but more so they could still hang on to their last foothold in West Berlin. I had for years been extremely interested in the history of the Third Reich, the Holocaust and the whole span of history that led from the beginning of the century, through the rise of communism and fascism, to the defeat of Hitler and the aftermath. I couldn't miss an opportunity to see Spandau gaol. Even though we stood behind an electric fence with its signs saying, 'Don't approach past this point, Guards have orders to shoot,' we were soon accosted by a mean-looking American military policeman, demanding to know what we were doing. Then the weirdest thing happened. When I explained why we were there, the guard's demeanour changed, his eyes lit up and he said with a faint hint of pride, 'As a matter of fact I saw Mr Hess myself for the first time today; he was in his garden tending his tomato plants.' We had quite a long discussion, in which he explained that all the American guards at Spandau were volunteers who had a special interest in guarding the war criminals.

I was fascinated and brought up the fact that Hess had tried to commit suicide a few months before, hoping he might tell us more about the incident. The guard assured me Hess was in much better spirits but, before he could say any more, we were all yelled at by a German policeman who had been watching from inside a small door cut into the massive gates of the prison and was now gesticulating angrily at our 'guide'. The MP apologised to us, saying 'Well, I guess you had better move on now and I must get on with my job.' I knew quite a lot about Hess, his role in the Third Reich, his strange flight to England, his weird antics and feigned amnesia at the Nuremberg Trials and his tomato patch in Spandau, but it was an eerie feeling to think that the man who had been second only to Hitler himself and deeply involved in creating the most evil regime in the history of the world was probably drinking his afternoon tea not more than 150 yards from where I was standing. Maybe that guard at Leavenworth had been warned about this crazy Englishman who had an obsession about prisons.

The week in Kansas City was over before I could catch my breath. During the long flight back to London I started to feel ill and by the time we got home I had come down with an evil bout of flu that kept me in bed for nearly a week. I felt like shit, but happy we had made so many new friends in KC.

* * *

Soon after the trip to Kansas City I met the playwright Julian Barry. That was in 1999 when I found myself both playing and 'acting' in his *Lenny* at the Queen's Theatre in London's Shaftesbury Avenue, where I had worked with Marlene Dietrich. Julian was a hard-nosed but generous Jewish New Yorker who, in a way I could never have foreseen, came to play a big role in my life. Along with trumpeter Guy Barker and drummer Clark Tracey, I was booked to work with a quintet in Julian's controversial play about the brilliant and legendary Jewish-American comedian Lenny Bruce. Julian was a great jazz lover. He had started on trumpet but now played alto sax and, like most jazz musicians who had been around in the sixties, was a big fan of Bruce's ultra-hip, hard-hitting satirical humour.

Julian had been in the theatre most of his adult life, making his living as an actor and stage manager in New York. Later he was nominated for an Oscar when he adapted Lenny from his play to the film of the same name, starring Dustin Hoffman. This led to him moving to Hollywood where he became much in demand as a screen and television writer, as well as travelling the world writing more plays, musicals and an opera. He told me his happiest years were the fifties. After the theatre closed each night he would hang out in the jazz clubs, listening to the greats and learning trumpet. After one of the shows where Julian was stage manager, Miles Davis used to drop by to meet Frances Taylor who later became his first wife and was working as a dancer in the production. Miles was surprisingly friendly and even gave Julian tips on playing his horn while he waited around for Frances to finish work.

Julian introduced himself at the very first rehearsal of *Lenny* and seemed to know quite a bit about me. I think he had some of my CDs. Anyway, he made a beeline for me and asked if I would give him saxophone lessons. He had switched from trumpet years before because of a recurrent hernia problem. We hit it off from the start, sharing many interests, especially our admiration for Lenny Bruce, and our friendship developed into a very close working partnership later. When I gave him his first lesson I discovered he could really play. His technique needed more work but he had great ears and a natural talent, and on the first lesson we were practising 'Stella by Starlight' in all the keys. I had to run to keep up with him.

One reason for my excitement over doing the play was that it

With playwright Julian Barry, librettist of *Zyklon*.

was to be directed by the great Sir Peter Hall, who had worked with Julian on other projects. The thought of trying to speak a few lines under his direction was both thrilling and terrifying, but Guy, Clark and I were told not to worry, that Peter would not expect miracles and would guide us through it all. His reputation as a director of theatre, film and opera is immense. He is famous for his involvement in both the Royal Shakespeare Company and the National Theatre, where his battles with authority were often headline news. He once got into a big fight with the media when Sir George Solti persuaded him to take a sabbatical from the National to direct Wagner's entire *Ring Cycle* at Bayreuth, a truly mammoth task and not one to take on just for a break from work.

He later told me a little about his Bayreuth experience. Apparently, everyone who has directed *The Ring*, even Wagner himself, has been crucified by the critics. Peter said that it was almost impossible to direct in the limited time allotted: a matter of ploughing through it as well as possible, often fighting endless battles with the ultra-conservative Bayreuth luminaries. Peter's controversial production was at first heavily criticised, like everyone else's. However, there is a kind of strange tradition in that shrine to the Wagner legacy that, after two or three years, each new 'disastrous' production there becomes the 'greatest ever' and then the next attempt has to endure endless comparisons with the last. Peter Hall's version of the *The Ring* is now accepted as one of the very best.

Lenny was originally performed in New York in the seventies, after Bruce's tragic death from an overdose of drugs. Later, Julian Barry was nominated for an Oscar for his adaptation of the play into a movie starring Dustin Hoffman. The nomination improved Julian's career prospects considerably and he moved to the West Coast where he was in demand as a Hollywood screen and television scriptwriter. He wrote for the first season of *Mission Impossible*, the long-running television series, for which Lalo Schifrin wrote the famous music score.

Working with Peter Hall was fascinating and he was surprisingly tolerant of my attempts at acting. I only had a few lines but threw caution to the wind and really put my heart and soul into it. I think it paid off because I soon found myself getting more lines. My main character was a junkie alto player, a part for which I guess I was eminently typecast. The character was based on a real musician who shall remain nameless, except to say he was well known in jazz circles and a good friend of Lenny Bruce's. The production started, in Peter Hall's typically audacious style, with Bruce, played brilliantly by Eddie Izzard, lying dead in his bathroom, stark naked with a tourniquet around his arm. He is 'woken' by a judge and we are back at one of his many trials. Because of his continual lampooning of America's politicians and its hypocritical moral righteousness, Bruce was constantly persecuted by the police and hauled up on obscenity or drugs charges, sometimes getting arrested while still onstage by police planted in the audience. In the first scene, he argues with the judge at one of his trials and I rush over, thrust a big joint in Lenny's face and excitedly blurt out 'It's Moroccan Red, Lenny!'

During rehearsals it must have got around that I had once been a drug addict myself because one morning Elizabeth Berkley, the beautiful and sexy actress who played Lenny's stripper wife, came over to ask my advice. She was having difficulty playing a scene in which she calls Lenny long distance and pleads with him to telegraph her some money. She is trying to hide the fact that she needs it for drugs and Elizabeth asked me how to play the scene. Knowing that situation intimately, I could give her insights into an addict's tormented and devious mind and how he would react. My first hand knowledge seemed to help her in a way that even Peter Hall couldn't, and she played the scene much better after that.

Elizabeth was a stunner and great fun. She had become quite an icon to many hot-blooded males who had seen her sexy role in the 1995 movie *Showgirls* and she loved thrilling the guys in the band every night with her striptease scene. One night I bumped into her outside the stage door. She gave me her usual warm welcome, throwing her arms around me and giving me a big kiss. I had to laugh when some of her male fans outside called out 'Wow! It's all right for some! You lucky sod!' It was just all in good fun though. She was a really nice person, and thought the world of my wife. They had a heart-to-heart talk one night at a party and Elizabeth listened intently as Linda gave her some motherly advice, saying that she was learning to be a good actress doing *Lenny* and should concentrate on developing that side of her talent, instead of wasting time on any more of those 'silly Hollywood sex roles'.

Poor Eddie Izzard had to do an erotic and totally nude love scene with her every night and she would really try to get him at it, much to his discomfort. We would watch with bated breath as Eddie tried to control himself. One night he almost didn't make it. We asked Peter Hall what would happen if he got a hard-on in public and he said that he, as the director, would get into trouble, not Eddie. Apparently the director can be prosecuted under the obscenity laws for the obscure crime of 'putting an actor into a situation that leads to an obscene act over which he has no control', or something similarly bizarre. Peter knew his obscenity law backwards, having been hounded by Mary Whitehouse more than once. In one famous incident he got into trouble when he tried to get round the law by hiring Soho strippers to play a nude scene at the National Theatre. At that time it was illegal to show pubic hair onstage, so he circumvented the legalities by having them wear pubic wigs instead, much to Whitehouse's fury.

In one brief scene, Elizabeth Berkley and I had to rush onstage snorting a line of cocaine together, before excitedly offering some to Eddie Izzard. Peter Hall wanted it as realistic as possible so we managed to find a white substance that looked like the real thing, but didn't make us sneeze when we sniffed it. I think Elizabeth rather fancied the 'method' school of acting because she really got us into the part in the wings before we went on, whispering things in my ear like, 'Oh man, this coke is great; I wanna get laid tonight!' Ha! I really enjoyed that scene, but it was weird to be snorting make-believe cocaine onstage in front of hundreds of people, after having spent so much of my life doing it for real behind closed doors.

I have always been interested in watching good actors work and I had some fascinating chats with David Ryall, a wonderful, elderly thespian who played the judge and was a good friend of Julian Barry's. David was fascinated watching the band improvise every night and wondered if actors could learn from the way we worked. Of course, they have to stick by and large to the script and are therefore quite limited in how much they can add to a part. Having said that, jazz and stage acting have a lot in common and Peter Hall often uses his considerable knowledge of jazz to explain elements of the actor's craft. One obvious parallel between the two disciplines is that each performance is different and highly influenced by the audience reaction and the way the actors or musicians feel on any particular night. Stage acting is a living, organic process, in the same way that jazz is, and on a night when everything suddenly clicks into place the performance reaches a higher level. When that happens the buzz is very similar to when a band suddenly hits an extra gear and really takes off.

Hall has strong views on actors' improvising. He usually insists his players learn every detail of the text and its unique rhythms and structure, before allowing any individual interpretation. For instance he often likens the iambic pentameter in Shakespeare's verse to the basic structure of a jazz tune. With jazz, you can only improvise properly once you thoroughly understand the underlying rhythmic and harmonic shape of the piece you are playing. He pulled the cast up once, in *Lenny*, for improvising too much. They were trying to pick up on what Eddie Izzard was doing. Eddie is a great stand-up comedian and a brilliant improviser so Peter gave him free reign in his individualistic variations on Lenny Bruce's comedy routines. However, he stressed that, to get the effect he wanted, the rest of the cast must stick closely to the written text. Only then could Eddie's part attain its full potential. Every night we marvelled at his flights of fancy. No one but him could have successfully added anything to Bruce's own hilarious routines.

I loved every minute of the three-month run. It was a fascinating experience and standing up every night, trying to project my lines as best I could, was good training. You have to speak a little louder to be heard at the back of the theatre and you learn this and a lot more besides, by listening and watching the real actors around you. It also helps train your speaking voice for when you have to make announcements on a gig. Julian quietly kept his eye on me and gave me the odd tip, like rolling my Rs even more, to get my American accent right. It always impresses me how actors can memorise a long role. A good actor friend of mine, Barry Foster, had told me it's easy to remember lines if the writing is good, but much harder if it's bad. I only had a few words to say but, even when you know your lines, it's surprisingly difficult to stand onstage and know what to do with yourself. You still have to act, even when you have no lines. Otherwise you just look ridiculous up there and ruin the scene. You have to learn when to respond to the other actors and when not to. We were so lucky to have someone like Peter Hall there to help us. He has an incredible eye for detail and that gives you confidence because, even with a minimum of stage direction, you know he will not let you go wrong. The whole thing was an amazing experience I shall never forget.

13

*'Of course you must finish it Peter .... Never forget, Wagner wrote
the entire* Ring Cycle *with no prospect of getting it performed'*
Sir Peter Hall

Sometime before I did *Lenny* I happened to watch a television
documentary series about science and warfare. One of the programmes looked at the history of poison gas and was mainly
about a German scientist called Fritz Haber. Haber was born a
Jew but converted to Christianity, as did many German Jews
during the early part of the last century. He was a chemist and
the man who convinced the Prussian military machine to use
poison gas in World War One, ostensibly to terrorise the enemy
into suing for peace, thus saving thousands of lives. He was
probably the first modern scientist to face the kind of moral
dilemma that surrounded the dropping of the atomic bomb in
Hiroshima. I found Haber's little-known story fascinating but,
when it turned out that he was also the man responsible for the
development of the lethal gas Zyklon B, I was stunned. He died
in 1934 but unwittingly created the means by which millions of
his own people would be annihilated. Furthermore, his first
wife, Clara, herself a brilliant chemist, had committed suicide by
shooting herself in 1915 with her husband's revolver when he
refused to stop his deadly research into poison gas for use in the
First World War.

The story was like a Greek tragedy and I became obsessed
with the idea that someone should write a dramatic work about
it. I never considered myself an opera lover but my fascination
with certain modern Viennese operas, like Alban Berg's *Wozzeck*
and *Lulu*, convinced me that only opera could create the dramatic power that such a story required. At first I just wanted to
get someone interested in the story, be it as an opera, a play or

even a film, and wondered who I could approach to develop the idea. After all, how could I think of writing an opera myself? I had no formal training. One thing was sure: the subject matter, given Haber's time and place in history, would never lend itself to a jazz treatment. He was a typical Prussian of the old school and inhabited that bizarre Teutonic world captured most brilliantly by Kurt Weil, Arnold Schoenberg or Berg, but not by anything that remotely resembled jazz. Prussian scientists and military men had some fine attributes, but swinging was definitely not one of them.

My first thought was to mention it to my actor friend, Barry Foster, an ardent jazz fan who sometimes invited Linda and me to plays he was performing in. Barry was interested in the story and offered to talk about it to Harold Pinter, a close friend. At dinner with Pinter one night he mentioned my idea. Pinter, I think, saw the possibilities but pointed out that he wrote exclusively fictional plays and certainly never librettos. So the whole thing remained a pipe dream for the moment. However, when I found myself doing *Lenny*, I decided to tell Julian Barry about it and, although he didn't seem too impressed, he asked me to lend him a video of the television documentary. That seemed to arouse his interest but he thought the story was more suitable for a play than an opera.

Time passed and one day I was sitting in a little cafe near the theatre when Peter Hall dropped in and joined me for a coffee. We chatted for a while and, just as we were about to leave, I took my courage in both hands and briefly told him about my new obsession. He seemed interested, wrote down Haber's name on a scrap of paper and asked me to email him a précis of the story.

The next day, with great excitement, I typed a short synopsis and emailed it to Peter, attaching some historical background on Haber. *Lenny* came to an end and I heard nothing until about three months later, when I suddenly received an email from Peter. He told me how much he admired talent, saying he thought I had it in abundance, and thanked me and all the guys in the band for our work in *Lenny*. He went on to say he had re-read the stuff I sent him and thought my idea had potential. He felt it should be an opera rather than a play and that I should try to get someone like Julian to help me with the dramatic structure. He asked me to let him know about future developments. I was thrilled that he had taken time to email me with such encouraging news and immediately called Julian. I was not expecting him to drop everything and agree to work with me, so I wasn't at all surprised when he asked me to just leave it with him while he gave it some thought.

Let's be honest. It was really nice to get encouragement from someone like Peter Hall, but I was not known as a classical composer and had never written anything more than a small scale string quartet piece before. I simply hoped Julian might do as Peter suggested and help with the dramatic shape of the story, in case I got a chance to take the project forward one day. A couple of days later Julian called and dropped a bombshell in my lap. 'OK, Peter, let's do it. I've rented a flat for a few months, so I can work with you and write the libretto, if you'll write the music.' He had actually decided to commit himself to working on an opera with me. It looked like I was actually going to have to write the music for this damned project, after all! Julian and I had become good friends and I began to worry about what I would be taking on and whether I could really handle it. I didn't want to let him down but he put my mind at rest, saying that he had nothing else planned for a while and had faith in me. He told me, several years later, that he decided to do it because of the strange intense look in my eyes when I played him a recording of part of an unfinished string quartet I was writing. He thought, 'Jesus this madman really wants to write classical music and he's transported by it.'

I had already decided to call the opera *Zyklon*. Apart from the obvious reason, it had an ancient Greek ring that seemed appropriate, especially since I felt the story had all the elements of a

Greek tragedy. All I had to do now was write about three hours of music. I had already estimated, from how long *Janus* took, that it would take at least three years to write, given a fair wind. My estimate turned out to be pretty well spot on. After a day or so Julian called to say, 'We have a problem with the dramatic structure,' The problem was this: Haber died in 1934, long before Zyklon was ever used to kill the Jews. Dramatically we didn't have an ending, just an empty black hole. Julian told me to wait until he could figure a way out of the problem. I saw Haber as a kind of fatefully misguided Faustian character, a victim of his own egotism who, in trying to help his beloved Fatherland, ended up destroying millions of his own people, both Germans and Jews. I suggested he should be portrayed as a ghost in the opera, but Julian was against the idea. I tried hard to convince him but he was having none of it. He thought about it though, and then came back with a solution to the problem. He suggested we start the opera at an office of the Nuremberg War Crimes Tribunal in 1946. A strange old man would shamble into the office and demand to be put on trial as a war criminal with the rest of the defendants. The old man is of course Fritz Haber. If Haber could then convince one of the army lawyers to listen, he could tell his story to him in a series of flashbacks. Right at the end of the opera, it would be revealed that the man was indeed Haber's ghost, seeking absolution from his perceived crimes. It seemed a great idea and the best way to handle the dramatic problem.

Using the Nuremberg trial would also enable us to place the horrors of the Holocaust firmly at the beginning of the opera and so establish the prime reason for Haber's guilt. Julian and I could also get our favourite arch-villains, Hitler, Göring, Hess et al, into the action. I had discovered we shared a fascination with the history of the Third Reich. Hitler even makes a brief appearance in *Lenny*, admittedly as part of one of Lenny's own famous sketches, and Julian wrote a brilliant black comedy, *The Matter of the Officers*, based almost verbatim on the minutes of

Hitler's meetings with his generals in his bunker as Berlin was about to fall. What made that play so funny was the way Hitler came out of it looking like the only sane guy in the bunker, as he and his henchmen argued about the trivial minutiae of retired officers' ranks and pensions, while the Third Reich collapsed around them. The play brilliantly captured the true 'banality of evil', to use the famous phrase coined by Hannah Arendt in her book *Eichmann in Jerusalem*.

Julian is a prodigiously fast writer – you have to be when you write for screen or television – so, after a few days, the first scene of the libretto arrived in an email. It was wonderful stuff. I envisaged a text close to natural speech, not a lyrical one, and he hit exactly the style I wanted, writing it almost like a play script, but with liberal use of blank verse. His libretto completely drove the musical form and inspired me at every step of the way. I had figured that the style would draw heavily on Bartók and Berg but, although those influences are there, the libretto became the prime driving force, suggesting how the music should go.

Once I decided to take up the challenge I buried myself in books about opera and singing and studied scores. I asked Lalo Schifrin for advice and he told me not to be scared; that a choral work was like any other form of composition, but I should avoid covering the singers with too much heavy orchestration. I was already familiar with Berg's *Lulu* and *Wozzek* and Bartók's *Bluebeard's Castle*, but followed Lalo's advice and also listened to Wagner's *Parsifal* and Debussy's *Pélleas et Mélisande*, both of which were inspiring revelations to me. I started work as Julian quickly sent page after page of libretto. It was to be three years of struggle but, in spite of serious doubts and times when I nearly gave up, I kept going, determined to finish the first draft of the score at least.

I wrote on my computer with a software music package that enabled me to record my own voice, so I could get some idea how the music might sound with the sung words. I have a lousy voice, yet I could sing in tune and, most importantly, capture

some of the emotion in the words. But every time I played Julian
the latest offering from the PC, my attempts at singing caused
much hilarity and me much embarrassment. In spite of this
handicap, we could get an idea of how the thing would sound
and, after a year of work, Julian made a proposal. If I could
finish the first act and record what we had with real singers, he
would put his own money into making a rough demo. The idea
was to give a copy to Peter Hall, who had offered to help if he
could.

Peter Watts from Miles Music worked with us to improve the
computer sound quality and I managed to find some excellent
singers. Finally we cobbled together a reasonable CD of the first
act, which I delivered to Peter Hall's house. Peter knew the chief
at the English National Opera and hoped to get *Zyklon* taken up
by their opera workshop. He advised us this was the best way to
start and invited me to meet him at Glyndebourne, where he
was directing a production of Verdi's *Otello*. Over lunch he told
me he had found the synthesized sounds off-putting in places.
But he was very encouraging and proposed we send everything
to the ENO, with a letter of recommendation from him. At one
point he rather threw me by asking what I wanted to get out of
the project. I said the first thing I wanted to know was whether,
now he had heard the CD, he thought I should carry on and
finish the opera. I told him it had become a bit of an obsession.
He gave me an earnest look and said 'Of course you must finish
it, Peter. It's very dangerous to give up on an obsession.' Then he
added, 'Never forget. Wagner wrote the entire *Ring Cycle* with
no prospect of getting it performed.' The last remark shook me
a bit, but I understood what he was trying to say.

I knew when I started that the chances of getting a full-scale
opera produced, let alone one by an unknown composer, were
virtually non-existent. Even the great operatic maestros often
struggled to get their work performed. Unless you are lucky
enough to get a commission you write an opera 'because you
have to'. Any other reason and you are doomed to disappoint-

ment. Peter was just letting me know how difficult it was, but that I should finish the good work and never give up. I made him a promise, there and then, that I would stay the distance and complete *Zyklon* whatever the obstacles. He could see I meant it and, many times when I was about to chuck it all in, his words would ring in my ears. I was determined not to let him, or Julian, down. Both of them were towers of strength and encouragement over the next years. I submitted a vocal score, the CD and the libretto to the ENO, along with a glowing letter of recommendation from Peter, and waited.

After many weeks I got a letter saying that, because of personnel changes in the workshop and financial restraints, the ENO could not take on any new works for the foreseeable future. My first reaction was that it was simply a brush-off and that they didn't like what I had sent. Peter was disappointed but assured me it had nothing to do with the quality but was indeed due to financial difficulties. There were to be big changes at the ENO and the head of the company later lost his job. Peter told me not to give up; he would see if he could find a new approach. Julian continued to send me each new section of the libretto as he wrote it. We knew he would be well ahead of me by the time he had finished, but that was to be expected as the music always takes much longer to write. After a few months the libretto was finished and Julian returned to the States while I carried on writing, sending him the latest tapes every so often.

A friend, Peter Morris of the Theatrical Management Association, put me in touch with Patrick Dickie of the Almeida Opera and, armed with a CD of the first act, I went to see him. He listened politely to the music, but he pointed out that the Almeida Opera usually performed fairly short chamber works and *Zyklon* was scored for a large orchestra and would end up about three hours long. By now we were getting feedback from various people about the work so far and some were criticising the rather slow pace of the opening scene. Julian and I agreed to cut out the whole first scene at the Nuremberg trial, including

Göring and Hess, and open the action directly in the office of the War Crimes Tribunal instead. We were sad to see the Nazis go, but sometimes you just have to make sacrifices, for art's sake! Julian also decided that instead of three acts, we should have just two longer ones. It didn't involve re-writing too much of the music and we both thought it gave a much better structure.

Zyklon took up most of my spare time but I still played the usual round of jazz gigs. It was getting harder and harder to find work though, and fees were becoming a bad joke. There were so many young guys around, chasing gigs with their home-produced CDs and their promotional expertise. Whereas in the old days you could just wait for the phone to ring for gigs at the regular venues three or four times a year, now you were lucky to get the same gigs once every two or three years. Promoters became so inundated with new groups that they filled their programmes several months in advance and if you didn't continually chase them you ended up with nothing. What was even worse, the cost of petrol, hotels and everything else had almost doubled since the eighties, but the fees stayed the same and this still applies today. I always try to entertain the audience and I believe no one owes you a living; but when I have to travel to a concert and back for anything up to ten hours, working for an hourly rate that a plumber or bricklayer would scoff at, I do get rather pissed off. Music has its rewards but you have to eat. I don't blame the promoters; they have a hard enough time making venues pay. But I do blame the serious lack of arts funding that seems the norm in today's world of cynical avarice.

* * *

Sometime in the late-1990s Alan Skidmore suggested that he and I should go to see Elvin Jones at Ronnie Scott's. Alan had worked with Elvin and knew him well as a friend. I jumped at the idea, having not seen him for nearly thirty years. Alan introduced me and, although he would not have remembered our previous meeting, Elvin was just as sweet and friendly as ever. After that we became friends and I would hang out in the dressing room with him and his wife Keiko whenever they came to the club. I eventually told him that we first met with Philly Joe in the late sixties but he just smiled and said knowingly, 'Oh! The bad old days, heh?' Keiko guarded Elvin with her life and didn't like people visiting him in his hotel, but she was his saviour, just the way Linda had been for me. We agreed that neither of us would have been alive to tell the tale if it hadn't been for the way our wonderful wives took us in hand when we were going off the rails all those years before. I loved that man. He was a beautiful, spiritual person and one of the few remaining giants of jazz. When I first met Elvin I hadn't really grasped the true significance of Coltrane's quartet, but later I soaked up every note they recorded. Every member of that band was a giant and none more so than Elvin. He recreated jazz drumming and took it to a level that has not yet been surpassed. I almost saw Trane's group once in London in the 1960s, but didn't go for some reason. I never got another chance as Coltrane died not long after. I was shocked and decided I was not going to let something like that happen again. That's why I always tried to catch Elvin when he was in town.

One September, he was booked at the Ronnie Scott Club with his Jazz Machine but one of the group, trombonist Delfeayo Marsalis, was unable to make the gig so Pete King asked me to go to the sound check and dep for Delfeayo. It turned out to be for nearly two weeks. I couldn't believe it: I was to play with Elvin Jones and that was as exciting to me as sitting in with Bud Powell. Elvin told me what he could afford to pay and that I should be getting a lot more. He was really apologetic about it. In fact it was more than I would normally get. Anyway, I told him, I would have played with him for nothing if I had to. The gig was one of my two greatest ever musical experiences; the other was playing with Bud.

Ravi Coltrane was on tenor. He seemed a sweet young guy and he played well too. It must have been tough being Trane's son and playing the same instrument. Elvin, as always, introduced each musician with a long, glowing eulogy. That makes you feel good, but not nearly as good as when he starts playing behind you. I talk a lot about that special relaxed feel. Well, Elvin was its greatest exponent: it felt so warm and comfortable that you couldn't help but play. Mind you, when he took a drum solo it could be very hard to come in again in the right place. He played extraordinarily complex cross-rhythms and certain patterns seemed to be speeding up or slowing down, except you knew they were all perfectly in time. Sometimes I had to watch Ravi, who looked as mystified as me, to make sure we came in together. Elvin told me his brothers, pianist Hank and trumpeter Thad, used to give him a hard time when he first started, and so did other musicians. They couldn't follow what he was doing and thought he was goofing around on the kit. But he always knew exactly what he was trying to do and eventually everyone began to realise what a genius he was. Coltrane must have known all along.

It's always nice to get someone else a chance to work with a great like Elvin and I was able to do this for Steve Melling. While we were at Ronnie's, Elvin asked if I knew a good pianist. He had a date in Germany right after and his pianist was leaving the band. I had given him a CD of my quartet that he seemed to enjoy so, when I suggested Steve for the job, he asked me if I could get him to do it. Of course, Steve took the gig like a flash.

Elvin and I would often chat in his dressing room or just sit and relax with a glass of his favourite red wine. He told me some funny stories. Like, when he was on the road doing concerts with Coltrane, Trane made the band wear dinner suits. Elvin used to sweat profusely, often changing into his bathrobe like a heavyweight boxer between sets, so I asked him how he managed. He told me 'Oh man, after a few days I would get to the hotel, dry off my suit and stand it up rigid in the corner!' He also told me a funny story about his brother Thad. Thad's big band was doing a date in Europe and part of the deal was they would record the gig. But there was no extra money for the recording.

The guys were all pissed about that, so tenorist Joe Henderson tried to get his own back. When he got up to take a solo he walked about ten feet away from the microphone, so he couldn't be heard on the recording. Apparently Thad got mad, came all the way down from the trumpet section, picked Joe up bodily and carried him across the stage back to the mike. The funny part was Joe just kept right on playing anyway!

Elvin was a beautiful man and his death hurt me as if I'd lost a close relative. I miss his lovely smile, his warm, friendly bear hug, his intelligent conversation and his awesome playing. No one will ever take his place.

Not long after I started work on *Zyklon* I went to Germany to play in a televised concert which was to feature Jessye Norman, the legendary African-American operatic soprano. She was to star in a television performance of Duke Ellington's *Sacred Music*. It had been Jessye's wonderful recording of Wagner's 'Prelude and Libestod' from *Tristan and Isolde* that first inspired me to record that music on the *Lush Life* album, and she got to hear about my recording and wanted to know more. Now, she is a true superstar, with the reputation of being temperamental and demanding, so I was, I admit, rather scared of her but, while we were preparing for the concert, she told me to call her room sometime and come up and play her the CD. It took me a while to get the courage but eventually I found myself in her luxury suite. She was lounging on a sofa in her dressing gown, watching a video of the day's rehearsal and telling the television director what she wanted changed for the next day. She turned out to be very approachable and suggested they should take a break from reviewing the rehearsal and listen to the track on my Walkman. Soon she was chuckling with delight, insisting the television director listen too and saying she loved it. She was so charming that I told her about *Zyklon* and asked if she would like to hear a bit of that too. She found time to listen to a short section of the first act; then she took her earphones off, smiled, and said 'Ah, I can hear Bartók's influence.' She was right because the first part of *Zyklon* is reminiscent of Bartók's *Bluebeard's Castle*. I said I hoped it wasn't a problem and she told me, 'Oh no! I like it. I just noticed that you love Bartók too'. I left her suite very happy as she wished me good luck with the project, gave me her secretary's email address and told me to get in touch any time. I never did, of course, even though I had harboured silly dreams that she might one day sing the part of Clara. That was never likely to happen. For a start she now sang mostly lieder recitals and rarely opera, and even if she had ever considered the role, I couldn't imagine a German Jewish lady chemist portrayed on-stage by a very large black woman, even if she was one of the world's greatest sopranos.

In March 2000 I got an interesting offer to tour with Roots, an all-star group led by American saxophonist Benny Golson. The band had already made a couple of extensive tours before but the regular alto player Arthur Blythe was unavailable, so I was approached to take his place. Benny, Nathan Davis and Odean Pope were on tenors and an old friend from my Paris days, Kirk Lightsey, was on piano, so I was really looking forward to the gig. We started at Ronnie Scott's and then toured Europe for almost three weeks. I was made to feel very much at home, the music was good and we had a nice time socially. It was quite a challenge to play lead alto with Benny, Nathan and Odean. All of them had enormous sounds on their horns, which I had to try and match and all three used big wide-lay mouth-pieces and rock-hard reeds. Benny had his reeds specially made, as he could only play on a number six. The hardest you could buy then was a five. I only use a three, but enjoyed trying to ring every ounce of sound out of my horn. It's more a matter of singing through the instrument than overblowing it and it felt good to be pulling my weight, blending with the tenors and making myself heard in the ensemble passages. Touring was pretty exhausting, however, with flights or long coach journeys virtually every day, as we travelled across Europe.

Work continued on the opera and I kept Peter Hall and

Left to right: Benny Golson, Nathan Davis (director), PK, Randy Brecker, Jon Faddis, Monty Alexander at the University of Pittsburgh 37th Annual Jazz Seminar and Concert, 2007. Photo courtesy Nathan Davis.

Patrick Dickie, from the Almeida Opera, up to date with progress, hoping they might still be able to help when the thing was eventually finished. The word was getting around and I got some coverage in *The Times* when Alyn Shipton interviewed me about *Zyklon*. That article lead to a new and unexpected development. I got an email from a lady who turned out to be Fritz Haber's granddaughter, Rowena. She had seen the paper and showed it to her mother, Eva Lewis. Eva was Haber's daughter from his second marriage and she was interested to know more about *Zyklon*. A very sprightly old lady in her eighties, she had appeared in the television documentary that first got me interested in the story, and she lived in Bath. I would have liked to have contacted her when I first started researching for the opera, so I was thrilled at the prospect of finally meeting her now. However, I was a bit concerned she might object to what we had written about her father. Rowena put my mind at rest telling me her mother was fascinated and just wanted to hear the music.

I called Julian, but he didn't share my excitement and strongly advised me to have nothing to do with her. He had had a bad experience in the past when one of Lenny Bruce's relatives had tried to sue him over something in his play. We finally decided I should test the water very carefully and on no account let her see the libretto. I went ahead and contacted Eva and she turned out to be very friendly and not at all concerned about the gist of our story, which was already covered briefly in *The Times* article anyway. So, after further discussions with Julian, Linda and I drove to Bath, armed with just a short synopsis. I needn't have worried, Eva turned out to be a real angel with a great sense of fun and we spent several fascinating hours with her.

She told us many things I wish I had known earlier. Haber did not actually invent Zyklon B himself, we discovered, but was in overall charge of its development, in his capacity as head of the prestigious Kaiser Wilhelm Institute. Zyklon was originally developed as a pesticide, but Haber knew only too well its lethal potential as a weapon and by that time Hitler was planning to defy the terms of the Versailles Treaty and re-arm in secret. In fact, we never state categorically in the opera that he invented Zyklon B. We simply suggest that he learned about the Holocaust in death and blamed himself for providing the means to implement it, even though he was in fact totally blameless.

Eva explained that her father's first wife, Clara, had suffered terrible depressions over her marriage. The relationship broke down long before her suicide, which happened only partly because she hated her husband's work on poison gas. She fought tooth and nail to stop him, believing in her sacred vow as a scientist to work only for the good of mankind. Haber's attitude was that that was well and good in peacetime, but 'in war science belongs to your country'. Eva also told us that Clara's very young son, Hermann, heard the fatal shot and ran into the garden to discover his mother lying dead. He broke the news to his father; a terrible thing for a child which had a devastating effect on him as he grew up.

Haber remarried and his new wife gave birth to Eva, who told us he was more like a grandfather to her than a father. He was always working so Eva didn't see that much of him, but remembered him as a loving father. She was used to seeing famous scientists around the house all the time and said that Albert Einstein often visited. He would put her on his knee and attempt to explain relativity to her, trying to put it into simple language, she never could figure it out. Eva was quietly supportive of the whole *Zyklon* opera project and put my mind at rest about any flack we might get from other quarters in the family, telling me not to worry about what was now just water under the bridge. After I got to know her, Julian also began to accept that she was on our side and would not cause us any problems.

* * *

After Charlie Watts finished a long tour with the Rolling Stones he contacted me about putting a new band together for the autumn of 2001. The old big band was great fun while it lasted but it had had its day. Instead Charlie fancied a ten-piece, which made more sense. Gerard Presencer and I helped him pick the line-up and he commissioned both of us to do the arrangements. Evan Parker came in on tenor with Alan Barnes on baritone. Charlie got Henry Lowther to join Gerard on trumpet, and we suggested the brilliant Mark Nightingale on trombone. With Anthony Kerr on vibes and the rhythm section beefed up with Brazilian Luis Jardim on percussion, we had a tight-knit group with enough different colours to make for interesting writing. Charlie picked most of the tunes and Gerard did a really hip arrangement of Mick Jagger's 'Satisfaction' to keep the Stones fans happy. We started with a stint at Ronnie's and then set off for a week at the Blue Note club in Tokyo, flying straight on to New York, for a week at the Blue Note there. The band sounded exciting and was for me the strongest jazz line-up Charlie had put together. We played to packed and appreciative houses at every gig and, as an added bonus, even had good reviews from the jazz critics for once.

In Tokyo I was able to meet up with my email friend Masaru Koike, the aerodynamicist with Mitsubishi. He came to the Blue Note and after the gig we hung out, talking about Coltrane and the latest news on the aerodynamics front, much to the bemusement of the guys in the band. The directors of Yanigisawa were also at one of the gigs to see me play one of their instruments. They had invited me earlier in the week to try out some altos. Their British distributors had already kindly given me my soprano and a new tenor, but I had always played the ubiquitous Selmer Mk VI alto and was perfectly happy with it. Anyway, they took me to try some horns and to my amazement I immediately fell in love with a Yanigisawa alto that had a superb tone quality, possibly due to its having a solid silver bell and crook and a bronze body. Gold plating inside the bell also helped to improve the sound. It was a beautiful instrument, exquisitely engraved by hand and became known as the 'Peter King Model'. I have played and promoted the horn ever since. It's head and shoulders above my faithful old Mk VI Selmer, and I was very happy to be able to repay Yanigisawa's generosity by genuinely singing its praises in their adverts. It's a good deal all round; I acquired a great alto and they seem very happy with the sales figures for that model, which is now much sought-after, I believe.

Flying to New York I crossed the International Date Line for the first time, arriving the day before leaving Tokyo, which was really weird. It was November 2001, just two months after the world shattering events of 9/11. I felt drawn to make the pilgrimage to Ground Zero, to see the aftermath for myself. Verne Christensen had flown in from Kansas and we both took the subway and managed to get to within a block or two of the scene. The images of 9/11 are burned into everyone's mind but nothing could prepare us for the overwhelming horror and annihilation that confronted us when faced with the actual site. We approached from upwind to avoid the awful smell which we were told still enveloped the area. But even two months after the event the site was still smouldering like some giant underground inferno. Wreckers tore huge lumps of masonry from what was left of the Twin Towers while smoke and flames belched forth from the very bowels of the earth below. At one point I saw what I thought were seagulls flying past, but realised they were sheets of paper fluttering down from the remains of what had, two months previously, been bustling offices. We did our best to face the awful scene but, after confronting some of the floral tributes and thousands of pathetic little photos and personal messages that completely covered the fencing around the site, we felt humbled and drained and made our way back to the hotel. I'm glad I went, but I couldn't help feeling uneasy as if I was some kind of vicarious voyeur. I think everyone who has seen Ground Zero must feel like this to some extent. It was a shattering experience and one that I'll never quite get out of my mind.

* * *

Back in England, I discovered that it's amazing how a five-second appearance in a movie can enhance your profile. Trumpeter Guy Barker called me to do a recording session for a new film, *The Talented Mr Ripley*, starring Gwyneth Paltrow, Matt Damon, Cate Blanchett and Jude Law, and directed by Anthony Minghella, who had won an Oscar for *The English Patient*. Jazz featured heavily in the story and Guy was to play in some of the scenes. However I was initially booked to record just a couple of tunes that would be mimed on screen by someone else. Minghella came up to me after one of my solos and asked if I could make it wilder and more avant-garde. On the next take I played it really wild and Anthony came in beaming. It was exactly what he wanted. He obviously gave the thing some thought after that, because he suddenly asked me during the coffee break if I was free the following month. He had decided he wanted me on-screen after all, to mime to my own solo.

I have worked in a few movies over the years but Anthony was the first director I came across who knew exactly how to film musicians. The general lack of musical understanding shown by most movie directors was typified by the 1992 film *Blue Ice* where one of the scenes had a tenor solo on the sound track but an alto player miming to it. By contrast, Anthony's attention to detail was amazing and the week after the recording I received a tape of the music, with a full transcription of my own solo and a polite request for me to memorise it. His approach was to insist that every movement of the musician's hands should be mimed exactly. This was very refreshing and we were all excited to work with him. Our scenes were supposed to be at the San Remo Jazz Festival in the sixties, but the appearance of the town and sea front had changed beyond recognition since then so, in his quest for accuracy, Anthony chose to film in Anzio instead, because it looked very similar to the old San Remo.

On the day of shooting Anthony warned us apologetically it would be a long day, but said that it would be worth all the effort to get a good result. We started at 4 p.m. and worked through till nearly four the following morning. There was only one hour's break and that was only because all the crowd scene extras were Italian and their union had strict rules about breaking to eat. It took all this time just to shoot maybe ten or fifteen minutes of film, because of the many different camera angles Anthony needed. We musicians enjoyed every minute though and had time to get to chat with Matt Damon and Jude Law when we weren't actually in shot. Matt and I both had lousy colds, so Anthony took trouble to make sure we both got a hot vitamin C drink every hour or so. That was the kind of guy he was. He worked you hard but really made you feel appreciated.

When we returned to London, we had to re-record some of the music because of an editing change, and Anthony Minghella was in the studio raring to go, having just flown in from Los Angeles. Guy Barker told me Anthony had been back and forth between New York, Los Angeles and London several times that week alone and had hardly any sleep, yet he was always wide awake and in good humour. His energy was frightening. You don't mind working twelve hours non-stop on-set for a guy like that. After the film came out and Linda and I had been to the French premier in Paris, people kept rushing up to tell me they'd seen me in the movies. The power of film! I mean I was only on for a couple of seconds, but the horrendous close-up of my ugly mug filled the entire screen. Apparently Matt Damon reckoned I was a 'real star', when asked about me in an interview, and the film director Mike Figgis once said I looked like the 'archetypal jazz musician', whatever that's supposed to mean.

I soon settled back into the 'real' world and the continual struggle to get work for my band. Occasional gigs with Colin Towns' orchestra helped too. Colin has a wild band, full of great players, but he writes the hardest parts I have ever seen. Before the first gig he sent me the music to look at. I freaked out when I saw he had written so many passages in the altissimo range, way above the normal register. Everyone struggled with the parts at first but, once you got to grips with them, the result was electrifying and very original. Colin is an amazing musician with a very wide-ranging knowledge of musical styles, from rock to classical, and his prodigious writing for television and films is very highly regarded. It's always a pleasure and a challenge to work with him.

I started travelling abroad again quite a lot, visiting new places. Dusko Goykovich, a Yugoslavian trumpet player who had worked a lot in the States, called me to play with his international big band in Belgrade. It featured musicians from all over Europe and we rehearsed all week for a concert and a recording. I had played a few times in Zagreb, now in Croatia, but never in the Serbian capital. In fact, the last time I worked in Zagreb was with Johnny Griffin and bassist Niels-Henning Ørsted Pedersen. Not long after the Belgrade gig I got a call from Nathan Davis who was also putting together an international band to do a concert and workshop at the American

University in Dubai. Brazilian trumpeter Claudio Roditi was on it, along with James Moody. It was great to see Moody again. He was in tremendous form and did a solo feature on *Moody's Mood for Love*, singing the famous lyrics to his own original recorded solo, instead of playing the tenor. He brought the house down, especially when he added a new 'rap' version as well and included a cute little dance routine. Moody and I are quite close, especially since discovering both our wives were called Linda.

In Dubai we were all invited for a trip into the desert. That turned out to be quite an experience. Two Arab drivers collected us, in top-of-the-range Toyota Land Cruisers and we set off on a motorway out of town. After only a few miles they turned off and we were suddenly in the desert. We stopped for what I thought was just a short break to take photos, but noticed our drivers were letting air out of all the tyres. The penny dropped: they were going to take us 'dune riding'. All we could see were massive sand dunes, some up to about 100 feet high. We rode those dunes for about an hour. It was amazing. I'm not a lover of SUVs, especially when the streets are clogged with women using them just to pick the kids up from school. This was different: this is what those vehicles are really made for. The drivers had incredible skill and it was astonishing to see how they handled the things over the soft sand, often reaching angles of forty-five degrees fore and aft and even from one side to the other. It was all very effortless and like doing aerobatics in a plane. There were about twenty SUVs in a convoy in case one of them got into difficulties and needed a tow out of the soft sand, so sometimes we would have to stop and wait for other drivers to catch up. Eventually we stopped in the middle of nowhere to watch the beautiful desert sunset from the top of a massive dune and that was followed by a barbeque in a Bedouin-style encampment, with belly dancers providing the entertainment.

* * *

Russia had always fascinated me. I had read Tolstoy and Dostoyevsky and quite a lot on Russian history, both under the Tzars and the period of the 1917 Revolution. I went on to read nearly everything by Solzhenitsyn, including every volume of *The Gulag Archipelago*, and this led me to study the whole Stalin era. I had flown over Siberia a couple of times on the way to the Far East and was mesmerised by the sheer vastness of the Russian Steppes, but I had never actually landed in the country, so I was very excited to get a call one day from a Russian tenor player, Oleg Kireyev. He had been on tour in the UK and now wanted me to play with him in his own country. The British Council had an office in Nizhni Novgorod (formally Gorki), and helped to set up a concert there, paying for my air fare. Oleg arranged more dates and after a few hassles getting my visa sorted out I was soon boarding an Aeroflot flight to Moscow.

After I landed, Oleg and I had to catch an overnight train to St. Petersburg. I had to get used to the punishing logistics of going on the road in Russia. Russian musicians seem to travel by train most of the time and think nothing of spending several days on the Trans-Siberian railway going to gigs as far afield as Vladivostok. I was told jazz audiences get better the further you travel east! St. Petersburg is a mere eleven hours from Moscow, but several times we had to sleep on the train straight after a concert, arriving at the place of the next gig just in to time to grab a couple more hours in the hotel. It was tough going but I wouldn't have missed the experience for the world. Oleg and the excellent Russian rhythm section quickly showed me the ropes on the trains. At the end of each carriage was an attendant and the secret was to order a sandwich, hot tea and plenty of vodka to help you sleep. You get used to it after a while and when you wake up in the morning you join the queue for the bathroom. It was strange to see businessmen, some still in pyjamas, waiting in line to plug their electric razors into a communal socket at the end of the carriage.

I had time to spare in St. Petersburg and was shown the city by a beautiful Russian girl who worked at the Hermitage Museum. I was fascinated to visit the historic cruiser *Aurora*, moored on a tributary of the Neva River. I stood on its deck, right by the actual gun that had been fired to signal the start of the 1917 Revolution. Even more amazing, a few minutes later I was standing right in the Winter Palace, now restored to its original magnificent splendour. Faced with Catherine the Great's huge and luxurious gold coronation coach and the incredible opulence of the Tsar's palace, it wasn't hard to understand why the revolutionaries stormed the place.

In Moscow we stayed in the Peking Hotel, a huge old edifice notorious for having been used regularly by the KGB in communist times. It still had a dowdy, menacing, Cold War look about it and on each floor a stern-looking woman sat at a desk from which she could watch every room. In the old days she would have been working for the secret police, but now her job was to keep our rooms secure from burglars instead. The rooms were huge, with high ornamented ceilings. I couldn't help scanning them for hidden microphones. Most of them were bugged in the old days.

Oleg was artistic director for the jazz club just across the snow-covered street from the Hotel Peking, but we had more travelling to do before we played in Moscow. There had been quite a lot of publicity about my trip but I was amazed at the reception we got. We played to large enthusiastic audiences in good-sized concert halls, performing in Kazan and Nizhni Novgorod and then flying to Ufa, in Bashkir province, just this side of the Ural Mountains and Siberia. I had never heard of Ufa before, but it was Oleg's home town and the great dancer Rudolf Nureyev was born in a little village nearby.

Kazan is the home of one of Russia's most respected aviation institutes and many Russian aeromodellers studied there before taking jobs in the industry. Another modelling friend Andrey Burdov, who was still living and working in Kazan, came to our concert. That was a funny scene because he brought his latest models with him to the gig. I spent the interval partly signing autographs, while Andrey's beautiful teenage daughter helped me spell the Russian names, and partly studying his latest models. The fans, ushered one by one into my dressing room by the promoters, took the strange goings-on in their stride and I had a great time exchanging pleasantries with some extraordinarily attractive Russian ladies, while also learning about Andrey's latest technical innovations!

Unfortunately, the gruelling schedule, the cold and the twelve-hour overnight train journey to Nizhni Novgorod finally caught up with me and by the time we arrived I had the mother of all viruses. I felt so bad they called a doctor and I nearly couldn't make the concert. It was embarrassing because all the British Council people were there. I was so sick I actually threw up and shat my pants at the same time; just before I was due to go onstage. Somehow I got through the concert and made the British Council reception afterwards and everyone thought I was a real hero for playing at all. We returned to Moscow and had a day off, during which time I recovered just enough to make the jazz club date and to play a concert at a large theatre complex very similar to the one the Chechnyan terrorists seized a week or two after I got home. That was frightening as it could well have happened at our gig instead!

Before I left Russia I just had to see Red Square, Lenin's tomb and the balcony where Stalin, Krushchev, et al, used to officiate over the annual May Day Parade, so Oleg took me out on the fabulous Moscow subway to see it all. We nearly froze to death walking around the snow-covered square, so we soon hurried into the famous Gum department store for a coffee, before returning to the hotel. I came home with my head full of fascinating images of Russia, not the least of which was that of the infamous Lubyanka, the prison where the old KGB had its headquarters and interrogation cells. I had read so much about the Stalin years, the Gulag and how so many innocent people had suffered torture in the Lubyanka, before being transported to

Siberia. It's just another building now and Muscovites pass it every day without a glance, but I could imagine what terror it must have struck into people's minds, in the days when a sudden knock on the door in the middle of the night would see you end up in one of its underground cells, followed by the inevitable journey into the terrifying abyss of the Gulag.

It was great working with Oleg and the excellent Russian rhythm section, but I hoped my groundwork over there could lead to a gig with my own quartet. A couple of years later Oleg put me in touch with Michael Green who, despite his English name, is Russian and the director of the Moscow Jazz Festival. Michael invited my quartet to appear at the festival where we played in the beautiful Hermitage Gardens. Oleg joined us as a guest and, as Steve Keogh was unable to make the gig, I used the Russian drummer who had played so well on my solo tour. I had a lovely surprise at the end of the show when Michael came onstage and presented me with a special 'Lifetime Achievement' award, something I have yet to receive in my own country. The quartet also flew with me on a dilapidated Bashkiri Airlines plane to Ufa where we played to a massive audience. I felt a bit like Norman Wisdom when he suddenly became a star in Albania. Ufa had remembered me and I seem to have become quite well-known there. I was even rushed away after the concert to take part as a special guest in a popular late night television arts magazine programme. I was so pleased to share the Russian experience with my own band. I am very proud of my current quartet but it's hard getting work for it abroad. However, the Russian trip was followed by a return visit to the Arab Emirates where this time the quartet was featured at the Dubai Jazz Festival.

By the end of 2003 I had nearly finished the first draft of the opera. Julian Barry came over to London for a few weeks so we could work together and it was quite a momentous occasion when I wrote the last notes in what had become over 650 pages of fully orchestrated score. I played him the last scene on the computer and he gave me a big hug saying 'You've done it. Man, you've written your first opera!' It was a great feeling. It had been a long slog, but in some ways that was the easy part. Now, if it was to be performed, it would require rewriting and the preparation of a final version of the orchestral score. I had written for a full-size opera orchestra, in a kind of compacted score which would need laying out properly, with bowings for the strings, expression marks, etc. I had kept it basic so I could get it finished quicker, but also because any future performance might need redoing for anything from a small chamber orchestra upwards. I would also have to prepare a full piano reduction for rehearsal purposes.

It felt strange to have finished it, at least for a while. For three long years I had slaved away, often late into the night, using nearly every spare hour I had and suddenly there was no more to write. I decided to put it out of my mind for a while, enjoy playing and write a couple of aeromodelling papers that I had been asked to contribute. Then I got a request through one of my rare saxophone pupils, a young Thai girl, Narisa, to play in Thailand. Her parents helped finance the trip so Linda could come with me. We flew to Bangkok and I played at a jazz festival in Hua Hin, where the King of Thailand has his summer palace, and at the Saxophone Club in Bangkok. The King is an extraordinary man, much loved by the people. I discovered he is a saxophone player and loves jazz, writing his own tunes and making records that sell in their thousands. Linda and I badly needed a break and a trip away together and our new Thai friends made sure we had a great time.

After we got back, film director Mike Figgis asked me to take part in a documentary. Martin Scorsese was producing a series of films about the blues, using several directors including Clint Eastwood, and Mike was to direct an episode about the British blues scene. I had worked with Mike before, playing alto on the soundtrack of his experimental and highly original film *Timecode*, released in 2000. He plays good trumpet and also writes his own musical scores and screenplays. For the blues documentary he hired Tom Jones, Lulu and Van Morrison, among others associated with the British blues scene, and the backing band included myself and Jeff Beck on guitar – quite a line-up and the series would be distributed worldwide. It was a challenge playing blues again, especially in its basic raw form as I did with Jimmy Witherspoon all those years ago, but it was great fun and got me some welcome international exposure. The DVD of the film had an optional 'Director's Take' that included a commentary by Mike Figgis and another solo version of 'Lush Life'. Mike suddenly decided he wanted me to play it on camera and also got Jeff Beck to do a solo guitar feature.

I tried to think of ways to take *Zyklon* forward. I believe Peter Hall tried without success to interest the Chicago Opera in the work when he directed a production of Verdi's *Otello*. But then two totally unrelated events happened that led to a breakthrough. Firstly, I met Dr Sheldon Saul Hendler, or Shelly to his friends. He contacted me because he was a friend of Red Rodney, who had told him about me years before. A professor of clinical medicine at the University of California, San Diego, he plays trumpet and flugelhorn and studied music with Henry Cowell and John Cage. He lived in New York during the fifties, often frequenting the jazz clubs, and he was to play a big part in the future of *Zyklon*. For a start, he knew a lot about Fritz Haber, some of his early research stemming directly from Haber's own work on reactive forms of oxygen.

The second unrelated event was a piece of pure serendipity. Julian Barry called me one day to say that he had been to an event at the City University of New York (CUNY) which was part of an ongoing project on 'Science and Art'. He had seen an opportunity and introduced himself to the people in charge, telling them about *Zyklon*, and they wanted to know more. So we cobbled together a package of stuff and sent it off, not expecting to hear any more. As the CUNY project was on a very small scale Julian didn't see how those running it could mount anything as big as an opera.

A couple of months or more passed with no news, but then CUNY got in touch, asking if we could give a short hour-and-a-half performance of *Zyklon*, with just a few singers and a pianist in Dec-ember 2004. It would be an enor-mous challenge to scale it all down so drastically and then find the right people to perform it, but how could we pass up such an opportunity?

Science & the Arts
The Graduate Center of the City University of New York
presents

Z Y K L O N

December 13, 2004 – 6 pm – Elebash Recital Hall

*Co-sponsored by the CUNY Center for Jewish Studies and the Barry S
Brook Center for Music Research and Documentation*

Programme for the first performance of the opera *Zyklon*, New York, 2004.

Julian persuaded CUNY to pay me $2,000 to cover my airfare to New York and some expenses. I could stay with him and com-mute to New York from his house in Connecticut and CUNY would provide a small amount to cover the cost of a pianist and some singers.

I had no idea how we were going to find singers. I knew no one who could handle it in London, let alone in New York, but Shelly Hendler came to our rescue, when he put me in touch with a brilliant opera soprano, Cynthia Aaronson-Davis. I sent her a rough draft of the vocal score and to my great relief she liked it and was really interested in singing the role of Clara for a very modest fee. Not only that; she helped me find just the right people to make up the rest of the cast. She advised me to approach Alan Johnson, a New York based pianist and vocal coach with whom she often worked. If we could get him on board, he would also organise the right singers for the job and rehearse them. I think *Zyklon* must have made quite an impression because Alan agreed to take on the task for a ridiculously small fee. There was no way I could have pulled things together without his help. One of the top guys in New York, with over twenty-eight world opera premiers to his name, he does everything: plays piano, conducts, coaches the singers and develops new works from initial stages right up to full performance.

Writing a proper piano-vocal score for the shortened version of the opera took me about a couple of months in London. In New York, Alan gradually put together a magnificent cast. It was quite frightening because he would send me each new singer's CV and these people were the top of their profession, many having sung starring roles in operas, from Mozart to Wagner. I couldn't understand why they would want to do *Zyklon* for the kind of money we were offering, so I mentioned it to Peter Hall's secretary one day. She simply told me 'They are not doing it for the money, Peter; they are doing it because they like the opera.' I was thrilled at the way things were panning out, especially when I heard how well the first rehearsals were going. Every so often, Alan Johnson would suggest small cuts or slight changes in vocal line to help the singers, but he always presented me with a well thought-out way of handling them with a minimum of re-writing.

Eventually, Linda and I set off for the Big Apple, settled into Julian's lovely house in the Connecticut woods and prepared for what was to be one of the greatest experience of my life. Alan Johnson had assembled a fantastic cast. The role of Fritz Haber would be sung by the young baritone, Chris Pedro Trakas and Cynthia Aaronson-Davis would sing Clara's role. Actress Valda Setterfield would narrate some of the plot to keep the action moving during the sections where music had been cut out. We also had Dan Illian to act the part of Major Sanders, the army lawyer to whom Haber tells his story, and the remaining characters would be sung by Kevin Massey, Calland Metts and

Cynthia Aaronson-Davis who sang the female lead in the New York production of *Zyklon*, PK, Shelly Hendler and Anthony Davis.

Andrew Martens, a brilliant young bass who would sing the role of Hitler.

I soon got over my nervousness when I met the singers, who were obviously excited to be working on the project. It was very strange to be suddenly pitched from a life of playing the saxophone into the role of working with singers on my own opera. Hearing it for the first time performed by top class singers, with Alan Johnson's fabulous interpretation of the piano score and his expert vocal coaching, was an unbelievable experience. I still had to keep kicking myself to realise I had actually written *Zyklon!*

I tried to prepare myself for a load of problems in rehearsal, expecting everyone to tell me this or that was badly written and needed changing, but the suggestions for alterations were just minor details. I assured everyone I wanted them to feel comfortable and was only too glad of any proposals to help the music work better. A good atmosphere resulted and everything quickly fell into place. Chris Trakas told me the music was challenging to sing. Although the harmonic style was predominantly tonal, it often moved chromatically and the vocal lines would constantly resolve onto new unrelated harmonies. Chris said that actually made it more difficult to get right than if it had been a completely atonal work, as the notes had to be pitched with greater accuracy. He explained that you could get away with mis-pitching the odd note in a twelve-tone piece without it being noticeable. Nevertheless, he and the others handled every tricky line with assurance.

They also needed to act and, despite having only about a fifth of the rehearsal time needed for a work like this, they acted their socks off too. Although they had to read the music as there was no time to memorise their parts, they still managed to bring all their acting skills to bear. At the first rehearsal Alan Johnson had the cast read through the whole opera, as if it was a play, to give everyone an overview of the plot before they sang a single note.

On 13 December we arrived at the Elebash Recital Hall on 5th Avenue and East 34th Street for the performance. I had recorded an album for Spotlite Records years before called *East 34th Street*. Many people thought wrongly that I had recorded it in New York, so it was an odd coincidence actually to be there now, exactly where the cover photo had been taken, for the premier of *Zyklon*. I couldn't help but notice the irony of the situation. For forty-five years I had hoped in vain to one day work under my own name in the Big Apple as a jazz musician. Who would have believed that my New York debut would be as an opera composer instead!

Waiting for the public to arrive, I got a severe attack of nerves. Would anyone show up? Would they hate what I'd written? CUNY had spent a lot on the venture and the thought of failure was terrifying. I was told that many of the audience would be interested in the scientific subject matter rather than the music, so there was not only the possibility of being criticised for my composition, but also about historical and scientific accuracy. In the event, we had a good attendance and the small hall was about three quarters full, but CUNY wanted Julian Barry and me to take seats in the front row, in case

East 34th Street CD (1999), recorded in London, January 1983.

we were called to take a bow at the end of the performance. This meant I couldn't see the audience and spent the whole first act frightened to turn round, in case I found that half of them had walked out. I was in a daze. But the interval came and I could hear applause. I turned round and to my intense relief the audience was still there. Several people came up to meet me, offering congratulations on the first act and peppering me with questions. We had survived so far. After the intermission I felt much more relaxed and was now able to just sit and enjoy the rest of the night.

The second act starts with Clara's suicide aria and Cindy Aaronson-Davis gave an awesome performance, filling the hall with her emotional and spectacular voice. Chris Trakas was giving his all to his role as Fritz Haber and Andrew Martens used his magnificent bass voice in a brilliantly sinister interpretation of Hitler. Haber sings one last aria and the opera finishes with him warning the audience that his spirit is alive and well, in the killing fields of war and in the minds of many scientists, still developing ever more vicious way to destroy innocent people. By the time of the performance Julian's libretto had taken on a new and terrifying pertinence, following 9/11 and Bush's new 'war on terror', and the audience must have been very aware of the warning implicit in the plot. They burst into loud applause at the end and Julian and I had to get up onstage to take a bow, as they gave us and the whole cast a standing ovation. We had pulled it off. I couldn't believe it. We had survived the first performance of *Zyklon* and in great style too!

People came up to congratulate us again and I was thrilled to hear some say how much they had been moved by the music. Even Patrick Dickie, who was in New York on business and had come to the performance, said he liked it. Although he still kept his cards very close to his chest, Shelly Hendler grabbed the bull by the horns and asked him point-blank whether he could put it on at the Almeida. Patrick just kept smiling and, still without revealing his real thoughts, said, 'Well, I guess that's partly why I am here.' I knew from experience it was another thing getting any kind of meaningful commitment out of him, but he did at least agree that the opera could be made to work with a small chamber orchestra and he told me to press on and see if I could take things further. I know it's a very hazardous business taking a chance on a new opera. I got the impression he would like to give *Zyklon* a try one day, but couldn't take a chance until the opera built up a lot more momentum.

In fact another person came into the picture in New York to give us a bit more hope. During a break in rehearsals one day, a lady came up to me asking if she could come in and see us at work. I discovered later that it was Rhoda Levine, the eminent opera director. She particularly liked works about controversial modern historical subjects and so was very interested in *Zyklon*. She watched our rehearsal with great interest and asked me to contact her with more information about the opera. Rhoda is a charming lady but will fight tooth and nail to get any project that takes her fancy produced. Ever since she has been tirelessly beavering away to get *Zyklon* performed in full. It's not easy but she is determined and she is our best hope so far. In any case, if it never gets further than the CUNY performance, we have at least managed to get a small version on in New York and people are aware of its existence. More recently, there has been an upsurge of interest in Fritz Haber. A gentleman we met in the audience at CUNY has written a play about him, new books have surfaced on the subject, and Ken Gordon interviewed me about him for the *New York Times*.

Eva Lewis also told me recently she was being interviewed for a new full-length German television film about her father. It all helps the cause. To add further impetus, a young up and coming conductor, Timothy Henty, came to see me with a view to playing a couple of short orchestral extracts from *Zyklon* that I had been lucky enough to get recorded. The recording came about because a friend of mine, Haydn Bendall, a brilliant sound engineer and producer, got an opportunity to test out a new studio in Berlin and, as part of the deal, had free use of a fine orchestra. He immediately asked me to provide a score and parts. It would only be a demonstration CD but, although I wasn't able to go with him and had to rely on the conductor to interpret the music, the result was excellent and proved to me that I was capable of producing a decent full orchestral score, on a scale way beyond anything I had ever attempted before. Tim included the same pieces in a London concert at St. John's, Smith Square, where his chamber orchestra, the London Kensington Sinfonia, gave them a fine first public performance in June 2005.

Another spin-off from New York came through one of Cindy's friends, Susan Tiefenbrun, Professor of International Law and Human Rights at the Thomas Jefferson School of Law. She was awarded the French Legion of Honour by President Jacques Chirac in 2003. In January 2005, Professor Tiefenbrun asked Cindy to sing Clara's suicide aria at the conference 'Law and the Humanities: Representations of the Holocaust, Genocide and Other Human Rights Violations' in San Diego. I wasn't able to attend but Cindy's sister, Stacy Ann Ralph, who accompanied her on piano, told me it was a very moving experience. Susan Tiefenbrun emailed me after the event, saying Stacy and Cindy's

At a diner in Connecticut with
Stacy Ann Ralph, August
2008. Photo Julian Barry.

performance of the aria from *Zyklon* 'added something really
special to the conference'. She went on to describe the music
as 'mesmerising, bitter and cutting edge'. Holocaust surviv-
ors spoke at the event and Cindy sang the aria right after an
impassioned speech by a woman who had suffered horrendous
'medical experiments' at the hands of Dr. Josef Mengele in
Auschwitz. I was very touched and humbled to have contributed
to such a prestigious and emotionally charged event.

I have been haunted by the history of the Holocaust for most
of my adult life and often wonder why I am so fascinated by its
horrors. I've had to wrestle with my conscience at times over my
morbid fascination, but now realise what drives my thirst for
knowledge about the subject. To come to terms with such pure
evil, you have to try to understand how an apparently modern
and civilised country such as Germany could allow itself to be
led into such depths of moral degradation. I have reached the
frightening conclusion that it could happen anywhere, at any
time. It's a gradual process, where apparently innocuous racial
prejudices combine with vague fears of danger to your country.
Apparently reasonable and intelligent people find themselves
becoming a minority and before they realise it, their decent
moral value judgements become obscured by dogma.

There was no single reason for the rise of Hitler and the Nazis.
It was a complex process that fed on Germany's humiliation

after the First World War and on a multitude of fears, economic problems and prejudices. We still need to learn the real lessons of the Holocaust and never more so than in today's climate of paranoia and religious polarisation. There is every sign that something very similar could rear its ugly head quite soon and on an even more massive and horrific scale unless we keep constant guard against the first tell-tale signs. I am an optimist though, in spite of everything, and I will continue the struggle to play jazz and compose, in the firm belief that sanity will prevail and that music still has the power to change hearts and minds.

At the Barbican, London, 2010. Photo Gill Vaux.

Coda

Writing this book has taken me on a journey back in time. I've had to confront some half-forgotten nightmares along the way, but have revisited some wonderful experiences too. Despite the destructive things I have done to myself in the past I have reached my seventieth year and still hope to improve as a saxophonist and as a composer. I have recently fulfilled a commission to write a jazz mass and may have another in the pipeline. I get a bigger thrill than ever from playing, especially with my quartet, and I still hope to fulfil my ambition to be accepted as a classical composer one day, especially if dental or other physical problems eventually force me to give up playing the saxophone. I would like to take up painting again too and I still haven't given up hope of being able to afford to take time out to fly model aeroplanes more and even win the world championships one day. After all, Bob White won the Wakefield Trophy in 1987, when well into his seventies!

I am a lucky guy. Music has been my saviour. In spite of the many disappointments and hassles it has brought me, it has filled my life with beauty and brought me into contact with some wonderful and uniquely talented people. I have now been in the business for over fifty years and hope to have a few more left yet.

Since completing the first draft of this book, I have had to deal with some rather traumatic events and I find myself thinking more and more about how frail our hold on life is. In 2005 my darling wife Linda suffered a cerebral haemorrhage. I nearly lost her and she was confined to a wheelchair, but she fought on bravely for another two years, finally making it to eighty-one before she contracted pneumonia and suddenly died peacefully in my arms at home in March 2007. Every day I relive the horror of witnessing her last dying breath. I fought all alone to bring her back to life until the ambulance arrived but, although they managed to get her heart going again, she never regained consciousness and finally died for the second time three days later.

The shock of her death and my worsening dental problems took their toll and I became ill myself. It turned out to be merely a nasty form of pneumonia but the doctors were convinced I had lung cancer and for nearly two months I had to face the spectre of failing health and my own possible demise. But, thanks to the overwhelming love and support of my family, friends, fellow musicians and my many loyal fans, I was able not only to come through it all but to also have the major dental surgery I so desperately needed to continue playing my horn.

Along with the help of so many wonderful people and the inspiration of Linda and her immense courage, I intend to make the best of whatever years I have left. After all, there is still so much more I want to do.

Appendix

FREE FLIGHT MODEL AEROPLANES

Most of today's aeromodellers fly radio controlled planes but I had never been interested in anything but competitive free flight. Although this branch of the hobby is now very small, it's still active and, at top international level, is a very exciting and high tec activity. Modellers from the old USSR blazed a new trail and were well supported by the communist state and aircraft industry. The new and radical techniques they developed dominated the sport from the eighties to the present day.

I. THE MODELS

There are three main classes of free flight models. F1B is the rubber powered class. F1A is purely a glider class with models of about seven feet span weighing around 420 grams: they are towed up on a 50-metre line then released to glide for as long as possible. F1C models are about the same size but weigh around 750 grams and have small but unbelievably powerful 2.5 cc motors which drive propellers at a staggering 32,000 plus rpm. These models are only allowed a short five-second motor run but climb vertically to over 600 feet before gliding for up to seven minutes.

All these models are phenomenally efficient gliders and the whole object is to get them to fly as long as possible. To do this they must be 'trimmed' to perfection by making small changes to the settings of the rudder, stabiliser and wing angles, etc. The object is first to get all the models to the maximum altitude you can using their respective power sources. Then the glide must be at the lowest possible sinking speed to give the maximum duration. The other equally important skill is launching the model into a thermal and avoiding a downdraft. This is a truly black art that you learn from years of experience by studying subtle changes in wind speed and temperature. Remember, once a free flight model is launched, you have no control over it and this is what makes it so much more fascinating to me than radio-controlled flying. We usually use highly sensitive thermal detection equipment, often taking the form of a chart recorder that gives a read-out with time of wind speed and temperature. The difficult part is interpreting the data, as the signs of thermal activity vary from place to place and from hour to hour. The best flyers can launch into a thermal ninety-five percent of the time.

At big competitions or championships we fly in rounds, from a designated set of poles on the flight line. There are usually seven rounds and you have to fly for just three minutes each one. A good model should be able to do this but, if you put it in a patch of sinking air or make a bad launch, you can easily do less and 'drop the max'. At a big international meeting as many as thirty or more flyers will make seven three-minute flights or 'max out' as we say. The competition then really starts, with a series of fly-offs, of increasing times, usually five, seven, or nine, and sometimes eleven minutes, before the winner is decided. As the day progresses, tension increases. In fact I get more nervous in the heat of competition than when I am playing a gig. The adrenaline rush gets bigger still if you are doing well, as one small mistake in air picking, a bad launch or a systems failure can mean a dropped flight and any hope of getting a top placing is suddenly gone.

In the early fifties the rules for the old Wakefield (Now F1B) rubber powered models allowed you to cram in as much rubber as you could. The models were restricted to 19 square decimetres of wing plus tail area and had to weigh 230 grams including rubber. This led to fragile models with airframe weights of only 100 grams, packed with 130 grams or more of rubber to drive the propeller. The best models were capable of flying around five minutes without thermal assistance. When I started again in the eighties the rules had changed and the newly named F1B models were only allowed a measly 40 grams of rubber, with the same 230 gram total weight. However, the new Russian designs were capable of flights of up to nine minutes, without thermal assistance and with less than a third of the amount of rubber.

With Linda Mk7, one of PK's
F1G (Coupe d'Hiver) models.
Photo Ron Pollard.

II. FLYING AN F1B MODEL

Most people have seen toy aeroplanes that use a twisted elastic band to drive the propeller, but the planes I'm talking about are a world away from these. They are quite large and made almost exclusively from ultra strong, light carbon fibre and kevlar. They are fitted with small mechanical or electronic timers that are pre-programmed to change the wing and tail settings during the flight to achieve the optimum flight path. The models are powered by special high energy rubber, wound to just short of breaking point. The propeller is about two feet in diameter and folds, after the motor has stopped, to reduce drag for the glide. Most of us now use Andriukov's special propeller technology that works like this: after winding, the propeller is blocked and feathered and the timer only releases it after you have thrown the model vertically to about 40 feet or more. At this point the motor bursts into action taking the model straight up to about 150 feet, after which the nose slowly drops and the timer trips a change in the tail setting to control the climb at a lower angle. Meanwhile, the rapidly diminishing torque of the rubber motor alters the pitch of the propeller, via a brilliantly engineered cam system, to optimise the efficiency at all points in the climb. While waiting for good air, you can also apply extra turns to keep the torque of the motor as high as possible.

The whole process of winding and launching is pretty nerve-wracking. You stretch the motor out to up to seven times its length, leaning back with all your weight at an angle of around 45 degrees. As you wind, you fight the rubber all the way in as it drags you towards the model. Often the motor can explode under the strain, propelling you head over heels backwards. If this happens you have another model prepared or frantically fit a new motor and start again. If you don't break motors sometimes, you are not winding the rubber hard enough. Next you fit the prop and move to the launch position. You watch for signs of thermal activity while adding even more hand turns to the motor. When you decide it's the right time, you signal your timekeeper you are about to launch, then with nerves jangling you hurl your model skywards. It's essential that all the various functions are double-checked for correct setup and that you throw it at exactly the right angle and straight into the wind. This is the most critical part of the whole flight and one tiny mistake can see the model losing half its potential height or even crashing to the ground under full power. If all is well, the plane moves into its lower-powered cruise phase and climbs more sedately to about 300 feet. At about 50 seconds the prop folds and the model glides, riding the thermal you've picked. After completing three minutes, the timer releases another trigger that moves the tail to a high angle, causing the model to go into a deep stall. We call this 'dethermalising' or DT for short. It then parachutes down quickly but safely to the ground, so you can get it back for the next flight.

III THE FLY OFF

At a big international championship the result often has to be decided the following morning, usually just after sunrise when thermal activity is low. In these conditions, ultimate model performance is the deciding factor. During the main contest rounds you usually trim the plane with a slight margin of safety as in thermal conditions the air can be quite turbulent. To get the maximum performance you have to go for broke. You adjust the trim right up to what we call 'the edge' and this requires a couple of check flights to get the model as close to the stall as you can get away with, as this gives the best glide, but allows very little safety margin. You also open up the glide turn so the model covers a large area of sky, in order to hunt for any slightly rising air that may be around. At this point even the best flyers in the world sometimes come unstuck and go too far, ruining their flight, but you have to pull out all the stops if you want to win.

We are talking ultra high performance here. These are definitely not toys! The best models also have a miraculous ability to find their own thermals. This miracle is achieved after many hours making tiny, subtle changes to the trim and Andriukov's models regularly glide in huge open circles covering a large area of sky for three or four minutes then, when they sense rising air, tighten up their turn to circle in it. It's amazing to watch, just as if the model is being flown by a real pilot. I have a couple that have this ability, but have others that do the opposite and seem to want to actively avoid lift. I never use those in important competitions.

IV POITOU, FRANCE 1991

When I flew against Andriukov in France in 1991 I was quite surprised to find myself in the fly-off, as picking air was difficult that day and many top flyers had dropped flights, leaving just three of us with a 'full house'. I had maxed out through all seven rounds, with many flights landing over a mile away, in seven-foot high corn or sunflower fields. Temperatures on the flying field shot up to over 40 degrees Centigrade, so it was an exhausting day, starting as it did at eight in the morning, and dehydration was a constant danger.

The fly-offs were interesting. One of my two models was still temporarily lost down wind, leaving me with only one. In the first five minute round I decided to wait and watch Alex, as he was the expert at picking the best air. I soon had to change this strategy as Alex, having the better model, just stood there calm as a cucumber, smiling at me. He only had to launch in the same air as me and his superior performance would win the day, so no way was he going to fly first. The tactics and gamesmanship at this level are pretty intense! He was just psyching me out, so I finally launched my model first, in what seemed to be a good patch of lift. I got it right because it was soon very high, in a powerful thermal. Alex had turned the tables on me and launched straight into 'my' air. My timekeepers and helpers told me I got the best of the air and had it been a one-off 'unlimited' flight, I probably would have beaten him and won, as the third flyer from Germany had a systems failure and was out of the contest.

We both easily made the five-minute fly-off so now had to go for a seven-minute round. This was a problem for me, as my only remaining model flew out of sight at about eight minutes and my retrieval team could not get it back in time for the next flight. It was finally found over eight miles away, along with the other model I had lost earlier. Alex sportingly persuaded the organisers to delay the seven-minute round, so I could fly but, after about half an hour, still with no model, I had to concede defeat. I was well pleased with second place though and was very happy when my helpers eventually brought both models back safe and sound with the help of the radio tracking system I had installed only a month or so before. This technology had just come into the sport and made retrieval much easier and quicker. Before this, we had to rely on a good compass bearing and orienteering techniques. Now we use a tiny radio transmitter weighing only three grams that sends out a pulsed signal from the model. Using a receiver fitted with a directional 'Yagi' aerial, we can now 'hear' the model and walk right to where it has landed.

Index

Jazz Books from Northway

Graham Collier, *The Jazz Composer – Moving Music off the Paper*

Chris Searle, *Forward Groove: Jazz and the Real World from Louis Armstrong to Gilad Atzmon.*

Mike Hennessey, *The Little Giant – The Story of Johnny Griffin*

Derek Ansell, *Workout – The Music of Hank Mobley*

Alan Robertson, *Joe Harriott – Fire in His Soul*, 2nd edition (forthcoming)

Ian Carr, *Music Outside*

Alan Plater, *Doggin' Around*

Coleridge Goode and Roger Cotterrell, *Bass Lines: A Life in Jazz*

Peter Vacher, *Soloists and Sidemen: American Jazz Stories*

Leslie Thompson with Jeffrey Green, *Swing from a Small Island*

Jim Godbolt, *A History of Jazz in Britain 1919–50*

Jim Godbolt, *All This and Many a Dog*

Ronnie Scott with Mike Hennessey, *Some of My Best Friends Are Blues*

John Chilton, *Hot Jazz, Warm Feet*

Vic Ash, *I Blew It My Way: Bebop, Big Bands and Sinatra*

Digby Fairweather, *Notes from a Jazz Life*

Ron Brown with Digby Fairweather, *Nat Gonella – A Life in Jazz*

Harry Gold, *Gold, Doubloons and Pieces of Eight*

Join our mailing list for details of new books, events
and special offers: write to Northway Books,
39 Tytherton Road, London N19 4PZ
or email *info@northwaybooks.com*
www.northwaybooks.com